MODERN MYSTICS

MODERN MYSTICS

BY

SIR FRANCIS YOUNGHUSBAND

K.C.S.I., K.C.I.E.

Essay Index Reprint Series

BOOKS FOR LIBRARIES PRESS, INC.
FREEPORT, NEW YORK

First Published 1935
Reprinted 1967

LIBRARY OF CONGRESS CATALOG NUMBER:

67-28774

PRINTED IN THE UNITED STATES OF AMERICA

CONTENTS

CONTENTS

PREFACE

IN my *Living Universe* I expressed my agreement with Bergson that the great mystics gave us an indication of the direction in which the human race would evolve. But, in spite of the works of Miss Evelyn Underhill and Dr. Inge, mystics are still suspect and mysticism is confused with mistiness. So to make clearer what I mean by mystics and the mystical experience I have in the present book taken examples of mystics of the present times about whose lives we have ample information. All, except one, have lived in my own lifetime; and besides reading about them in books I have been able to inquire about them personally from those who knew them. So we are able to get into closer touch with them than we can with the mystics of long past and see how the mystical experience came to them, what it was like and what effect it had upon their lives. And I have drawn examples from the East as well as from the West in order to show how widespread is this mystical experience.

Lastly, I have tried to show how naturally the mystical experience fits into that view of the universe which science and philosophy are now coming to hold, namely, that it is a coherent whole of diverse parts interdependent upon each other and manifesting the existence of a Personality energizing, controlling, and directing all.

I have drawn most copiously from the biographies of these mystics, repeating their very words, or the words of the biographers who have known them, in order to make their experiences as vivid and the record of them as exact as possible. I, therefore, express my very special indebtedness to the authors of the following books : *The Life of Keshub Chander Sen*, by P. Mazoomdar ; *The Life of Sri Ramakrishna*, published by Advaita Ashrama ; *The Dawn Breakers*, by Shoghi Effendi ; *Saint Thérèse of Lisieux*, translated by Rev. Thomas N. Taylor, published by Burns, Oates & Washbourne ; *The Life of Evan Roberts*, by Rev. D. M. Phillips.

F. E. Y.

February, 1935.

INTRODUCTION

ACTIVITY unceasing is what we everywhere see when we look out around us. And the same when we think of ourselves. Even in our sleep it ceases not : our hearts continue to beat, our blood flows, our lungs breathe, our stomach digests, our brains still work. Wherever and whenever we look it is the same. Always and everywhere there is activity. And how universally prevalent it is, both in time and in space, and how intense only science can tell. Even solid rocks are theatres of intensest activity. They, the mountains, the seas, the stars are built up of ultimate particles of matter which are not hard bits of material but simply centres of energy, centres of activity, radiating out influence in every direction. Activity is universal in time and in space—in every tiniest part and in that great whole which comprises stars as numerous as the grains of sand upon the seashore. Space itself is active. It is perpetually vibrating.

But this unceasing activity is not chaotic : it is controlled and directed. The sun is the scene of the fiercest activity ; but it is round. So also is the Earth. And the plants and animals which have sprung from the Earth and which are conglomerations of innumerable groups of atoms are held together in definite forms and patterns—in patterns of molecules, crystals, amœbæ, jelly-fishes, fishes, birds, animals,

1

trees, flowers, men. The orderliness and intelligibility of Nature is recognized by all scientific men. It is the basic faith upon which they pursue their laborious investigations.

And each of these forms—each man, animal, plant, rock, mountain, planet, sun, star, as well as every minutest particle of which each of these is composed, is connected with every other part and therefore with the whole, and affects and is affected by every other part, so that a pin-drop sends a tremor through the universe. Everywhere there is interconnection, interrelation and interdependence. Isolation is unknown and impossible. And so connected are we ourselves with our surroundings—surroundings which include the whole universe—that it is hard to see where our bodies end and the environment begins. Apart from breathing our bodies are continually radiating out rays and being bombarded by them, and at the rate of millions a second. A man's body is not clear cut : its influence extends to the confines of the universe just as it is affected by the whole universe.

Progressiveness is also observable. There is evolution. What we see to-day is found to be gradually derived from what went before. The activity is a creative activity. It is a process. It looks as if behind it there were some Power with an aim in view, ordering all this activity and directing it towards some end. And what we are irresistibly drawn to inquire into is what is the nature of that Power and what is it driving at.

In this creative process we ourselves are so immersed and so irresistibly borne along in its mighty impetus that we appear to have little control over our destiny. We seem to have nothing to do in the matter. We had no say about our birth. We could not choose our parents. And having been born, neither they nor we can stay or accelerate our growth. Our parents might like to keep us dear little children. We ourselves might like to jump into real grown-up manhood. Neither they nor we can add a cubit to our stature. We grow up in spite of ourselves. And sooner or later we are bound to die. Do what we may we cannot live as long as an oak. We cannot even sleep when we want to, or keep awake when we want, or remain without food for more than a month. In many most important ways we have hardly any control over ourselves but are carried impotently along in the whole creative process proceeding all about us. We are involved in a universe, which is dynamically developing about us. We cannot get away from it. It is constantly affecting us, as we see if we think only of the weather. And we have to be continually making the most delicate and varying and often very complex adjustments to that mighty whole which originally brought us into being and with which we are indissolubly connected for all the days of our life.

Not only that, we are born with certain insistent appetites which we are compelled to satisfy on pain of death or of acutest suffering. The desire to live is imperative within us and hardly less domineering the desire to reproduce ourselves. So we have to exert ourselves to obtain and eat food—and the right food—or we shall die. And we have to seek a mate or suffer lifelong pangs of desire.

Our destiny seems settled for us from the time of our birth. And all that seems to be left to us is to let the wheels go round. Yet, with all our apparent impotence we are far from being mere automatic machines. The fact that we grow and reproduce

3

ourselves differentiates us from a machine. Far more important is the fact that we do have some power of choice. We do have some say, while a machine has none. Swept along as we may be in the great creative process we can choose what we shall eat and drink and who shall be our mate. And by choosing the right food and eating the right amount of it, and by choosing the right mate we may satisfy our inborn appetites and because of that satisfaction experience pleasure, or by choosing the wrong food or the wrong mate fail to satisfy those appetites and suffer pain. And by thus experiencing either pleasure or pain we are again widely differentiated from a machine.

Then besides these bodily desires and the power of satisfying them we are also born with certain spiritual cravings which no less need satisfaction. The chief is companionship. No man could live by himself without even the companionship of an animal. And when he craves for a mate it is not only, or chiefly, for bodily satisfaction. Much more is it for companionship. And inside the longing for companionship is a deeper craving to make that companionship as perfect as possible—to make it the most perfect love.

All this increases our craving to know what and what like is the driving power of the creative process, and what it is driving at.

Now some men are exceedingly sensitive to its operation. There are highly impressionable persons peculiarly receptive of impressions from the creative process proceeding all around them. And some of these highly susceptible persons are finely discriminative of these impressions—which they shall receive and absorb and which they shall reject. And a few exceedingly rare persons are not only impressionable and discriminative, but expressive also. They are thus able to communicate to others the most valuable of the impressions they have received from the operating of the creative process ; and we thus have the means of judging something of its essential nature and what it is proceeding to create.

From time to time in different countries there appear men and women who have experience in rare moments of a more exalted state of living than we know of in the common everyday life of our time. Such persons are not necessarily better, or more heroic, or more saintly than many of their fellows who have never been favoured with such an experience, though they are always men and women who undoubtedly have set their affections on things above, on the higher things of the spirit, and have striven and suffered and sacrificed in order to attain their goal. But they have had the good fortune, through some happy combination of circumstances, to have been caught up in a rapture and to have experienced in a supreme moment a mode of living intenser, more joyous, more assured, and far more vivid than ordinary life. Their experience has been to them so sacred that they have recoiled from speaking of it to a single other soul. And, even if they would, they fear that to put it into words would be at once to lose its precious fragrance. Yet, with all their hesitation they would long to proclaim their discovery to all the world, that others may share it with them.

The persons who have enjoyed this experience are usually known as mystics. The experience itself is known as the mystical experience. The state of life which is experienced is called the mystical state.

The Hindus call this experience *Samadhi*. It is a

5

well-recognized condition among them, though anyone who has attained to it feels it too sacred a matter
to speak of except perhaps to a few fellow-seekers
after the higher things of the spirit.

Among Moslems those who have this experience
are known as *Sufis*, though as a rule no Moslem who
had enjoyed it would call himself a Sufi. With the
same religious reserve as characterizes all true mystics
he would not refer to it even among his friends.

These mystics and the state of being of which they
have experience we will now examine because they
have had experience of direct correspondence with
the Power behind the Creative Activity—with the
Spirit of the Universe—with God. They reveal to us
the conditions of that higher mode of life into which
the human race is evolving. Their experience is the
peak experience of the race, and a pointer of the
direction in which it is developing. Their consciousness has reached a higher pitch of awareness of the
world about them than ordinary men attain. What
they have to tell is therefore specially worth hearing.
And in this present work examples will be chosen
from among mystics who have lived in the present,
or quite recent times, because we have ample means
of knowing the conditions under which the experience
came to them, and because present are more stimu-
lating than ancient examples.

But in the examples which will now be given of the
mystical experience emotionalism to a degree unbe-
lievable by those who have never witnessed it will be
described ; and to many readers this may be highly
distasteful. And it may be admitted that even the
friends of some of these mystics thought them mad.
Yet there is the fact that they have since profoundly

influenced men. And when identical experiences have come to such different persons living in such different circumstances as a Moslem merchant in Persia, a Hindu villager in India, a Roman Catholic nun in France and a Baptist miner in Wales, we should be disposed to take it seriously. And distasteful as this extreme emotionalism may be to many, perhaps these will reflect that it is only through strong emotion that the deep things in life are reached and that it was due to strong emotion in their parents that they themselves came into being. If their parents had been cold, unswayed by emotion they themselves would not now be in existence.

Further, it will be found that it was through these tremendous emotional experiences and as a resultant of their purging and purifying effects that the mystics were able to reach that abiding serenity which can only come from complete spiritual satisfaction—from the satisfaction of the whole self and the deepest foundation of the self.

There should indeed be no objection to strong emotion in itself. Intensity of emotion in a man is only the counterpart of intensity of activity in every ultimate particle of matter. And it is eminently desirable that we should be capable of the utmost strength of feeling. No love of beauty or love of a mother for her child could ever be felt with too deep an intensity.

The fact that the mystical state is a highly emotional state must therefore be accepted. Nevertheless, that fact makes it all the more necessary to examine and test it in the light of pure reason if we are to learn from it. Mystics themselves would also profit by such examination. Their experience will be all the more profitable to them if it is purified by understanding. They have convictions—and indeed invincible convictions—but they would have more weight with others if they were reasoned convictions. Reason alone and wisdom alone would never have produced these experiences or brought such certitude any more than reason or the very highest wisdom alone could have put the young man in love with the maiden, or the patriot in love with his country. These things lie above the domain of reason. Nevertheless, after the experience has been experienced it may be interpreted, tested and sifted in the light of reason, so that it may be properly understood and its true value be appraised. Though reason may never be able to give that experience, yet that experience must be fitted into a reasonable view of the universe. Or perhaps it would be truer to say that the experience and the reasonable view of the universe must be fitted into one another.

Now when mystical experiences are examined in the dry light of every day they may very easily be brushed aside as unimportant or even as harmful. The passionless scientist might dispose of them as mere hysteria, hallucinations, pathological symptoms of no validity or worth whatever. This is perfectly possible, and in fact has been done. And it may be admitted that there are cases which resemble but are not the true mystical experiences which might be so condemned. But the higher mysticism, the real mystical experience, cannot be so airily disposed of. It is scarcely probable that men of great intellect like St. Thomas Aquinas in ancient times and Father Poulain and Dean Inge in the present day would have devoted so much intellectual energy to its interpretation if in their opinion it had not possessed real worth. Nor would the keen minds of India, Persia and Arabia during long centuries have discussed its manifestation among Hindus and Moslems, and devised systems and codes and rules of life by which others might acquire it, if they had not regarded it as a supremely valuable experience. And if some psychologists disparage the mystical experience there are others of the highest eminence who regard it as normal and healthy and who note this much in favour of the mystic that he is the better and not the worse for his experience. A drunkard certainly delights while he is drunk. But the next morning is the worse, not the better for it. So also is the person with an hallucination. The mystic, on the contrary, finds his whole being saturated with the joy he has felt. It has become a lasting possession to him. And it alters his whole attitude to life. The mystical experience has stood the test of centuries of criticism and opposition among Hindus, Christians, and Moslems in every country ; and if it is still valued to-day by men of acknowledged sense it may fairly be presumed that there is something in it worth serious consideration.

As to the objection which has been made to the mystical experience that it is purely subjective—a mere excogitation of the person's own self—it may be replied that no mental state whatever is purely subjective. Every mental state is produced by outside stimulus as well as by internal urge. The external and the internal go together—the internal responding to the external. For every man exists in relation to his fellows and to the whole universe. No man, no living thing, no stone or speck of dust is isolated. All are bound up in one whole, as integral parts of that whole. All are necessary to that whole. And all are affected by that whole. That whole being, of course, the whole universe. Not this Earth alone, or the solar system alone. But that totality of things, the entire universe. The mystic, like everyone else, is thus a working part of the universe as a whole. He is in relationship with the whole universe. The mystic's state must therefore be due not only to what is going on within himself but also—and perhaps chiefly—to the impacts on him of influences from outside. The mystical experience is never entirely subjective : it is always objective as well. It is subjective-objective.

And the " outside " to whose influences mystics, like the rest of us, are exposed, is the whole universe —nothing less. When we are testing their experiences in the light of reason and of accumulated scientific knowledge we have to see how they fit in with as reasonable a view of the universe as science and philosophy combined can afford. So it is important to consider them from the point of view of the universe and not from a merely terrestrial standpoint. For it may have been from the universe as a whole that came the stimulus which gave rise to these experiences. Mystics, in any case, are very sensitive and receptive of soul. And what elevated them to the exalted state they experienced may have been something impressing itself upon them from the universe at large—from the universe and not from the solar system alone.

The most primitive people sense a Mysterious Power at work in the world about them. They have odd ideas as to the nature and mode of operation of that Power. But this impression on their minds cannot be brushed aside as nothing but superstition. Some superstition there may be. But there may be more truth at the core than cooped-in townsmen may think. These primitive folk's close and constant communion with their fellow-men, with animals, with plant-life, and with physical nature may have enabled them to sense something at the heart of things which the more sophisticated townsman may have missed. They may not have been able to form a clear intellectual conception of that which they sensed. But they may have reached nearer the truth when they believed it to be a living Power than the sceptic reaches who can see nothing but chance behind the happenings in this world or than the man who sees the world as a machine and nothing more.

Proceeding then on the assumption that this planet is an integral part of and organic to the universe as a whole, and that unceasingly raining in upon it are living influences from the universe outside it, we will in this present work study the experiences of those living beings on this planet who, by the delicate sensitivity of their nature, are most susceptible to these impressions. We would assume that those impressions, while they may come proximately from living beings in this planet and perhaps other parts of the universe, derive ultimately from the Central Power of the universe—much as the impressions which the cells in my brain give to the muscles of my toe derive ultimately from me. And we would assume further that these impressions would be transmitted from one part to another in the same way as the impressions from a living being in Broadcasting House are transmitted all over the world. Then by studying the impressions which these most susceptible persons receive we would try to form some conception of the essential characteristics, not only of that Mysterious Power which must be behind the whole evolutionary process

11

and therefore also of what It is driving at—of that higher mode of life, or state of being, into which man must be gradually developing and for which he is being slowly fitted.

And this should be valuable. For science tells us that life on this Earth may last for many millions of years yet, and presumably develop. In round figures it has existed on this planet for about a thousand million years and in all probability it will last for another hundred thousand million years. But out of the thousand million years during which life has existed on this planet man has existed for only about one million years—for only one out of the thousand. He is a very recent product. He is only in his babyhood. He may develop into something beyond our utmost imaginings. Yet just as we can trace in the simplest form of life faint inklings of ourselves, for example a tiny power to choose what it will absorb, what it will reject, what it will respond to, what it will repel, so may the most developed of ourselves have in us delicate indications of those beings into which man may develop a thousand million years hence.

And we may be aided in making our forecast by considering the stages through which animal life has gone in arriving at the human stage. During the course of development upward from amœba to man there have been certain very definite steps taken. One particularly we will dwell upon : the step from the water on to land. During by far the greater period of life-development living beings were found only in the water. None—either plant or animal— existed on the land. The land was bare and uninhabited. Then, gradually, there emerged from the waters living things who adapted themselves to life

12

on land in the air and the sunshine. They had entered upon a new state of being. In the waters the sunshine penetrated but dimly, and they could see only a short distance around them. The stars and any life in the starry realm would be unsuspected. Now a prodigious change would have taken place. They must have suffered much from the dry air, from the alternating heat of the noonday sun in summer and chill of the night hours in winter. But as they acclimatized themselves to the new conditions they found themselves entering upon a wider, fuller, intenser state of being. The sunshine entered their souls. Instead of being cold and fish-like they became warm-blooded. Their eyesight developed till it pierced to farthest horizons. And their hearing developed as their eyesight. To the very varying conditions of their surroundings they adapted themselves in an equal variety of ways. Consequently, the rate of their development rapidly increased. In the last hundred million years they accomplished more than they had in the whole of the previous nine hundred million years. Life became infinitely more vivid and intense.

A like change is now before the human race. As living things came out of the water on to land so are they now coming out of planetary life into universal life. They are emerging into the air and sunshine of the universe as a whole. They will not go about the universe in the body. They will live the life of the universe on the wings of the soul. But they will embody and manifest in ever higher and completer degree that Central Living Power of the universe of which we ourselves are just faintly becoming aware.

It is into this higher state of being that a few of the more finely developed human beings are delicately feeling their way—throwing out tentacles, reaching upward, scarcely able to endure the higher conditions yet irresistibly attracted to them. These are the great poets, the great musicians, the great thinkers, and most especially the men of sensitive intuition who divine their way ahead, the great religious leaders, the great mystics. All these in their most exalted moments have caught glimpses of a higher and far more beautiful state of existence which we Christians have been taught to speak of as the Kingdom of Heaven, and which may be experienced in some measure even here and now. For, though beings more fitted to experience and endure it will doubtless develop in the future, yet that higher state is all about us at this moment—as the sunshine and air of land life was always there for those livers in the waters to enjoy if only they had the enterprise and the organs to avail themselves of it.

We may suppose then that mystics, in the great moments when they are enjoying the mystical experience, are being to a special degree acted upon by the Central Power of the universe which is both in them and around, beneath and above them. Under the pressure of the creative urge within them and stirred to a glowing fervency of activity by the spiritual impact from without—under the pressure of the Creative Spirit within them acted upon by the same Creative Spirit around and above them, they have burst forth into a new kind of life.

They may be taken as resembling fledglings beginning to fly. So far the young birds have not ventured out into the wide world which surrounds their nest. Their wings are not strong enough to support them. Then comes a day when their wings have developed and when they are driven by a deep instinctive urge within them and are called by their mother and the air and sunshine without them to make the critical plunge, trust to their unused wings and fare forth into the unknown. A fearful venture of faith it must be to the young swallow. But once it is made he skims through the air and soon is rising and falling, turning and twisting in a rhapsody of joy in the new world he has found. So also, I suggest, is it with the mystic who has found the wings of his soul.

A more likely resemblance may be to a butterfly. The caterpillar tied to the ground crawling slowly and laboriously along is a thing of no great beauty and leads a dull, uninteresting life nibbling at leaves. But after a period something working within it produces a wonderful change. It is slowly transformed into a chrysalis. Inside the chrysalis the transforming process continues. And then as the outside warmth and light acts upon the chrysalis the transformed creature inside it gnaws through the outer covering and emerges as a resplendent butterfly with gorgeous colouring, soon ready to fly where it will through the air and feeding itself by sipping nectar from the flowers.

The new being that the caterpillar had become and the new life it found as a butterfly are typical of the mystic. And just as the same world was all the time round the caterpillar as was round the butterfly—only the butterfly could avail itself of it while the caterpillar could not—so does the mystic discover and live in a world which is yet all the time about us ordinary men.

And recognizing that this may be so have we in our ordinary experience of life anything which will help us to form an idea of what the extraordinary experience of the mystics is like ? I think we have.

The full glory of the new condition of life can be known only to the greatest mystics—and perhaps even to them only in part. Yet we ordinary men and women may have had just a glimpse of it in those high moments in our lives when we have been in love. The young man and maiden in the highest transports of their love for each other have felt themselves wafted up to a world of beauty far above the ordinary world. What they experienced then they do not speak of. And no one is rude enough to inquire. It is recognized by them and by others as too sacred for speech. And even the finest literature, the most delicate poetry, the most entrancing music has not been able to convey any real impression of what they have experienced in the deepest recesses of their being at the culminating moment of their love. But what they then knew they knew as probably the greatest experience in their lives and as more truly real than anything else. And this it is which may give the many who have known it some inkling of what the mystical experience is.

And this is the more likely because what lovers feel is all part of, and in direct line with, the great creative urge of the world. Besides being felt—and felt with tremendous intensity and from the foundations of their beings—by men and women of every race and every age and of every degree of culture it is felt also by birds and by animals from the highest forms to the lowest and simplest ; and it has been so felt through all the stages of development from the amœba upward. What a man and woman feel in the most exalted moments of their union, and what they regard as so precious and intimate, they in reality share with all creatures. It is part of the creative urge which drives the world and which has created them and ourselves and every living thing about us. It would seem therefore as highly probable that what it gives rise to at its highest is an indication of what it will bring forth in the ages to come. What the most perfect lovers in the most perfect moments of their love have experienced may give at least to them a glimpse of the world to be—of that higher state of which the great mystics tell us.

And perhaps an illustration of the way in which a living whole may affect one of the parts of which it is composed may further help us to understand the wonderful way in which a mystic is affected.

How the mystic is related to the Creative Spirit of the universe, and how the Creative Spirit works in and upon the mystic may be inferred by observing a patriot in relation to his country. Take a Frenchman and France. In ordinary times the love of a Frenchman for France and of France for him is scarcely noticeable. He goes about his daily business feeling nothing in particular going out from him to France or coming in to him from her. Then suddenly comes a national crisis. His country is in danger. And instantly he is aflame with passionate love for France. He feels her calling to him and with his whole heart he responds to the call. He may be a poet of delicate physique and highly strung nerves. But he goes gladly forth to suffer incredible physical hardships and risk his precious life under the most torturing conditions. Pain and agony of mind and body are his lot. Yet moments come of supreme exaltation when he finds himself lifted high above the squalor and the mirk and the torture, and he glows with the love he bears his country and which his country bears him.

Or, again, this Frenchman may have devoted his life to the service of France. He may be an Ambassador of France in a foreign country. It will have been his business and his delight to represent France as she really and truly is—to represent the real France —to the country to which he is accredited. To do this effectively he will have had to study his own country more minutely and intimately than he might ever have done if he had always remained in France. And comparison with the foreign country in which he was working would have helped him in the study. He would seek to catch the fundamental and lasting spirit of France so as to be able accurately to interpret it to these foreigners. And he would have laboured year after year, in small ways and in great ways, in rough times and in smooth, to cultivate and preserve and consolidate a lasting friendship between the two countries. Then the time would arrive when his labours would be over. When the time for his departure home would come and he would be able to stand back and see the result. All that he had hoped may not have been achieved. Frictions and discords may still remain. Yet much may have been done. He may have won the affection for himself personally of the country he was working in. And because his own country sees he has gained this esteem and affection she will welcome him home with gratitude. To one who has so faithfully served her she will pour out her love. And in the silence of his own heart at the end of his service there will be an inner glow of proud satisfaction. He will have loved his country and will have felt his country's love for him. And in that culminating moment of his life he will have discovered both what he had it in himself to be and what his country might be at her best. The Frenchman will have had a foretaste of the France to come.

Thus this Frenchman has been born of France. He has breathed the air of France. He has lived the life of France. He has loved the love of France. In the spirit of France he has lived and moved and had his being. And in like manner has the mystic been born of the universe, breathed the air of the universe, lived the life and loved the love of the universe. In that mysterious Living Power which actuates all the activity of the universe he has lived and moved and had his being. He has entered into that Creative Urge and it has entered into him. There has been a mutual interpenetration. And when they are interpenetrated to the full the mystic intuitively senses what the Mysterious Power essentially is. He divines what the driving Power of the world is like and has a foretaste of what it is driving at.

And if this be really so, then once more we see how valuable this experience is to us in forecasting the next step upward in the progressive development of the human race. The mystic has had experience—direct and immediate experience—of the inmost working of the universe. His soul has been in actual correspondence with the soul of the universe. Having entered deeply into the spirit of the universe and having been even more deeply penetrated by it he has known something of what the essential nature of the universe really is. And if he knows what is the essential nature of the universe he knows also what it must eventually become. For all things in the end become what they at bottom are.

And the progress which mystics disclose may prove

to be something very different from what is generally considered to be progress. To most men, not only of the present day but of every age, progress is looked upon as synonymous with the improvement of material conditions. A civilization which can produce motorcars, aeroplanes, railways, steam-ships, telephones, telegraphs, radios and cinematographs is generally regarded as advanced. But the enlightened few in every age have seen that true civilization is something more than material development—that it is spiritualization—that all these material things are only instruments for giving the leisure and opportunity for the development of the spirit. Just as the progress of a plant is towards something more than the very necessary and useful stalk and is towards the fulfilment of its essential nature in the flower, so the progress of the human race must be towards the fuller actualization and manifestation of the Central Spirit of the universe. The nearer the human race approaches to that Spirit the further it will have progressed. And the value of the mystical experience will be found in showing us that towards which we should aim at progressing.

We start our investigation, then, with the assumption that we are born out of and always remain part of a universe which is a living universe and animated with Spirit—that at the core is Spirit. That dynamic urge which permeates the universe from centre to circumference we have in ourselves and by it we are being continually acted upon. It burns within us. And we are bathed by it as by the sunshine from without. But there are times when this Power is peculiarly insistent and urgent within us. And there are times when it presses upon us with peculiar urgency from without. And there are rare occasions

when in rare individuals the urge from within and
the pressure from without meet and correspond.
That within an individual is reaching upward with
peculiar insistency. And the spirit from without is
pressing upon the individual with unusual potency.
There is interaction between the individual and the
whole. The individual rises to meet and respond to
the pressure of his environment. He is enthralled
by it. He enjoys the mystical experience. And in
that moment he is entering on a new state of being.

Before that he had led a pre-natal existence. Now
he is being born into the world of light and air and
sunshine. Before that he was enclosed in the bud.
Now he has burst through the bud and opened out into
the full-blown flower, enjoying the light and air and
sunshine which had all the time been acting on him.
He resembles those venturous precursors of his who
crawled from the sea on to the land and first experienced the thrill. As they ventured forth from the
dullness of the sea to the brightness of the land so
does he rise from the grey life of ordinary existence
into the glowing realm of the spirit. His unaccustomed eye may be unable long to bear the glory.
But once having experienced the thrill of the larger
existence he will want to communicate it to his
fellows. And what he has to tell us we have now to
hear so that we may have some faint inkling of what
is that higher state of being towards which we are
being propelled, but for the creation of which we
ourselves also bear responsibility.

CHAPTER I

HINDU MYSTICS

KESHUB CHANDER SEN

IN the year 1875 there met in Calcutta two of the greatest Indians of that century; and they immediately leaped to each other. Strongly contrasted as they were in a hundred particulars, each instantly recognized in the other the same craving for God; and each saw that the other had had a like experience of God. There was an affinity between them which flashed at once from the one to the other. They aroused feelings in one another which none else could. They gave a joy to each other which nothing else could excite. There were differences between them; and these differences were strong and fundamental. Yet they only served as contrasts showing up the essential characteristics of each: they were not oppositions. They did not sever the two men: they only went to unite them. And it is because of these differences which united instead of severing them that I describe these two remarkable men in their friendship.

Keshub Chander Sen was then in the height of his renown. He was a commanding figure, with a perfect knowledge of the English language and highly cultured in Western learning. Also he was one of the finest orators of his day, and his eloquence on

22

the public platform had attracted the most prominent men both in India and England. Viceroys had publicly acknowledged his gifts. In India he was the leader of a religious movement among the most cultured in the land. He had visited England and created a deep impression there, being received by Queen Victoria herself.

Ramakrishna was very different. He was only known to the smallest circle. He had no knowledge whatever of Western learning and spoke no English. He had been no farther than Benares and Calcutta. He never spoke in public. He rarely or never read. And he had no organized following.

Yet these two had a strange attraction for one another and " fell in love " with one another at sight. They were both fired with the same zeal for God—for getting right down to the heart of things—for climbing the highest heights of spiritual attainment. They each sensed that the other had experienced things of the spirit of which most men knew nothing. And they both felt that they could excite each other to the enjoyment of yet richer experience.

The meeting of these two men, each at the summit of his powers—Ramakrishna thirty-eight and Keshub thirty-six years of age—has been described in some detail by eye-witnesses. While Keshub and some of his followers were performing their religious exercises in the Belgharia garden in Calcutta a rickety hackney carriage drove up and a scantily dressed man of dishevelled appearance got out. He was accompanied by a younger man—his nephew, Hriday—who went forward to introduce him. His appearance was so unpretending and simple, and he spoke so little at first that not much notice was taken of him till, after having returned to consciousness from a state of trance into which he had been thrown while singing a hymn, he burst forth in a torrent of words which went straight to the heart of his listeners. What he said was so profound and so beautiful that they soon perceived that he was no ordinary man.

This first acquaintance with Keshub quickly matured into intimate friendship, and the intimacy between these two intensely religious men had a powerful effect on Keshub's catholic mind. These two fine Indian religious spirits instinctively leaned towards each other. They were both great learners. Both were incessantly trying to acquire all they could from other leading men. And both saw how much each had to learn from the other. Few could assimilate the inner thoughts of Ramakrishna like Keshub or benefit more by him. Especially did the remarkable tenderness with which Ramakrishna cherished the conception of God as Mother appeal to Keshub, for he himself had already conceived of God in that manner. On the other hand, none did more than Keshub to refine the exuberant religious life of Ramakrishna.

Consequently, Keshub and his followers would often go to see Ramakrishna in his temple at Dakineshwar, about six miles above Calcutta on the banks of the Ganges ; and Ramakrishna would frequently visit Keshub in Calcutta. Keshub has recorded that God had endowed his spirit with such sensitivity that the moment he drew near a saintly soul he imbibed his goodness, and as soon as the saint had left he could distinctly feel that he had poured virtue into his life : he seemed, he said, to become like the saint. Ramakrishna had the same feeling—only perhaps to an intenser degree. The very sight of Keshub, we are told by one who knew them both, was sufficient to cause an upheaval in the highly emotional soul of

Ramakrishna. His heart would be captured by the Infinite in such a manner that he would fall into a deep trance. And when he had recovered from it he would speak with such force and rapidity that the other could hardly find time to utter a single word. Thought after thought would rush into his mind, and he would have to stop the other that he might give expression to all that he had in him. It would be an unbroken flow of spiritual truth and experiences welling up from the perennial spring of his own devotion and wisdom. And the similes, the metaphors, and the illustrations would be as apt as they were original.

One occasion when Keshub went by steamer to visit Ramakrishna in his temple has been graphically described by a follower of Keshub. It was during the Maghotsav festival. The steamer was decorated with flowers. The sky was clear and blue. A delicious air was blowing. The broad bosom of the Ganges was dancing under the evening sky. Keshub and his party were chanting the name of Hari all the way; and the devotees, their hearts filled with enthusiasm and love, were performing a mystic dance round Keshub himself. At that time Ramakrishna was sitting in his simple room at one end of the temple conversing on religious subjects with a few select devotees. Suddenly he stopped and with uncontrollable emotion exclaiming, "Here comes Keshub with his party: who can sing such Kirtan but Keshub's party?" he rushed out of the room to the river bank. By now the steamer had reached the landing-place and the singing rose to a climax. It was impossible to control Ramakrishna. He dashed on to the steamer and folded Keshub into his bosom, ejaculating, "Thou art my Shyam, I am thy Radha. Thou art my Shyam, I am thy Radha."

After the first greetings he began to speak of the various ways in which he used to perform his spiritual exercises, but suddenly pulled himself up, saying there were things about secret exercises which should not be told : it was impossible to express in language the ecstasy of divine communion when the human soul lost itself in contemplation of the Deity. Then he spoke of Nirakar (formless) Brahman, and repeating the word Nirakar two or three times he quietly passed into Samadhi as the diver slips into the fathomless deep.

In this state of Samadhi his whole body relaxed and then became rigid. There was no twitching of the muscles or nerves, nor any movement of the limbs. Both his hands lay in his lap with the fingers slightly interlocked. The sitting posture of the body was easy, but absolutely motionless. The face was slightly tilted up and in repose. The eyes were nearly, but not wholly closed. The eyeballs were not turned up or otherwise deflected, but they were fixed and conveyed no message of outer objects to the brain. So far his body was inexpressive. It was in the smile that all the power of expression was concentrated. The lips were parted in a beatific and indescribable smile. And there was something in that wonderful smile that could never be reproduced.

Keshub and his party gazed in silence for several minutes on the motionless form of the saint. Then Keshub's singing apostle began to sing a hymn to the accompaniment of a drum and cymbals. And as the music swelled in volume Ramakrishna slowly opened his eyes and looked round him as if he were in a strange place. The music stopped. He asked who those about him were. Then he vigorously slapped the top of his head crying out, " Go down, go down ! " He gradually became fully conscious, sang a hymn and then gave a lucid exposition on how the voice should be trained. And no one made mention of the trance.

How did these two men, so unlike in many respects and leading such different lives, come so near each other in the end ? What was the initial disposition of each ? And by what way, and through what struggles and sacrifices, had the two converged towards the same spiritual summit ? These are the questions we have now to answer. And first we will study the character and career of Keshub Chander Sen.

Keshub Chander Sen was born in Calcutta in 1838. The Sens are of Vaidaya caste, of high position in Bengali society, wealthy and cultured. As a boy he was gentle, shy and reserved, though conscious of his own importance. He was good-looking, had great intelligence and at school worked hard and won prizes. But in those early years among his boy companions he was not warm-hearted, he made no bosom friends, and was not religious. He showed no precocious spirituality.

His education was received at the Hindu College, Calcutta, a good school of the aristocratic type. And there he already showed a decided turn for initiation and leadership—his self-will and indefatigability in overcoming opposition early displaying themselves. He had always been fond of making up *jatras*, popular semi-theatrical performances. More for entertainment than for any religious purpose he would make up the Ram Jatra representing scenes from the great religious poem, the Ramayana. And later he established classes for reading, reciting, and playing scenes from Shakespeare—he himself taking the leading part, and being more particularly fond of the part of Hamlet. To Shakespeare he was particularly addicted,

27

though he also read Milton, Bacon and other English writers, and much philosophy.

He has given a picture of himself as he was in those days of dawning manhood. The background was of deep, intense black. In sorrow, anxiety, asceticism his religious life began. All the pleasures which youth enjoys he shunned as poison. To his body he said : " Thou art the road to perdition : I will rule thee, or thou wilt lead me to death." To be worldly was, in his eyes, sinful. To be fond of his wife was sinful. He did not weep, but he lived on without a smile. Though he was married at eighteen his wife, then a girl of ten, had not yet come to live with him. Now, when he was twenty and leaving College she was coming. He was about to enter the world. Danger was ahead. The end was to be in joy ; but the beginning was in melancholy. He resolved never to be over-fond of his wife or of the world.

His biographer, Muzoomdar, describes him at this time as tall, thin, lanky, bony, morose, sad, and stern. Novel-reading was an abomination to him. Love-songs he abhorred. He ate neither fish nor meat, and was, indeed, for the rest of his life a vegetarian. He spoke little. His neighbours blamed him for being a proud, contemptuous, unsociable young man. And though he read much, he read only austere books of moral philosophy or fiery Christian sermons by Blair and Chalmers. He matured his morality before he began his religion.

How his religion began it is not easy to trace. It seems to have come through prayer. He did not know what the right religion was, or what the true Church. But he felt the supreme necessity for prayer.

" Why or for what I prayed I did not know," he wrote. " But in the first glimmer of light I heard the voice, ' Pray, pray ; without prayer there is no other

way.' . . . I felt a longing for something higher.
The consciousness of sin was awakened within me.
But I felt that I had a Heavenly Friend always near
to succour me. God Himself told me this—no book,
no teacher but God Himself in the secret recesses of
my heart. He gave me the secret of spiritual life, and
that was prayer. And to this I owe my conversion."

He at once began composing forms of prayers for
every morning and evening and used them daily,
although he was not yet a member of any Church and
had no clear conception of God.

His elder brother who was his intimate guardian
tried to ridicule him, to argue him out of this melancholy state, and to put him down with a high hand,
as elders can do in an Indian household. But nothing
availed with Keshub. It seemed as if he was under
the operation of impulses he could not control. Soon
he began to feel the need of communion with friends
from whom he could receive spiritual assistance and
comfort, and with this object in view, in 1857, while
he was still at the Hindu College, he established a
little Society which he called the Goodwill Fraternity.
In speaking before this little brotherhood he found a
wholesome vent for his sombre moods. And in reading to it a sermon on Inspiration by Theodore Parker
he showed that beneath his brooding melancholy an
intense fire was hiddenly burning. One evening five
or six young men with Keshub in the lead gathered in
the Sen family mansion doors, and in the dim light of
an oil lamp each one poured forth his innermost yearnings in sincere prayer. Keshub spoke and they all
wept and ejaculated aloud. A nameless solemnity
filled every heart. For the first time the Eternal
Spirit of God seemed to them a hallowed presence.
This Goodwill Fraternity continued its activity for

a couple of years. Keshub would often preach extempore in English. All his intelligence, energy and
moral earnestness were set aflame by the zeal that was
burning so fiercely within him. He would speak loud
and long, pouring forth a torrent of words. And
many young men were drawn by them.

And now there appears upon the scene a stately
figure who was to play a decisive part in Keshub's life.
Another of the great families in Calcutta are the
Tagores (of which the poet Rabindranath Tagore is
the most famous representative). In Keshub's time
the chief was Davendranath Tagore, a typical, digni-
fied head of a household. And this princely personage,
attended by liveried servants, once appeared at a Good-
will Fraternity meeting, thus greatly encouraging the
young men. For with all his worldly appearance he
was a man of profound religious feeling. He was leader
of the Brahmo Somaj, a small but important religious
body which had been founded a quarter of a century
previously by that great reformer, Ram Mohun Roy,
and had attracted to its ranks many of the Western-
educated and more liberal-minded men of the time.

To this body Keshub himself had lately been
attracted. A pandit had lent him a small publica-
tion of the Brahmo Somaj, and in a chapter of it
entitled " What is Brahmoism ? " he had found that
inner correspondence of spirit which for him amounted
to a revelation. He privately signed the Brahmo
Somaj covenant. Davendranath Tagore, who always
tried to persuade young men of influential families to
join the Somaj, was much gratified to hear of Keshub's
spontaneous adhesion, and it was to show his interest
that he had come to the Fraternity meeting.

But trouble lay ahead for Keshub with his family
over this adhesion to an unorthodox religious body.

And the opposition of his family is a terrible thing to
a young Hindu, for the head of a family is believed
to be given that position in trust from God. He looks
to God for guidance in the discharge of his duties;
and he expects implicit obedience.

And as the strength of Hindu family ties will be
often referred to, a word or two about the Hindu
family is needed. The Hindu marriage is not a con-
tract but a sacrament. It is the union of souls. The
wife worships her husband as her Lord, and the husband adores her as the Divine Queen. The wife
thinks that the husband reincarnates in her son. The
son looks upon the father as God incarnate and his
mother as a goddess. An atmosphere of reverence is
thus engendered. And every member of the family
is regarded as of divine value. All are expected to
work together for the common happiness. And servants are regarded as part of the living whole—a whole
dominated by religion. All rise early, perform their
ablutions, enter the worship room, prostrate themselves before God, sing hymns, make offerings, salute
the family priest and each of the family; and it would
not be until these religious ceremonies had been performed that food would be taken. The day's work
would thus start under a religious impulse.

Probably in the case of Keshub's family many of
these customs may have fallen into abeyance. But
the family tie was still strong; and so also was the
influence of the family priest. And at this time—
about 1858—the family priest of the Sens appeared
in the family house to celebrate the rites of initiation
in religion over the young, absolution from sin over
the old, and spiritual efficacy over all. Keshub was
among the young who were marked for the ceremony
of initiation. He had expressed his disinclination to

his mother. But his guardians were determined that the initiation should take place. Great preparations were accordingly made for the ceremony. The guardians, headed by his fiery old uncle, the terror of the whole family, were assembled. Keshub's cousins went submissively through the ceremony, and the time for Keshub himself had arrived. It was a crucial moment in his life. The fatal question was put: "Wilt thou accept the ceremony of initiation as the other young men have done?"

Quiet and self-possessed he gently but firmly replied: No. More than once the question was asked and with increasing firmness. But Keshub was immovable, and the powers of orthodoxy were unable to prevail against his steady determination.

Davendranath Tagore sent to inquire the result of the dread contest, and the congratulations he sent to Keshub on hearing of the stand he had made were the basis of the remarkable friendship which grew up between these two men, and which, in spite of a soul-racking difference on Brahmo Somaj affairs, lasted until Keshub's death.

In accordance with Hindu custom Keshub now had to earn his living, and for that purpose entered the Bank of Bengal as a clerk in 1859. But two years later, in the face of strong remonstrances from his family, he resigned his clerkship in order to write tracts and deliver lectures for the Brahmo Somaj.

In his first tract he showed the baneful influence of the godless education given in the Government schools and he urged young Indians to turn to God and pray to Him for those spiritual blessings which are essential to the sustenance of the soul. And in a second tract he spoke of God as an ever-present and ever-living Reality that can be seen and felt.

Then he started a little Society named the Sangat Sava, mainly for religious conversation. Strange earnestness characterized every proceeding, says Mazoomdar, the devoted friend and biographer of Keshub. All were young men. They met frequently and with fiery zeal for self-reformation, laid bare their whole hearts, courted mutual aid and criticism, and under Keshub's guidance made genuine progress. They would sit up the whole night in Keshub's room. And though religion was new to them and they were new to each other, a burning repentance for past sins purified their hearts, joint prayers knit them together, and Keshub's eloquence and example fired them as they fired him.

Keshub also began a correspondence with Theists outside India, especially with Francis Newman and Frances Power Cobbe in England. And realizing the value of a newspaper as a means of influencing the Hindu community on religious and educational matters he started the *Indian Mirror* in 1861. Not content with this he proceeded to establish the Calcutta College in 1862. And such a reputation had he already won that in the same year, at the age of twenty-four, he was appointed Minister of the Brahmo Somaj, Davendranath Tagore saying of him at this time : " Whatever he thought in his mind he had the power to express in speech ; whatever he said, he had the power to do ; whatever he did, he had the power of making other men do."

Nevertheless, all was not running on oiled wheels without friction. And the occasion of his installation as Minister found him faced with another of those terrible obstructions which age-long Hindu traditions set up in the path of progress. He and other young Brahmos had been educating their wives and trying to instil into them the same views on religion that

33

they themselves held. On the grand occasion of Keshub's installation they determined to invite them to take part in the festivities. And Keshub went to fetch his wife from her father's house and take her to the house of Davendranath Tagore. But to this the guardians strenuously objected. The ladies of the two families had never been on visiting terms. And the guardians specially objected to giving any countenance to his accession to the Brahmo Somaj Ministry. So when he and his wife—then only about fifteen years of age—were preparing to set out for the ceremony they found the way barred. All the elder brothers, uncles and cousins residing in the family house of the Sens had come out to object. Servants and gate-keepers were posted at various points. And the big outer gates were bolted and barred. Keshub and his young wife walked past the angry relatives, who had imagined that their mere presence would deter him. And when the gate-keepers refused to let him out he simply ordered them to withdraw the bolt and unlock the gate, and, compelled by his commanding presence, they obeyed.

This was not, however, the end of the matter. Keshub had still more to suffer. The ceremonies of the installation had scarcely finished when he received a formal letter from his uncle and elder brother forbidding him to re-enter the family house and telling him that since he had deliberately outraged the feelings of his guardians he might in future shift for himself and expect nothing further from them.

To a young married couple without any means of subsistence this was a cruel blow. It was mitigated by the kindness of Davendranath Tagore, who nobly invited Keshub to live in his house as long as he liked. But it was at the cost to Keshub of domestic ostracism and the severance of his dearest family ties that the way was opened for that freer life which the women of India have since then won for themselves.

His next great enterprise was a tour through India. His ideas were expanding. He would embrace all India in the Brahmo Somaj. He lectured everywhere. And it is noteworthy that he used the English language. He seems to have been more at home in it for the expression of his ideas. And through it he was able to exercise a wider influence than he ever would have been able to exert through the medium of his own native Bengali. He was well received by Sir Bartle Frere, the Governor of Bombay, and by Dr. Wilson, the veteran missionary. And he attracted large audiences.

And he was already beginning to press for those social reforms, such as permitting the marriage of widows, and intermarriage between castes, which he had so much at heart for the rest of his life. Here, however, he came up dead against his noblest friend and patron, the generous-hearted Davendranath Tagore, who could never reconcile himself to the idea of widows marrying, still less to the marriage of persons of different castes. Such revolutionary ideas were abhorrent to this old Hindu. And many of the more staid, elderly members of the Brahmo Somaj were with him. They, too, were alarmed at the new ideas and new measures which Keshub and the young men round him were introducing. Keshub was of an aristocratic family, and from long-inherited tradition reverenced the sacred caste of the Brahmins. But he was burning with youthful ardour ; and deeper still was the fiery ambition to establish a new society and found a new religion. The sensitive elders quickly divined these hidden intentions. They had already gone far in breaking with the ancient Hindu forms of worship by discarding idolatry. But they were still strict observers of the rigid caste customs regarding marriage. And they were not prepared to approve of members of the different castes mixing together, eating together, marrying together and even occupying the pulpit hitherto reserved for the sacred Brahmin caste alone.

All this feeling antagonistic to Keshub's revolutionary ideas had intensified during his absence in Bombay and Madras. And when he returned he soon sensed the trouble that lay before him. He had sincere reverence for Davendranath. But he did not open his heart to the elder, who complained that he kept his own counsel and hid behind an impenetrable reserve. There was no drawing together between the two men. There was, indeed, a drifting apart. Keshub with all his shyness and all his reverence was inflexible in purpose. And when he insisted on reforms and Davendranath opposed them, a break was sure to come.

It came over a trivial incident. A cyclone had damaged the old building of the Somaj, and the weekly Divine Service had to be held in Davendranath's private house. This was in November 1865. When Keshub arrived he found that the assistant minister who had been deposed for retaining the sacred thread of the Brahmin caste had been reinstated by Davendranath a few minutes before Keshub's arrival and was installed in the pulpit. Keshub warmly protested against this irregularity. Davendranath replied that as the Service was being held in his private house he could make what arrangements he liked. Keshub insisted that worship was public. He declined to join in the Service, and left the house. Thus began the act of secession from the parent Somaj.

Keshub did not actually at the moment mean to make a definite break. He proposed a separate day

36

of public worship in the Somaj building for himself and his friends. And he endeavoured to arrange united festivals during the anniversary. But Davendranath was inexorable. Old Hindus can be very stubborn. And young Hindus can be very fiery. There was no prospect of reconciliation. The warm Indian affection between the two remained—and remained till death. But in the matter of reforms the breach was final.

Having thus broken away from the old Somaj, Keshub now went ardently and resolutely ahead with his new idea and in 1866 established a Brahmo Somaj for all India with a constitution by which the members might control their own affairs and elect their own officers and thus be free of the autocratic rule of a few favoured individuals. Membership was to be open to men and women of every race or community who wished to join. Selections from the Scriptures of all nations were compiled in a text-book of devotional lessons. And for the first time extracts from the Bible, Koran, Zend-Avesta, and the Hindu Shasters stood side by side as the Scriptures of the Brahmo Somaj.

He also now came out in startling prominence as a speaker. At Calcutta, in March 1866 he announced a lecture on " Jesus Christ, Europe and Asia." The hall he engaged was packed with both Europeans and Indians.

" Verily, Jesus was above ordinary humanity," he said. "And was not Jesus an Asiatic ? I rejoice, yea, I am proud that I am an Asiatic. Christianity was founded and developed by Asiatics in Asia. And when I reflect on this my love for Jesus becomes a hundred-fold intensified. I feel Him nearer my heart and deeper in my national sympathies. . . . In Christ we see not only the exaltedness of humanity but also the grandeur of which Asiatic nature is susceptible.

The more this fact is pondered, the less I hope will be the antipathy of European Christians to Oriental nationalities and the greater the interest of Asiatics in the teachings of Christ."

This striking lecture aroused both resentment and approbation. The parent body of the Brahmo Somaj from which he had seceded looked upon it as an indication that he was seeking shelter under the Christian missionaries and congratulated themselves that they had weeded him out. And Keshub keenly felt the criticisms made upon him. On the other hand, the Viceroy, Lord Lawrence, was so pleased with the lecture that he intimated to Keshub that he wished to make his personal acquaintance when he returned to Calcutta.

Along with these outward activities great internal changes were taking place in Keshub. In his early religious development there had been plenty of faith and enthusiasm, asceticism and moral rigour, but not much joy or love of God. In the beginning of 1867 his nature took a sudden change, according to Mazoomdar. The separation of tender ties with Davendranath Tagore, the unpopularity following upon the lecture on Jesus Christ, the absence of worldly resources, and even of a place of worship, the vacillations and differences among his own companions, joined perhaps to a sense of his own sins and shortcomings, created a crisis in Keshub's soul. And about this time he began to hold daily Services in his house in order to find spiritual comfort in his trials. At these Services the emotions of his powerful nature were stirred to the depths. Hitherto he had had an abundance of moral austerity, acute intelligence, and fiery enthusiasm. Now he had an extreme tenderness of devotional sentiment. And he hailed this ecstasy of a new life with all the ardour of his nature.

To add to the intensity of his fervour he imparted the spirit of the Vaishnava religion into the Brahmo devotions. Vaishnava hymns (Sankirtan) adapted to Vaishnava tunes and sentiment were introduced ; and the Vaishnava drum, cymbals and violin were used. A new world of religious feeling was thus opened up, and a new spiritual relationship made with the popular Bengali prophet, Chaitanya.

And a tremendous impetus to the musical development was given by the adhesion of Trylokynath Sanyal—afterwards known as the singing apostle. He would improvise tunes, and compose new hymns to suit Keshub's sermons and prayers. And his melodious voice would touch the hearts of his hearers.

This new phase culminated in the Festival in God of November 1867. Keshub on this occasion threw himself rapturously into the excitement. It came to him as a strange inspiration which he could not resist. He loudly sang, though his natural shyness had never allowed him to do this before. Never before had he wept, but now streams of tears ran down his face. He had become a new man.

A few months later—in 1868—he went to Monghyr, where unexpectedly and unsought a veritable Revival took place. He held the ordinary Services in a little bungalow which he had rented. These Services were from the first numerously attended. But week by week the congregation increased. Often the members were moved to tears, and sobs, and to ejaculations that were almost hysterical. The women vied with the men in expressing their devotions. Even people from the bazaar were attracted. Processions perambulated the streets by night, as well as by day, and sang at the ghats by the riverside. The whole town was in a ferment. Some danced. One or two fell into fits of unconsciousness. Not a few saw visions. Several left their worldly vocations and joined the missionary body.

It was a new experience. And the love of the members for one another was unusually developed. They embraced and fell at each other's feet. And these feelings were intensified to the utmost pitch in relation to Keshub. They prostrated themselves before him. They talked of him in extravagant terms as "lord," "master," "saviour." And they openly alluded to him as one of the prophets like the Buddha, or Chaitanya.

This caused alarm to some members. They wrote to the papers charging his admiring disciples with worshipping Keshub, and accusing Keshub himself of conniving at it. And in this accusation there may have been a grain of truth. Privately, the shy, reserved Keshub revolted against anything of the kind. But he, also, was never wanting in a consciousness of his destiny or of his great powers. He was convinced that men would have to recognize his unique place in the Brahmo Somaj and that they would have to give him unquestioning honour. And in this present Revival he felt that his opportunity had arrived, his mission had been revealed to him, and that the response he had long waited for had been inspired in those about him by the grace of God. It was testimony that the Spirit of God was with him, and that his work was true and his time had come.

This Revival at Monghyr did, indeed, make deep and abiding impressions upon Keshub. He saw the direction in which the religion of the Brahmo Somaj could be made popular in the land. And it created for the first time that mystical feeling and that faith in an active special Providence which from now onward ran as undercurrent in all his activities. He felt assured, too, that the lop-sided intellectual education which the rising generation had so deeply imbibed, the scepticism which it generated, and the materialistic and irreverent tendencies which Western civilization daily spread could be counteracted only by those violent upheavals of the devotional sentiment towards God which are so characteristic of India.

From these intensely spiritual gatherings Keshub was now called to the more matter-of-fact business of helping the Government of India to draft a law regulating Hindu marriage. In the previous winter he had met Lord Lawrence, who had indeed attended one of his eloquent lectures. And now the Viceroy had invited him to Simla as his guest. Keshub assisted the Government officials in their work. But for his deeper self the Himalaya was a greater attraction. He saw the great mountains for the first time. And he thought of the ages when they were the abode of the holiest and wisest men of India. He felt himself the descendant and successor of these saints. And he wrote an exhortation under the title "A Voice from the Himalaya," urging men to rise from their death-like sleep and let their ears hear the joyful sound of salvation and their eyes drink the sweet light of the new day.

From Simla he returned to Calcutta. The Brahma Mandir, his new place of worship, was formally opened in August 1869. It was, he declared, founded with the object that all quarrels, all misunderstandings, and all pride of caste might be destroyed, and brotherly feeling perpetuated.

Suddenly, at the end of 1869, he announced that he was going to England. He left Calcutta in February 1870 and reached London in March. It is not necessary to say much about this visit, for we are con-

cerned especially with his spiritual history. We need
only note that he had a phenomenal success—all the
more remarkable considering he was still only thirty-
two. Lord Lawrence, who had by now retired from
the Viceroyalty, prepared the way. The British and
Foreign Unitarian Association organized a meeting of
welcome at which Dean Stanley and several Members
of Parliament were present, and speeches of good-
will to the Brahmo Somaj were delivered. He
preached in Unitarian Churches. He delivered lectures and made speeches in many places. And so
fine was his oratory that he was compared with
Gladstone and Bright. He was received with special
graciousness by Queen Victoria, he breakfasted with
Gladstone, he was visited by John Stuart Mill, and he
most favourably impressed Lord Shaftesbury.

An impression of him at this time has been given
by Miss Frances Power Cobbe, who then saw much of
him. She describes him as the most *devout* man with
whom she had ever come in contact. What profoundly impressed her was not so much his intellect
as his goodness. He seemed really to *live* in God and
to feel the joy of prayer as quite the greatest thing
in life. He told her, indeed, that when he prayed he
felt that his union with God was eternal. In outward
appearance he seemed to her to be the ideal of a great
teacher. He had a tall, manly figure (always clothed
in a long black robe), a handsome square face with
powerful jaw. His complexion and eyes were like a
Southern Italian's. And he had all an Eastern's
gentle dignity of manner. He spoke English quite
perfectly and made long extempore addresses without
error of any kind, or a single betrayal of foreign accent.

Keshub, on his part, was not so deeply impressed
by what he saw of Christianity in England. The

spirituality, the imaginativeness, the faith, the enthusiasm, and the asceticism of the East he saw could not be bound within the cold creeds and catechisms of Europe. They would burst their way through.

Yet he was evidently stirred by the vigour of the West. Westerners might not be so spiritual as the Indians. But they were more practical. So he returned to India bursting with reforming energy. By November he had established an Indian Reform Association " for the social and moral reformation of the Natives of India," which was divided into sections for Cheap Literature, Charity, Female Improvement, Education, and Temperance. The intelligence and refinement of the women of England had impressed him, so he established a Normal School for Native Ladies. In 1871 he was much occupied with the Brahmo Somaj Marriage Bill. And in 1872 he formed the Bharat Ashram for family life, a kind of religious boarding-house to which the wives and children of Brahmos from the interior were sent for training. He had noted the good points of the English home and he hoped to reproduce some of them in this institution.

But his views on women were still a little uncertain. Favourable as he was to liberating them from many social trammels he could never tolerate the idea of an artificial, strong-mannered or strong-minded womanhood. Perhaps he had been scared by some of that genus whom he had seen in England. He would rather err on the side of over-caution than of laxity. He was strongly against the University education of women. He protested against women being taught as men. They should be given an artistic, poetic education, with a practical training in domestic duties, elementary science, and the laws of health. He repudiated the popular custom of the seclusion of women, but he believed in the retirement of women. There was a mysterious zenana where the inner glories of God were made manifest.

As a reformer of caste, of the position of women, of marriage customs, of intemperance, and as a social reconstructor and educationalist his reputation was now great. He held a unique position in Calcutta. He was a member of all important Committees. And the Viceroy, Lord Northbrook, visited him in his own home.

Yet he had his critics. A number of his followers suspected that his main motive was the establishment of his own autocracy. They objected to his teachings on Special Providence, arguing that it was unreasonable to suppose that God should be specially gracious. The more rationalistic among them were also greatly shocked at his doctrine that the Holy Spirit directly commanded and guided devotees on all important emergencies of life. They protested, too, against some of his social reforms, while, on the other hand, they complained that he was not sufficiently favourable to the emancipation of women. Holding these views, they contemplated starting a rival organization. And though this idea did not take form they gradually ceased to attend the Mandir.

All this pained Keshub beyond measure. And perhaps, after all, the true bent of his nature may not have been so much towards those practical social reforms which his literary and personal contact with the West had stirred him to inaugurate as towards those deeper underlying reforms of the spirit so much nearer to his own Indian nature. At any rate, from now on he thought far less of social reform and much more of religious reform, and threw his whole soul towards foundational things of the spirit.

In 1875, the very year that he met Ramakrishna,

and when he was still only thirty-seven, he suddenly became melancholy again as he had been in his youth. He was saddened at the sight of so much worldliness. He insisted that his missionaries must practise asceticism and strict discipline. An intenser course of spiritual life was required, more renunciation, a stricter poverty, longer hours of devotion.

Brahmoism so far had been somewhat free and easy. Keshub now introduced Vairagya (asceticism), and there was an unceasing development in that direction in 1876. He returned to the point he had reached in 1869 before he went, at Lord Lawrence's invitation, to Simla and afterwards to England. He became in a word less English and more Indian. He once more fervently embraced Vaishnavism with its enthusiasm and excitement, its *Bhakti* (love of God), its vehement singing and dancing and its street processions.

His ideal of piety became an intoxication and madness in God. There were three natures in him, he said—three persons—the one a child, the second a madman, the third an inebriate. And in this union, he affirmed, he had gained wonderful wisdom and holiness. The more a man sought God the more childlike he became; the more a man communed with God the more like a madman he appeared; and the more he tasted of Heaven the more inebriate he grew. He liked to go where devotees, like madmen, sang and danced in the excitement of God's name. And he had the same passion as an inebriate. An inebriate always increases his dose. So did Keshub. Formerly his devotions took five minutes. Now they took five hours. Formerly any kind of wine did for him. Now he wanted strong wine, such as was drunk by Jesus and Chaitanya. And he waited for the day when the whole East and West would become

45

maddened and inebriated by the love of God. So he said in his autobiography, the Jeevan Ved.

And he would not only sing ; he who was formerly so shy and reserved would join with those who *danced* in their enthusiasm of singing the name of God. He would laugh and cry in the ecstasy of his devotions. He would not allow his reasoning powers any authority over his devotional fervour ; and he expressed the greatest contempt for the intellect in regulating the relations between the devotee and his God. Reason was out of court there. Relationshipwith God was the province of faith and love, and he willingly allowed himself to be carried away by the impulses of his love. Men laughed at him, but he laughed back and said they didnot know what it was they were laughing at.

Direct and immediate intercourse with the soul of God was the distinctive feature of his religion. He subordinated every act of his life and every duty to his prayers. From now to his death the best part of the day was spent in the daily service of his household sanctuary. That sanctuary became the darling object of his heart. He adorned it in every conceivable way. After his early morning ablutions he would go into the garden, pluck the best flowers and place them by the pulpit. The firstfruits of the year were also placed there—and the drum, the cymbals and the one-stringed violin of the singing apostle.

As in his early youth so now he had a wonderful faith in the efficacy of prayer. Through prayer a man gained new wisdom, new insight, fresh flow of heart, and greater force of will. And he not only prayed ; he wanted and waited for answer to his supplication. And he went by the answer he received. He believed in divine command (Adesh)— though not a few of his friends ridiculed such an idea.

He assiduously cultivated the habit of realizing the Spirit of God in everything. He would address flowers, trees, fire, water—everything that was beautiful or grand. To him they were all symbolical. And he seemed to commune with some hidden personality in them.

Woman also he spiritualized. And it was now that he acquired the idea of the Motherhood of God.

Solitary commune with God was a necessity to him. He would sit under some favourite tree and keep talking as in a trance after which, with kindling face, he would rejoin his friends.

Especially did he love the Himalaya, for there he perceived affinity between himself and the great Indian sages of the past; and he had an intense desire to establish a hermitage there and spend in it the remainder of his days. On the occasions when he went to Simla he would spend much time in absorbed communion with God. This absorption would at times become an ecstasy. He would be conscious of the presence of a Supreme Loving Personality. He would be enraptured. He would violently cry and laugh, and would talk vociferously. His friends would be alarmed at these strange excitements. But he would steadily persevere, finding in this practice the chief consolation in his physical and mental sufferings.

Describing these experiences, he wrote that this consciousness was of the soul and the Supreme Soul in one—a spiritual unification—duality in unity. The Hindu devotee with his untutored nature yet trained eye would see a Person behind all the wonders and beauties of creation, and therefore he believed, trusted, loved, and adored all at once. And what happens in a small measure to ordinary humanity,

bursts like a flood of light upon great geniuses, said
Keshub. And he illustrated the vision from the
experiences of Moses in the burning bush, and Jesus
in the heavens opening and dove descending. "To
see in an instant the very God of the Universe in a
flying bird, not only as an inspiring vital fire, but as
a blazing personal Divinity was," says Keshub, "a
feat of spiritual perception to which only the Son of
God was equal."

Yet, in addition to these solitary communings, there
was a deep necessity in his nature for ceremonial.
He intensely sympathized with the warmth and
imagery of popular Hindu worship. He was stirred
by the flowers, the lights, the music, the fragrances,
the prostrations, the joyous, enthusiastic singing of
the Hindu worship. He discarded idolatry. And
he never went to any Hindu temple. But he liked
to adopt what he could of the æsthetic features of
Hindu worship.

All this ferment of spiritual life culminated in 1878
when, at the age of forty, he again urged a Revival ;
but this time on the lines of a new revelation, a new
life, an altogether new departure—as he eventually
termed it, a New Dispensation. He felt he must
establish nothing less than a New Religion. He would
harmonize all religions. The Scriptures of Hindu,
Christian, Moslem and Buddhist were to be united in a
blessed harmony. There was to be an international
fellowship of Asia, Africa, Europe and America.

In his ideal of a National Church the religion of
Christ formed a large element—perhaps more than
half. There was to be unity of spirit but diversity
of forms. Thus India should sing the glory of God
with Indian voice and with Indian accompaniments.
And so should England and America. But all the

voices should commingle in one swelling chorus—a universal anthem proclaiming the Fatherhood of God and the Brotherhood of Man.

The greatest obstacle he met with was in regard to his doctrine of Adesh, or commandment of God. Protests were made against this idea of Divine Inspiration in the ordinary emergencies of life—as, for example, when he declared he had divine authority for agreeing to the marriage of his daughter with the Maharaja of Kuch Behar, though she was still under age. He was charged with setting himself up as a divine guide—as on a footing with Jesus or St. Paul.

This hostility roused him to intense excitement. And he proceeded to make his position clear. Inspiration, he defined as "the fire of divine life as a response to man's earnest prayers." He emphatically disclaimed any pretensions to be a prophet, but as emphatically claimed to receive inspiration.

"In my creed all precepts begin with, 'Thus saith the Lord.' But how do I know His voice ? There is a ring, a peculiar intonation in the spirit voice of the Lord. Those who have heard it often can recognize it at once. It was my God who said to me long ago, 'Thou shalt become a Theist.' It was He who said, 'Thou shalt give up all secular work, and take no thought for the morrow.' It was He who said to me, 'Thou shalt lead a simple life, and devote it to missionary work.'"

"'Tell me, Father,' he prays, 'if Thy voice is a sound, and whether it comes to us as a sound.' The response is thus worded : 'I do not speak as men speak. Yet have I a voice which all true devotees can hear. It is the Spirit's voice audible to the spirit's ear. There is neither sound, nor language, nor gesture. It is the language of the heart. Neither Hebrew, nor Greek, nor Sanskrit, nor English ; but the plain vernacular of the heart, the natural instincts, and the feelings.' "

At all times he unflinchingly maintained that conscience was the direct voice of God. And he wrote:

" We must not regard inspiration as God speaking by fits and starts, but as the perpetual breathing of His Spirit. It may be realized in individual conscience now and then, here and there, by this man or that. But the Spirit of God is ever working in us, and the flowing current of His inspiration knows no rest. Whether we hear Him or not, He speaks always. Whether we catch the rays of His inspiration or not, He shines eternally and sends forth His light for the redemption of mankind. Our position as frail beings amid the temptations of this world, renders it necessary that God should ever speak, so that we may hear Him whenever we wish, and receive inspiration whenever and wherever we need it."

This doctrine of inspiration was the foundation on which he laid his New Dispensation. And he maintained it vehemently against all opposition.

His doctrine of the Motherhood of God also received severe criticism. God addressed as Mother, and represented as speaking to the devotee as the mother would speak to her child—God regarded as the Queen of the Indian nation, proclaiming the will divine as a queen would make her proclamation to her loyal subjects, were new and startling forms, even to the Brahmo Somajists. And they were unpopular in England as well as India. But he wanted to discard the formalism and remoteness which theologians had interposed between the soul and God. He wished men to approach God as a child would approach his mother.

After long brooding and intense thought he therefore, at the anniversary meeting in January 1881, formally announced the New Dispensation with full sacramental solemnity. In March he ordained Apostles of the New Dispensation. In April he instituted a Sisterhood. And for all he formulated a definite Code of Conduct and Laws of Life. Further, he advocated the production of New Dispensation Drama and New Dispensation Dancing.

He maintained that the New Dispensation was practical, was in line with scientific development, and was ready for criticism. But he balanced these practical " European " traits with emotional " Asiatic " traits.

" The New Dispensation was profoundly emotional. It hated dryness. It was the religion of tender love and sweet affection. It afforded the fullest culture to all the highest impulses and emotions of the heart. It represented the golden age of religion, when all looked bright and joyous. The New Dispensation was transcendentally spiritual. Its eyes were naturally turned inward and saw vividly the spirit world within. It preferred the soul-kingdom to the kingdom of the sense. It abhorred materialism. It spiritualised everything it touched. It drank inspiration."

According to this New Dispensation the devotee stands face to face with the great and beautiful in nature.

" The force that bursts upon his vision is one in which all that is in the effect is summed up as in the primitive cause—power, intelligence, love and beauty. He sees himself and the universe, the *me* and the *not me*, living and moving in a central will-force—in an intelligent and loving personality. And as his cognitive faculties apprehend this almighty, all-wise, and all-good Person, his heart overflows with emotions and gratitude ; trust, reverence, wonder, love, joy and enthusiasm all surge up and sweeten his vision. And all this takes place instantly. Faith, intellect, and feeling form in a moment one eye, and the observer observes with scientific accuracy, with firm faith and with abounding joy.

"Such God-consciousness grows in vividness and joy as the mind is concentrated more on it. The massive doors of the universe are now flung open. All objects, animate and inanimate, open their inner sanctuary. The temple doors are suddenly unlocked and the Deity within shines upon the devout eye of the observer. Hitherto a thick curtain has hung over the face of the universe, veiling the wondrous secrets. Now, the curtain rolls up and the veiled God is immediately unveiled before the clear vision of the devotee. The observer and the observed, the subject and the object, the soul and the All-soul, the son and the Father hitherto stood separated. Now the observer at once removes the obstruction, pulls down the barrier and advances unimpeded to his God. A Divinity previously cognised mediately is now perceived immediately. An absent God is now a present God. The separated two thus stand before each other, face to face. Then union takes place through spiritual affinity as they approach and flow into each other. At first there is mutual attraction, then communion, then inter-communion, then absorption.

"Constant intercourse consolidates union and makes it more and more real and sweet, till at last the bond of union becomes indissoluble."

Or, again, and in what Keshub considered a higher way, union with God is obtained subjectively instead of objectively. In place of observing Nature the devotee finds his way to the unseen through depths of his inner nature. The process is thus described:

"All is tranquil and hushed within. Only a sense of self fills the soul. The devotee calls out to it to disappear. And it vanishes away. Then the Infinite bursts upon his view. He shines as something tremendously real—a burning reality. From the depths of his being this Presence surges up as the fountain of reality. From above it descends like a continual shower of inspiration. From all sides it draws near as the presence of one who is nearest and dearest. And the deeper the insight the brighter the illumination and the sweeter the Presence. The mere Presence is soon transformed into a Person with Intelligence, Love and Holiness. As the union ripens and develops the spirit-bonds become lighter and more and more of the Infinite is drawn into the finite soul. Gradually the Almighty overpowers, captivates and entrances the devotee's little soul. Father and Mother, Friend and Guide, Teacher and Saviour, Comforter and Gladdener are all combined in this one Person. And if there is any such thing as a spiritual smile it plays on His lips."

Such was the spiritual absorption into which Keshub habituated himself. But his health was failing. His forty-fifth birthday was celebrated on November 19, 1883, with great pomp and rejoicing. He received visits from the Bishop of Calcutta, Ramakrishna, and Davendranath Tagore. And we like to hear that he still, in spite of very deep differences, looked upon Davendranath as his spiritual father. He bowed his head at Davendranath's feet, and took his hand and put it on his head as if courting his benediction. On his side Davendranath lovingly embraced him, and talked to him of the mercy of the Heavenly Father.

But this proved to be his last birthday celebration. His illness increased, and in January 1884 he died.

And he died at the top of his fame. Even his most ardent admirers were astonished at the unexpected testimony to the esteem in which he was held. From

the Queen of England and the Viceroy of India down
to the humblest member of his flock condolences
poured in on his family. And public meetings were
held to commemorate his achievements.

This great tribute from the West as well as from
the East was given to Keshub Chunder Sen. Yet, as
a fact, he had been steadily moving from the teachings
and traditions of the West towards the deeper traditions and more congenial ways of life and thought of
the East. Shakespeare, and science and English
philosophy so prominent in his youth, faded away in
his middle age. Jesus indeed remained ; for Jesus
was an Asiatic. But in place of the great English
writers had come Chaitanya, the sweet saint of Bengal,
and Ramakrishna, the very personification of all that
was distinctively Indian.

II

RAMAKRISHNA

On hearing of the death of Keshub, Ramakrishna
was deeply afflicted and said : " The death of Keshub
has taken half my own life away. He was like a
great banyan tree. He gave comfort and shelter to
thousands of souls. We are so many palm trees
incapable of sheltering a single soul."

Whether or not the difference between these two
religious geniuses is best expressed by comparing
Keshub to the umbrageous banyan tree and Ramakrishna to the thin palm tree, the two were very different from one another, yet also with a semblance.
A banyan and a palm, different as they may be, are
both trees—and both tropical trees. Ramakrishna and
Keshub were both Indians, and both Bengalis and both
tropical in the exuberance of their spiritual growth.

Unlike Keshub, Ramakrishna was religiously disposed from childhood. He was of the priestly Brahmin caste. Both his parents were genuinely religious. And he himself, from his earliest days, showed strong religious proclivities.

He was born in February 1836 in the small Bengal village of Kamarpukur. He always had a wayward spirit, with strong likes and strong aversions. But he was a sweet-natured, healthy, intelligent, vivacious, graceful little boy with great fascination. Women especially adored him—and evidently did their best to spoil him. But at the village school he was beloved by both boys and masters. A highly attractive boy he must have been—though with a will of his own, and with these strong aversions. At school, for instance, and right up into his manhood, he could not endure mathematics. Such study was wholly against his grain. On the other hand, he loved mythological stories from the sacred books and not only seeing, but acting in sacred dramas.

The performance of religious drama is easier in India than it is in Europe. There is no need there for elaborate staging. In those days strolling minstrels would pass through the villages reciting stories from the Hindu epics and the Puranas ; and the villagers, without any stage-setting, would act them. Ramakrishna would listen with rapt attention and mark every pose of the actors. And so wonderful was his memory that he would repeat these dramas almost verbatim. He would study the lives and characters of spiritual heroes. And he would gather the folklore of his own and neighbouring villages. Also from the potters he would learn the art of moulding images of gods and goddesses and from the painters he would learn how to paint them.

This was his real education, and how highly impressionable he was to nature as well as to art is exemplified in the well-known story of the effect upon him of the sight of a flight of cranes. It is told in his own words :

" One day, when I was six or seven years old, I was walking through the rice-fields, and on looking up I saw a sombre thunder-cloud rapidly spreading over the whole sky. In front of it flew a flight of snow-white cranes. And they presented such a beautiful contrast that my mind wandered off to far away regions. Lost to outward sense, I fell. And some people finding me in that plight carried me home in their arms."

This was the first of the trances of which an account has already been given. His people were greatly alarmed. But he was quite well when he regained consciousness. And he reassured them that he had only lost consciousness because his mind had been overpowered by an inexpressible joy.

Soon he found a new source of pleasure—consorting with itinerant holy men. The village was situated on the road to Puri, a great place of pilgrimage. And pilgrims, wandering monks, and others would frequent the rest-house which had been built for them. Ramakrishna loved to go there and hear their prayers and songs, listen to their stories of the saints, and hear of the different holy places. He knew of their strange life, their indifference to bodily pain or pleasure, their renunciation of the world, their devotion to God, and their contentment with whatever food was offered them. And he delighted to hear their religious discussions, learn their songs, join in their prayers, sometimes even partake of their food, and often assist them by fetching water and fuel.

Thus did he, while still very young and as malleable as melting wax, have imprinted on him the ancient traditions of the Hindus. He was born a Hindu. He was now growing up and was to remain for all his life a Hindu of the Hindus. Keshub was brought up under strong Western influence. But Ramakrishna in his upbringing had not a trace of anything but Hindu culture.

Another incident shows his impressionability to this Hindu culture. He had set out with a party of women to worship a goddess who was held in great veneration by the people of a neighbouring village and was singing songs in praise of the goddess when suddenly he was overcome with religious emotion, his body became stiff and motionless, tears rolled down his cheeks, and he made no response to the frightened women when they called upon him. Some splashed water in his face. Others fanned him. There was no result. Then they called upon the goddess. And after repeating her name only a few times the boy showed signs of returning consciousness. Presently he was himself again and no harm seemed to have been done him.

He was now nine. The time had come to invest him with the holy thread of the Brahmins. He then became a true Brahmin, and was supposed from henceforward to enter a new life—a life of purity and great restraint. Also he was entitled to worship the family god, Raghuvir. And this filled him with joy. When he sat down to worship the god he thought of him not as a stone figure but as God incarnate—the Creator, Preserver and Destroyer of the world. And the hours passed in worship elevated his mind and often brought him remarkable visions.

One day he was called upon in an emergency to take the part of the god Shiva in a dramatic performance.

While his friends were dressing him for the role his mind soared above the ordinary consciousness, so that when the time came for him to appear his countenance was grave and he seemed to be the living impersonation of Shiva. He had completely lost himself in the divine glory. Calm, sweet and oblivious of the pains and pleasures of the world, the great God appeared before him as the ideal of serene contemplation.

The boy stood lost in the sublimity of Shiva, dead to the surrounding world. Some village elders approached him and found him unconscious. He would have been taken for dead but for the stream of tears which fell from his eyes and for the radiance of his countenance. His friends were alarmed and tried to restore him, but in vain. The performance had to be stopped. And he did not recover consciousness till the next morning.

When questioned about these trances which were becoming more and more frequent the boy said that meditation on any deity brought the real form before his mind, and the emotion evoked thereby caused him to lose outward consciousness. His mother and relatives were at first much concerned, but his unimpaired health and bodily vigour gradually set their minds at ease. And though he was thus overpowered, there was no interference with his daily routine.

One of his occupations was producing sacred plays. He passed much of the day in company with a group of other village boys. Their favourite retreat was a mango grove. Here, Ramakrishna selected a number of young boys who could sing and formed them into a dramatic company ; and they would perform episodes from the *Ramayana* or *Mahabharata*. He would select the part of each actor and take that of hero for himself. His favourite themes were the various incidents in the life of Krishna, especially his sports with cowherds and the milkmaids of Vrindavan. With his fair complexion and flowing hair, with a garland about his neck and a flute at his lips, he would take the part of Krishna himself and he would be overwhelmed with emotion and fall into frequent trances.

Then, again, he would cheer the women-folk by his lively and amusing ways. He would act plays for them and sing religious songs which he had picked up. His natural ways and adaptability made them forget his sex; and his nature at this time became amazingly feminine.

Often in fun he would go about in the guise of a girl carrying a water-jug ; and though he walked with people who knew him from birth they would scarcely recognize him. And his merriment and jests were enjoyed by all.

Now, as throughout life, he had an astonishing capacity for getting inside the very nature of others —for entering their inmost selves and becoming them for the time being. It was a capacity for deep insight. And with it went great directness and outspokenness. His nature was genuine to a degree, and he would speak his mind with utter frankness.

He was more serious, too, than appeared. He was beginning to feel that he was destined to fulfil some great mission in life. He did not know what. But the monastic life had a great attraction for him. Even as early as this, to experience God seemed to him the only purpose worth holding. If it had not been for his mother and brothers he would have liked to renounce everything, take the begging bowl, and fare forth like the Sadhus of whom he had seen so much.

But he had to do something towards earning a living. The difficulty was that he could never bring himself to attend to school teaching. Book learning, apart from the sacred plays, was wholly repugnant to him. All that could be done for him was to take him off to Calcutta where he might help his eldest brother in the performance of his duties as a family priest. And this indeed he did. He showed great diligence and conspicuous devotion. Still he would not study, though he was now seventeen. And when his brother admonished him he replied : " Brother, what shall I do with a mere bread-winning education ? What I want is that wisdom which will illumine my heart, and having won which I shall be satisfied for ever." He looked about him in the great city and saw everyone running after the transitory pleasures of the world. Survival of the fittest was the principle that guided men. Precious human life was being wasted. Spirituality was ignored. The holy books were looked upon as mere superstition. And the education which was offered Ramakrishna tended in the same direction. He looked at his brother's books. He looked at the scholars. He asked himself : " Shall I obtain piety and divine fervour by pursuing this education ? Will it enable me to be as God-fearing a man as my father ? Shall I be able to escape from clinging to the senses ? " To all of which questions he replied, No. " Then what shall I do with this education which cannot help me to see God or to transcend the miseries of the world ? I would rather remain ignorant all my life than throw away my cherished ideals."

So he said to himself. But it was a hard position for his eldest brother who, now the father was dead, was, in the severe Indian fashion, responsible for the family. And even when two years later he was able to get for Ramakrishna a position as priest to the newly erected Dakshineswar temple, Ramakrishna was not entirely satisfied and was at first averse from committing himself even to priestly duties. He was convinced that there was nothing worth doing except conquest of the flesh, renunciation of wealth, and the attainment of God-consciousness—or, as we might better express it, direct experience of God. And he supposed that the ceremonial duties expected of a priest would not leave him sufficient time or freedom for this main object of his life. However, arrangements were made by which his nephew, Hriday, would assist him, and he accepted the position.

The temple is dedicated to the goddess Kali, and is situated on the banks of the Ganges about four miles north of Calcutta. And by this sacred river of the Hindus Ramakrishna was destined to remain for the rest of his life with only a few brief intervals for pilgrimage or for recuperation in his native village. Except perhaps in the Himalaya, a more perfect spot for leading a spiritual life could hardly be found ; and Ramakrishna availed himself of it to the full. Much of his time was spent in worship of the goddess, but much also in meditation in a grove close by the temple and in the temple garden. In addition, he had opportunities of converse with those who came to worship and with itinerant monks who came to enjoy the hospitality of the temple. And we Europeans must remember that the hot, humid atmosphere of Bengal, enervating and exhausting as it must be to us, is to the Bengalis exceedingly well adapted for commune with nature. It is not so scorchingly hot as is the hot weather of Northern India. Nor is it so piercingly cold in the cold weather. Life can be lived in the open air all the year round. All the year round the vegetation is beautiful. And ever rolling by were the majestic waters of the Ganges, impressive enough even to a stranger but full of inspiration to a Hindu.

Here was Ramakrishna installed for life. And it was soon observed that his mode of worship of the goddess differed from that of the ordinary Brahmin. He would look upon the image as the veritable representation of God and treat it as such. When he seated himself for worship a veil of oblivion would separate him from the rest of the world. He would be wholly unconscious of those attending the service. Sometimes he would sit motionless for hours ; and it would be with difficulty that he could be recalled to ordinary consciousness. While uttering the various mantras he would distinctly see those phenomena which to the ordinary priest were but phantoms of the imagination.

Thus while chanting the mystic syllable *Rang* which directed the priest to conceive of a wall of fire around him, Ramakrishna would really feel himself in the midst of a circle of fire guarding him from all evil influence.

Again, he would actually feel the mystic power called the Kundalini, or " the coiled up," rushing from its place of rest at the lower extremity of the spinal column, along the spinal cord to the thousand-petalled lotus of the brain. The radiant glow of his face at the time of worship, his deep concentration and the atmosphere of purity about him suggested to the onlookers the idea that the very spirit of Brahmanahood was being manifested there before their eyes. No one had ever before seen such intensity of devotion.

Besides this worship in the temple Ramakrishna spent long hours in meditation. His friends were troubled by his love for solitude and growing indifference to the world. Instead of taking part in the festivities of the temple he would pass his leisure hours in the groves, sitting silent under a tree far away from the bustle of life. Worse still, he would take solitary walks in the quiet of the early morning along the banks of the Ganges. And worst of all, he would disappear at night. What he did then no one knew, so his nephew followed him once to see. He found he went into the grove. At first Hriday dared not disturb him there. Eventually he summoned up courage and entered the jungle, and was startled to find Ramakrishna under a tree in deep meditation, and without clothes or the sacred thread. He asked him why he had thus given up his clothes and the sacred thread. There was no response. He might as well have addressed a statue. But when Ramakrishna returned to ordinary consciousness he told Hriday that one should be free of all ties in thinking of God. The sacred thread meant that he was a Brahmin, and therefore superior to all. When calling upon the Mother one must set such ideas aside. A remarkable speech for a Brahmin to make.

And at this time he was deeply affected by the death of his eldest brother. He was young when his father had died, so did not much feel it. But he had been very deeply moved when he was a little older by the death of a brother's wife. He was of an exceptionally affectionate nature. These domestic afflictions hurt him cruelly. And the last happened to come at a time when he was in a state of spiritual upheaval. He had been impressed with the transitory nature of the phenomenal world. And he was wanting to devote all his energies to the search for something that was real and imperishable. He was convinced that man could transcend the miseries and evils of life only by reaching the sweet perennial fountain of all bliss ; and his yearnings to experience God were becoming insistent. While those about him were wasting time in all kinds of frivolity he was burning day and night with a consuming thirst for God.

Kali had now become his favourite deity. Every day at the time of worship he would decorate her image with flowers and sandal-paste. This image was a rare piece of sculpture with its lovely figure and divine expression. She was arrayed in a gorgeous robe of gold brocade and decorated with precious ornaments from head to foot. From her neck hung a garland of skulls and round her waist was a girdle of human arms, made of gold. In her lower arms (she had two right arms and two left arms) she held a decapitated human head—also made of gold—and in the upper a sword. With her lower right hand she offered boons to her devotees. With the upper she symbolised, "Fear nothing." The skulls and the sword represented her terrible side. And her right hand offered boons and fearlessness. And to Ramakrishna the image was not inert stone : it was the Mother herself—the Mother, like Nature, both terrible and sweet, alternately destroying and creating.

This was the goddess whom Ramakrishna worshipped. The Preserver as well as the Destroyer. And to him she was always the loving Mother. Full of power, but also of motherly solicitude, and sweet and tender. The Mother, who with loving care protected her devotees from harm. And to her he offered a whole-souled devotion, regarding her as the only true guide in times of doubt and darkness. Thus the vision of the Divine Mother became the one passion of his life. This was how he would experience God.

But he had a strange way of worshipping. The singing of devotional songs was one of its features. These seemed to open the flood-gates of his heart and he would weep like a child separated from its mother, and cry : "Oh ! Mother, where are thou ? Am I a wretch, that thou dost not reveal thyself to me ?

Wealth, pleasures, friends I want not. Only thee, Mother, do I desire." He would rub his face against the ground in his agony. And in the evenings he would cry : " Another day of this short life has passed and still I have not realized the Truth. Another day is spent in vain, Mother, for I have not seen thee." His plaintive cries would attract people and move them to tears, and they would whisper : " Poor young man ! Has he really lost his mother ? "

" Oh ! what days of suffering I passed through," said Ramakrishna, years afterwards. " I knew that the Mother, full of a bliss compared with which all earthly possessions were as nothing, was then quite close to me. So how could I be satisfied with anything else ? I had to seek her. And I became mad for her."

People did indeed think that he was really becoming mad. He was ridiculed at first. But even though they regarded him as unbalanced they respected and admired him on account of his steady devotion. As for Ramakrishna himself he was quite indifferent to what people said. He directed all his energies to the great goal he had set himself. And in time his devotion had its reward. The longed-for vision came.

" I was suffering excruciating pain because I had not been blessed with a vision of the Mother. I felt as if my heart was being squeezed like a wet towel. I could not bear the separation any longer. Life did not seem worth living. Suddenly my eyes fell on the sword that was kept in the temple. Determined to put an end to my life, I jumped like a madman and seized it, when suddenly the blessed Mother revealed herself to me, and I fell unconscious on the floor. What happened externally after that I do not know. But within me there was a steady flow of undiluted bliss, altogether new. I was feeling the presence of the Divine Mother."

Another description he gave of the same experience was this :

" The buildings with their different parts, the temple and all vanished from my sight, leaving no trace whatever. In their stead was a limitless, infinite, effulgent ocean of Spirit. As far as the eye could reach, its shining billows were madly rushing towards me with a terrific noise. In the twinkling of an eye they were on me. I was completely engulfed. I panted for breath and fell down unconscious."

As soon as he regained consciousness he called aloud, " Mother, Mother."

Thus at last did he gain his heart's desire. And it is to be noted that it was his tremendous faith, his intense conviction that God alone was the source of bliss, that carried him through and sustained him in all his trials and afflictions. Without a teacher or helper, with no great knowledge of the Scriptures, and even without passing through the usual course of asceticism he obtained the vision.

Ramakrishna had realized his ambition. He might now have been content. But he was still unsatisfied. His constant prayer was for a repetition of the vision. He would roll on the ground, crying : " Mother, be gracious unto me. Reveal thyself once more." So bitterly would he cry that people would gather about him to see what was the matter. He said afterwards that he scarcely realized their presence, they looked more like shadows or painted pictures than real objects ; and he did not feel at all abashed at displaying his feelings before them.

" But the moment I lost outward consciousness,"

he said, "in a paroxysm of pain at separation from the Mother, I would find her standing before me in her matchless radiant form, granting boons to her devotees and bidding them be of good cheer. I used to see her smiling, talking, consoling, or teaching me in various ways."

Though he now lived in the world, he belonged in reality to another realm and held communion with strange, invisible beings. He was often seen conversing with the stone image of Kali as if it were really conscious. And people naturally thought him mad.

As his experience deepened, the vision of the Mother became continuous. Formerly, at the time of meditation he with difficulty gained a glimpse of her beautiful hand, feet or face. Now he saw her entire form as she spoke to him and directed him in his day's work. Formerly, he regarded the stone image of Kali as possessed of consciousness. Now the image disappeared and in its stead there stood the Living Mother herself, smiling, and blessing him. "I actually felt her breath on my hand," said Ramakrishna, "though at night when the room was lighted I never saw her divine form cast any shadow on the walls, however closely I looked."

His nephew Hriday has told of Ramakrishna's acts at this time.

"Whenever I entered the temple," he says, "I would feel a thrill, especially when my uncle was worshipping, as though there were a living Presence there. I used to watch him, and his strange manner of worship filled me with wonder and reverence, though I often questioned his sanity, for his actions were contrary to the Shastras. With eyes and chest flushed, he would move like a drunkard to the throne of the goddess, touch her chin as a sign of endearment, and begin to sing; or, taking the image by the hand he would talk, joke, laugh and even dance. Again, at the time of worship he would become so deeply absorbed in meditation that there would be no sign of external consciousness."

During this period of divine madness he could not bear to associate with ordinary men of the world; but he loved to be with devotees and join with them in their worship and song. And occasionally he would visit neighbouring temples.

His eccentricities were, however, causing much concern to the lady who had built the temple, and to her son-in-law who managed her affairs. They were devoted to Ramakrishna; but they feared for his mind, and thought a deviation from the rigid observance of continence might be beneficial to him. So they hired two women of ill-fame to enter his room and tempt him. But the moment he saw them he fled for shelter to the goddess. His chastity must never be sullied.

His mother also had now become distressed at his behaviour. She heard that it was to all intents and purposes like a madman's. She thought that in the country his strained nerves might be soothed. And she invited him back to his village. He obeyed her call. But he was gloomy and sad. His former companions had no more interest for him. His buoyancy had left him. And he used to frequent the cremation grounds, which in India are regarded as sacred, and there he would spend whole days and a great part of the night in worship and meditation.

He was now twenty-three and his mother and elder brother planned a marriage for him. Once married, his mind would not soar so high. And the responsibility of maintaining a family would steady him. A young girl was found—young indeed, for she was only five years old—and he was married to her forthwith, though the marriage ceremony did not amount to much more than a betrothal ; and it was not for some years later that she came to live with Ramakrishna at Dakshineswar.

He stayed for about two years at his native village of Kamarpukur. Then, perhaps urged by the poverty at home, he took leave of his aged mother and struggling brother and young wife and returned to Dakshineswar.

There, in 1861, he again took charge of the worship of Kali and was immediately plunged anew into the intoxication and madness of communion with God. Again he felt the same repugnance to all worldly matters. Again he prayed and meditated day and night. And again he felt those painful burning sensations of the body and suffered the same insomnia.

" Oh, through what states of mind I passed in those days," he afterwards said, " the slightest impression from outside stirred the depths of my spirit. Even a street girl appeared to me as Sita going to greet her victorious husband. An English lad standing cross-legged against a tree brought me to the thought of Krishna and I sank into deep meditation. The idea of caste lost all meaning to me. I would eat food cooked by low-caste people. In the grove I would sit, in deep meditation, with my body perfectly still, and lose all consciousness of the outside world. Birds would perch on my head. Often snakes would crawl over my motionless body. The ordinary man would not be able to bear a fraction of the tremendous fervour I felt. His body would be shattered by a quarter of the emotion. Only by seeing the Mother in some form or other could I forget my indescribable pangs. Without that vision my body could not have survived."

Now he entered a new phase.   A remarkable woman came to Dakshineswar.   She was a Sannyasini of high spiritual attainments.   He called her the Brahmini. She assured him that it was because people did not understand his blessed state that they called him mad. And this greatly comforted him.   The relationship of mother to son sprang up between them.   Both passed a great part of the day in the grove in religious conversation.   And his questions about his various spiritual experiences she would be able to answer because she had dived deep into the Scriptures and could quote the authority of similar experiences by previous seekers after truth.

Every day he would go into a trance, as they talked on spiritual matters.   And from this loss of outward consciousness, from his ecstasies during the singing, and from various other symptoms she was convinced that he had scaled the loftiest heights of the spirit. She found a strange analogy between his life and the life of Chaitanya.   Both had experienced the same tempest of divine emotion raging in their souls.

Hitherto Ramakrishna had strictly avoided association with women.   Now he actually accepted the Brahmini as his guru—his spiritual guide—in practising a difficult course of Tantrika spiritual exercise. The Tantras teach the motherhood of God and the glorification of woman.   The woman's body was looked upon as sacred, and the woman was treated with reverence, as a goddess in whom the Mother of the Universe was manifested.   The attraction between a lover and his beloved was taken as an example to emulate in the search for God.

Ramakrishna began his new course only after he had sought and received the permission of the Divine Mother.   Then he placed himself in the hands of the

Brahmini and she put him through all the prescribed exercises.

" At nightfall she would ask me to come to one of the seats. I would go, and after performing the worship of the Mother Kali, begin to meditate according to her directions. But as soon as I began to tell my beads I would be overwhelmed by divine fervour and fall into a trance. Wonderful visions I would have. Some of the exercises were so dangerous that a devotee might lose his footing and sink into moral depravity. But by the infinite grace of the Mother I was brought through unscathed."

These Tantrika rites tested his self-control to the full. But the impression they made on his mind was always one of divine bliss unalloyed by any worldly taint. To him there remained no evil as he floated in a limitless ocean of divine beatitude.

" Something rises with a tingling sensation from the feet to the head," he says. " So long as it does not reach the brain I remain conscious ; but the moment it touches the brain I am dead to the outside world. I try to relate what I feel when it goes beyond the throat, but as soon as I think it over, up goes the mind with a bound and there is an end of the matter."

Ramakrishna had again experienced God. And now devotees would come to Dakshineswar and exchange ideas with him. The tale of his tremendous experiences would fire them also. Spiritual fervour is contagious in the extreme. And they would wish to catch it from him. His holiness, his unspeakable blissfulness, his unstudied wisdom, his childlike peacefulness, his affection towards all men, and his consuming love of God deeply impressed men. And he would guide each along his respective path. Like all great teachers he would not upset their modes of thought or try to make them think alike. He would supplement but not supplant. Each should be devoted to his own ideal. Each should have sympathy for all others.

Not content with receiving devotees, Ramakrishna would also go forth to find other seekers after God and ascertain how far they had progressed towards their goal. Usually devotees are satisfied if they have experienced God in one aspect. Ramakrishna yearned to know him in every aspect. Nothing fully satisfied him. His whole life was spent in seeking God and experiencing Him in different aspects.

Now he wished to experience God in the relation of parent to child and of a girl to her lover. And while he practised these forms of worship he became possessed with the idea that he was a woman. His inherent tenderness was a help to him. And he would so forget his masculine nature, and his speech and gestures would so resemble a woman's, that the women of the household of the owner of the temple would accept him as one of themselves. He would feel the love of a mother for her child.

Then he took up the highest form of Vaishna worship—the relation between a maiden and her lover. in this worship, as the devotee becomes more intimate with the object of his adoration only the sweetness of the relation interests him. The devotee thinks of his Beloved with the same intensity with which a maiden dwells on the charms of her lover. As the maiden pursues her object with the whole energy of her soul and is happy only when she has attained her end, so also should the devotee pursue God. This is the phase of spiritual practice developed by Chaitanya and now to be practised by Ramakrishna.

A beautiful expression of this is found in the Vrindavan episode in Krishna's life, when the milkmaids of Vrindavan were madly in love with Krishna, the embodiment of beauty of every kind. They sought no personal ends, they cared not for their own happiness. Their one object was to please Krishna.

When Ramakrishna had decided to undertake this spiritual exercise he borrowed a complete outfit of women's clothing and impersonated a Gopi—a milkmaid—of Vrindavan madly in love with Krishna. And he spent six months in this state, at no time lapsing from the part he had assumed.

What is considered by most Hindus as the highest spiritual experience of all, namely, the Nirvikalpa Samadhi, now came to Ramakrishna. It did not, however, come to him naturally and spontaneously as so many other of his spiritual experiences had come to him. He was "initiated" into it by a guru.

There came to the garden of Dakshineswar, in about the year 1866, an itinerant monk noted for his experience of Brahma. He was believed to be a Punjabi by birth and had renounced the world while still young. For a time he had belonged to a monastery of the Nago sect at Ludhiama in the Punjab—a sect which is renowned for their austerity and power of endurance. He was tall and of robust constitution, and had always led an out-of-door life. Like other members of his sect he considered fire particularly sacred. Wherever he might be he would keep a lighted fire by him. In the dead of night he would brighten the fire, and taking his seat by it, sink into deep meditation. All he possessed was a water-pot, a pair of tongs, a skin to sit on, and the sheet in which his body was wrapped.

He seems to have studied the Vedanta and he had

received spiritual instructions from his guru at a very early age. Man since birth is fettered by shame, hatred, fear, caste, pedigree, honour, etc. He was taught to rid himself of these impediments, little by little. Then he had wandered forth and practised spiritual exercises on the banks of the sacred river Nerbudda till, after a rigid discipline extending over forty years, he had at last attained to the Nirvikalpa Samadhi.

Then he set out to visit the sacred places of India. He had already been to Puri and Gangasagar, and on his return journey along the Ganges halted at Dakshineswar.

There he noticed Ramakrishna, seated in an abstracted mood, and his bright face at once attracted his attention. He asked Ramakrishna whether he would like to learn Vedanta. Ramakrishna said he must first ask the Mother ; and her permission having been obtained he returned to Totapuri. Totapuri then told him that he must give up the insignia of his present state of life, such as the sacred thread and the hair-tuft which marked him as a Brahmin. He must begin a new life. In the last half-hour of the night guru and disciple entered the meditation room. The guru chanted the holy mantras and the disciple repeated them as he put oblations one after another into the sacred fire, renouncing as he did so all desire for enjoyment, here and hereafter, and giving assurance of safety to all creatures. After the burning of the hair-tuft and the sacred thread, Ramakrishna accepted from his guru the emblems of a new life, the loin-cloth and the ochre-robe.

Then, prostrating himself before his guru, Ramakrishna took his seat to receive instruction.

" Brahman is the only Reality," said Totapuri,

"beyond the limits of time, space and causation. When a seeker is merged in the beatitude of Samadhi he does not perceive time or space or form. Pierce through the maze of name and form. Dive deep in the search for self and be firmly established in it through Samadhi. You will then find the world of name and form vanishing into nothing, and the puny ego merging into the cosmic consciousness. You will realize your identity with Brahman."

All that day he argued with Ramakrishna and tried to persuade him to withdraw the mind completely from all objects and dive into the Atman—the Universal Soul. But try as he would Ramakrishna could not cross the realm of name and form and bring his mind to the unconditioned state. He could withdraw it from all objects except the all too familiar form of the Blissful Mother which appeared before him as a living reality preventing him from passing beyond the realm of name and form. In despair he said to the guru, "It is hopeless. I cannot raise my mind to the unconditioned state."

"What! You can't do it! But you have to," said the guru sharply, and finding a piece of glass he pressed the point between Ramakrishna's eyebrows and told him to concentrate his mind on that point.

"With a stern determination," relates Ramakrishna, "I again set to meditate and as soon as the gracious form of the Divine Mother appeared before me, I used my discrimination as a sword and severed it in two. There remained no more obstructions to my mind. It at once soared beyond the relative plane. And I lost myself in Samadhi."

Thus far is Ramakrishna's own account of his great experience. His biographers say that he then passed

into the ineffable glory of Nirvakalpa Samadhi. In
that rapture his senses and mind stopped their
function. The body became motionless as a corpse.
The universe rolled away from his vision. Even space
melted away. Everything was reduced to ideas,
which floated like shadows in the dim background of
his mind. Only the faint consciousness of "I" repeated itself in dull monotony. Presently that too
stopped, and what remained was existence alone. The
soul had lost itself in the Self and all ideas of duality,
of subject and object, had been effaced. Beyond
speech, beyond experience, and beyond thought he had
experienced the Brahman—he had become the
Brahman.

Totapuri sat for long watching his disciple. Finding him absolutely motionless he stole out of the room,
locking the door behind lest anyone should intrude.
Then he waited a call from Ramakrishna. But none
came. Day passed into night, and no call reached
him. Three days went by and still there was no call.
Alarmed at this silence Totapuri opened the door and
entered. And there sat Ramakrishna, in the very
same position as he was in when he left him. In the
body there was no sign of life. But the countenance
was serene and radiant. The disciple was dead to
the objective world. His mind was absorbed in the
Self, without a flicker—absolutely steady.

In breathless wonder Totapuri gazed at his disciple.
"Is it really true?" he said to himself. "Is it possible that this man in a single day has attained to
that which it took me forty years of strenuous practice
to achieve?" In an access of joy he cried, "Great
God, it is nothing short of a miracle!"

Then he took steps to bring the mind of Ramakrishna back to the world. The little room in the grove

rang with the holy mantra, Hari Om, uttered in deep and solemn tones. Little by little Ramakrishna returned to consciousness. He opened his eyes and saw his guru tenderly watching him. And the guru replied by locking him in his embrace.

"When the Supreme Being is thought of as inactive—not creating, sustaining or destroying—I call Him Brahman the Impersonal God," said Ramakrishna. "When I think of Him as active—creating, sustaining, and destroying—I call Him the Personal God. But really the distinction between an Impersonal and a Personal God is a distinction without a difference. The Impersonal and the Personal are one and the same Being, even as milk and its whiteness. They are one like the gem and its lustre. Similar is the relation between Brahman and the Divine Mother."

Referring to this period he used to say:

"For six months at a stretch I remained in that state from which ordinary men can never return. After three weeks the body fell off like a sere leaf. I was not conscious of day or night. Flies would enter my mouth and nostrils just as they would in a dead body, but I did not feel them. If it were not for the ministrations of a monk my body could not have survived. He understood my state of mind: he also realized that my body must be kept alive at all costs, as it was meant to do great good in the world. So he would bring food regularly, and even if he had to beat me with a stick he would try to bring my mind back. As soon as he found me a little conscious he would press food into my mouth. But only a little would reach my stomach, and there were days in which all efforts would fail. At last I received the Mother's command: 'Remain on the threshold of relative consciousness for the sake of humanity.' Then I was laid up with a terrible attack of dysentery. An excruciating pain in the stomach tortured me day and night. Only gradually did I become a normal man. But before I did my mind, on the slightest provocation, would fly back again and merge in Nirvikalpa Samadhi."

It was now eight years since he had been back to his native village, Kamarpukur ; and it was thought that a change would improve his health. So in May 1867 he returned there accompanied by his nephew, Hriday, and by the Brahmini, his former woman guru. Here he stayed for six or seven months, and it is a relief to hear from his biographers of signs of common human nature after the strained life he had now for many years been leading. He found, we are told, relaxation by entering into the joys and sorrows of the simple village folk. Also he sent for his wife. The last time he had seen her she was seven years old—too young to understand her position. Now she was fourteen. And after a few days' stay with him she was eager to serve him with all her love and devotion. He on his part began to train her in spiritual matters and took special care that she had an all-round training in the discharge of her household duties, in making good use of money, and above all, in behaving according to circumstances, relying solely upon God.

This development, however, disturbed the equanimity of the Brahmini. And here again we see some human nature. We are told that, though she was highly advanced spiritually she had not attained perfection. Already she had been greatly put out at Ramakrishna's acceptance of Totapuri as guru. She could not bear to see Ramakrishna associate with any other teacher or devotee. As one who had taught Ramakrishna she came to consider herself a supremely important personage whom everyone must either obey or be accursed. And now she did not take at all kindly to the idea of Ramakrishna's doing his duty to his wife. Perhaps she feared this would endanger his celibate life. Ramakrishna instructed his wife to look upon her as her own mother-in-law and serve her with love and respect. But the Brahmini grew very peevish and often rebuked the ladies of the household. The position soon became intolerable. This she herself came to recognize and then her remorse was keen. One day she approached Ramakrishna with sandal-paste and garlands of flowers, adorned him with these as an Incarnation of Sri Gauranga, implored his forgiveness and bade farewell.

Ramakrishna's health being restored he returned with Hriday to Dakshineswar. And by this time, as a result of his spiritual experiences, his mind had acquired a wonderful breadth, so that he accepted the different forms of religion as so many ways of reaching perfection.

A former Hindu having been attracted by the spirit of universal brotherhood obtaining in Islam, had become a Moslem. He was a lover of God and probably a Sufi. He had now taken up his residence at Dakshineswar and his devotion soon attracted the notice of Ramakrishna, who argued to himself that, since Islam was also a way to experiencing God, he would see how God blessed devotees who worshipped Him that way. He decided, therefore, to be initiated by this man, Govinda by name, and become for the time being a Moslem. And while he was practising the Islamic faith he lived outside the temple precincts and was willing to eat Moslem food, though he was persuaded by his Hindu friends to be content

79

with having it cooked by a Brahmin under the direction of a Moslem.

"I used to repeat the name of Allah," says Ramakrishna, "wear my cloth in the fashion of the Moslems and recite the Namaz regularly. All Hindu ideas being wholly banished from my mind, not only did I not salute the Hindu gods, but I had no inclination even to visit them. And after three months I realized the goal of that form of devotion."

First of all he saw a radiant Person with a long beard and of grave appearance, and then his mind, passing through the experience of the Brahman with attributes, was finally absorbed in the Brahman without attributes.

Christianity also he practised. A certain man named Sambhu who, though not a Christian had studied the Bible, used to talk to Ramakrishna about Christ and Christianity. One day, in the year 1874, Ramakrishna was in a garden-house, on the walls of which were many beautiful portraits, one of which was of Christ. While he was looking attentively at the picture of the Madonna and Child and reflecting on the wonderful life of Christ, he came to feel as though the picture were animated. Rays of light were emanating from the figures of Mary and Christ and, entering into him, altogether changed his outlook.

When he realised that his Hindu ideas were being pushed into a corner by this onrush of new ideas he tried his best to stop it. He eagerly prayed to the Divine Mother (Kali) : " What is it thou art doing to me, Mother ? " But in vain. His love for the Hindu gods was swept away by this tidal wave. In its stead a deep regard for Christ and the Christian Church filled his heart and opened to his eyes the vision of Christian devotees burning incense and candles before the vision of Jesus and offering unto Him the eager outpourings of their hearts. Returning to Dakshineswar temple he was so engrossed in these thoughts that he forgot to visit Kali.

For three days these ideas held sway. On the fourth day he was walking in the grove when he suddenly saw an extraordinary-looking person of serene aspect approaching, with his gaze intently fixed on him. He knew him at once to be a man of foreign extraction. He had large, beautiful eyes, and, though the nose was different from an Indian's, it in no way marred the comeliness of his face. Ramakrishna was charmed, and wondered who it might be. Presently the figure drew near. Then, from the inmost recesses of Ramakrishna's heart there went up the note, "This is the Christ who poured out His heart's blood for the redemption of mankind and suffered agonies for its sake. It is none else than that Master-Yogin, Jesus, the embodiment of Love."

Then the Son of Man embraced Ramakrishna and became merged in him. Ramakrishna lost outward consciousness in Samadhi and experienced his union with the Brahman with attributes.

After some time he came back to normal consciousness and was convinced that Jesus Christ was an Incarnation of the Lord.

About Buddha he shared the general notion of the Hindus that he was an Incarnation of God, and used to offer him his sincere devotion and worship.

Early in 1868 he started with a party to what is now the United Provinces of Agra and Oudh. He was greatly distressed, and shed tears at the abject condition of the people and sat with the poor villagers till, at the sight of his compassion, his friends ordered food to be distributed. As he approached Benares he had a strange vision. The sacred city actually appeared to him to be made of gold as it is described in the sacred books. From Benares the party moved to Allahabad, where all bathed in the sacred confluence of the Ganges and Jumna. Then they went to Vrindavan, so rich in sweet memories of Krishna, and tears rolled from their eyes. After visiting Muttra they returned to Calcutta.

Ramakrishna's wife had not accompanied him when he had returned to Dakshinswar. She had gone back to her father's house. But in 1872 she and her father set out for Dakshineswar. Convinced after a few days that his attitude towards her was unchanged, she decided to remain and give herself over to his and his mother's service. And she lived with his mother, who had for some years resided at Dakshineswar.

In May, on an auspicious night for the worship of Kali, he made special arrangements for the worship in his own room and asked his wife to be present. He took his own seat and then beckoned her to the seat which was reserved for the goddess. In a semi-conscious state she reverently watched the proceedings and took the seat. During the ceremony she went into Samadhi. Ramakrishna also, when he had finished the mantra, fell into a trance. Priest and goddess were joined in a transcendental union in the Self. Hours passed. At dead of night he partially recovered consciousness. And then he surrendered himself and the fruits of his life's spiritual exercises at the feet of his wife, and reverently saluted her.

In the worshop of Woman his series of spiritual exercises reached their consummation. He had dedicated his all to the Mother of the Universe manifested through the living symbol of his wife. In his vision everything in the universe became a symbol of God.

His wife continued for a time to live at Dakshineswar, and has thus spoken of her experience :

" I have no words to describe my wonderful exaltation of spirit as I watched him in different states. Under the influence of divine emotion he would sometimes talk on abstruse subjects, sometimes laugh, sometimes weep. Or again, he would become motionless in Samadhi. This would continue through the night. There was such an extraordinarily divine Presence in him that I used to shake with fear and wonder how I could survive the night. Then he discovered that I had to keep awake the whole night lest he should go into Samadhi and he asked me to sleep in another room."

One night, finding his wife asleep by his side, he said to himself : " Here is a woman's body which the world holds dear. But he who takes pleasure in it is confined to the body and cannot experience God. Tell me frankly whether you want this or God. If the former, then here it is." His purified mind answered the question by plunging into a Samadhi so deep that it lasted the rest of the night.

Months passed in this way, but not once did their minds come down to the plane of sense. And Ramakrishna used to say, that after marriage he anxiously prayed to Kali to root out all sense of physical enjoyment from her mind ; and that his prayer had been granted he knew from contact with her at this period.

When, after the lapse of a year or more Ramakrishna felt not the least trace of a body-idea in his mind, and continued to look upon his wife as the manifestation of Kali and sometimes as the Atman or

Brahman, he understood that Kali had brought him successfully through the ordeal, and that, through her grace his mind was able to remain without any effort on his part on the highest plane of spiritual realization. And at the end of 1873 his wife returned to her village.

It was two years later that the meeting with Keshub took place, of which a description has already been given. And his personal appearance at that time has been thus described. He was of dark complexion and wore a beard. His eyes never opened very wide and were introspective. He was of medium height, slender almost to leanness, and very frail-looking. He had an excessively nervous temperament and was acutely sensitive. He spoke in very plain Bengali with a slight but pleasing stammer.

So far he had thought chiefly of his own spiritual development. But now, having attained the acme of individual personal development, a remarkable change took place in him. He began to think not so much of himself as of others. What he had himself enjoyed he wanted others to share. He had no such urge as had come to Keshub to go all over India preaching—or even to go as far as Calcutta only four miles off. But there did arise in his mind a tremendous longing to pass on his experiences to a few devotees. "There is no limit to the yearning I had then," he afterwards said. "I looked forward wistfully to the day when my beloved companions would come. I hoped to find solace by conversing with them and telling them of my experiences. A mother has never longed so intensely for the sight of her child, nor a lover for his sweetheart, as I did for them." But it is noticeable that he was not to go to them : they were to come to him.

Shortly, the devotees began to come. In 1880, came a young man who afterwards as Swami Vivekenanda was to become his most famous disciple. And an account of his life will show how Ramakrishna carried out the new object he now had in view.

III

VIVEKENANDA

SWAMI VIVEKENANDA'S original name was Narendra Nath, and at the time he met Ramakrishna he was one of the most brilliant members of the Brahmo Somaj. He was born in 1863. He was keen-minded and of great vigour, both of intellect and body. But he was also endowed with a deep religious disposition. Even as a child he would purchase clay images of gods and play at meditation before them. Later on meditation became his favourite occupation and, unknown to others, he used to spend a great part of the night in this way.

As a young man he acquired great power in debate. In society he was a brilliant though somewhat caustic conversationalist, free and unconventional in manner ; somewhat peremptory but vibrant and sensitive. In his college days he had drunk freely of Western philosophy but had been shocked by its, supposedly, agnostic doctrines. He believed that the creed of Universal Reason called on him to suppress the yearnings of his artist nature. But his senses were acute, his passions imperious, his susceptibilities tender, and to suppress these was to kill himself. A pale, bloodless reason could not save him in the hour of temptation. He wanted a flesh and blood reality, a hand to save and uplift—in short, a guru or master who, by embodying perfection, would fulfil the yearning in his soul. He had approached Davendranath Tagore and asked him if he had seen God. But the answer he received did not satisfy him. And it was at this critical point, when he was seventeen years of age, that he met Ramakrishna, then forty-four, at the house of a friend in Calcutta.

He sang a few songs, and Ramakrishna became keenly interested in him, found out all about him, and invited him to visit Dakshineswar at an early date.

Vivekenanda passed the examination for which he had at that time been preparing. And his stubborn refusal to marry having convinced a cousin of his of the sincerity of his religious disposition this cousin took him to Dakshineswar to see Ramakrishna. It was a momentous meeting. And fortunately both Ramakrishna and Vivekenanda have left accounts of it.

" He seemed careless about his body and dress," says Ramakrishna. " His eyes bespoke an intro- spective mind as if part of it were always concen- trated upon something within. I was surprised to find so spiritual a man coming from the material atmosphere of Calcutta. He sang a few Bengali songs at my request. They were the spontaneous outpour- ings of a devout heart desiring union with the Self. And he put such pathos into the song that I could not control myself, and fell into an ecstasy."

" I sang the song," says Vivekenanda, " but shortly after he suddenly rose, and taking me by the hand he led me to the verandah, and shut the door behind him so that we were alone. Then, to my surprise, he began to shed tears of joy as he held my hand, and addressing me as one long familiar to him, said : ' Ah, you come so late ! How could you be so unkind as to keep me waiting so long. My ears are wellnigh burnt through listening to the profane talk of worldly people. I have been panting to unburden my mind to one who can appreciate my inmost experiences.' Thus he spoke with sobs.

" Then he stood before me with folded palms and addressed me, ' Lord, I know you are that ancient sage Nara, the Incarnation of Narayana, born on earth to remove the misery of mankind,' and so on. I was altogether taken aback by this conduct. He must be stark mad, I thought. But I kept quiet and let him go on. Then he seized me by the hand and said, ' Promise that you will come alone to me at an early date.' At this importunity I had to say ' Yes,' and we returned together to my friends.

" I sat and watched him then. I could see nothing wrong in his words, movements or behaviour towards others. Rather, from his spiritual conversation and ecstatic states, he seemed to be a man of genuine renunciation, and there was a marked consistency between his words and his life. He said, ' God can be experienced. One can see and talk to Him as I am doing with you.' As I heard him say these things I could not but believe that he was saying them not as an ordinary preacher would but from the depth of his own experience. Even if insane, this man is the holiest of the holy. With such conflicting thoughts I bowed before him and begged his leave to return to Calcutta."

About a month passed before Vivekenanda again visited Ramakrishna. This time he went alone.

" I found him sitting alone on his small bedstead," says Vivekenanda. " He was glad to see me, and calling me affectionately, made me sit beside him on the bed. (The two would be sitting cross-legged beside each other.) The next moment I found him overcome with emotion. Muttering to himself, with eyes fixed on me, he slowly drew near. I thought he might do something queer as on the previous occasion. But in the twinkling of an eye he had placed his right foot on my body. The touch at once gave rise to a curious experience within me.

" With my eyes open, I saw the walls and everything in the room whirl rapidly and vanish into naught. The whole universe, together with my individuality, seemed about to merge in a mysterious Void. I was terribly frightened. I thought I was facing death. For the loss of individuality meant nothing short of death. Unable to control myself, I cried out : ' What is this that you are doing to me ? I have my parents at home ? '

" He laughed aloud at this, and stroking my chest, said : ' Let it rest now. Everything will come in time.' The wonder of it was that no sooner had he said this than the strange experience vanished. I was myself again, and found everything within and without the room as it had been before.

" All this happened in less time than it takes to relate. Yet it revolutionised my mind. I began to question whether it was hypnotism. But that was not likely, for hypnotism acts only on weak minds, and I prided myself on having a mind just the reverse. So what might this sudden transformation be due to ? I could not come to any conclusion. But I thought, how could a man who metamorphosed at will a strong mind like mine be dismissed as a lunatic ? So I was in a dilemma about my experience. My rationalistic mind received an unpleasant rebuff at its failure in judging the true state of things. But I was resolved to fathom the mystery."

During his third visit Vivekenanda fared no better. From the first he was determined not to be influenced. But again he lost consciousness. Ramakrishna invited him into an adjacent garden, and after strolling there for some time they took their seats in the parlour (not on chairs probably, but cross-legged on the floor). Soon Ramkrishna fell into a trance, but as Vivekenanda watched him he was suddenly touched by him and immediately lost all outward consciousness. And when he came to, Ramakrishna was stroking his chest.

Vivekenanda was now fully convinced of the extraordinary nature of that power which was working through Ramakrishna. He had not been a believer in the necessity of having a guru for experiencing God. How could a man, necessarily weak and short-visioned, be the unerring guide that he had to be in order to command another's implicit obedience? But now he realized that such a man could indeed exist and that his personal influence could be of inestimable value in bringing a man nearer to God. Still he was determined not to accept anything about Ramakrishna without testing it by his own experience or reason.

Vivekenanda was a sceptic, with no faith in Hindu gods, and he laughed at many of the injunctions of the Hindu Scriptures. But Ramakrishna instructed him with infinite love and patience. He was full of admiration of his pure character and strength of mind. He knew the boy was endowed with rare potentialities. But he saw that if his tremendous energy were not directed into a proper spiritual channel he might perhaps found a new sect but not fulfil his real mission, which was to be God's instrument in bringing about the spiritual regeneration of mankind. Naturally, therefore, Ramakrishna was anxious to direct his mind to experiencing God.

But Vivekenanda was not easily handled. Ramakrishna wanted him to read the Advaita [1] treatises, and these to Vivekenanda, a staunch member of the Brahmo Somaj, appeared to be heretical. He would

[1] *Advaita* is the principle that the only reality is *brahman*—that the dualism set up between the self and the world, between spirit and matter is the result of *maya*-illusion.

therefore rebel, saying there was no greater sin than to think of oneself as identical with the Creator. I am God, you are God, these created things are God —what could be more absurd than this! Ramakrishna would be amused at this bluntness, and simply tell him to go on praying to the God of truth and believe in that aspect of Him which He might reveal to him. But Vivekenanda would not give in easily. Whatever did not tally with reason he would consider as false. And it was of his very nature to stand against falsehood.

Ramakrishna was equally sure that Vivekenanda would in the end come to appreciate the doctrine of Advaita and be led to the highest experience. He would therefore make a point of constantly talking of it before him. One day he had been trying to convince Vivekenanda of the identity of the individual soul with Brahman but was unable to succeed. Vivekenanda and others then laughingly discussed the question among themselves while Ramakrishna went into a semi-conscious state. After a time he came out of this state, asked smilingly what they were talking about and then touched Vivekenanda. Immediately Vivekenanda was plunged into Samadhi.

"That magic touch of the Master immediately brought a change over my mind," said Vivekenanda. "I was stupefied to find that really there was nothing in the universe but God. I saw it quite clearly, but kept silent to see if the idea would last. That influence did not abate in the course of the day. I returned home but there, also, everything I saw appeared to be Brahman. All the while, whether eating, or lying down, or going to college, I had the same experience and felt myself always in a sort of comatose state. There was no sensation in my limbs and I thought I was becoming paralysed. I had no satisfaction in eating, and felt as if somebody else were eating. My mother became alarmed. She was afraid I would not live long. This state of things continued for some days. When I became normal again I realized that I must have had a glimpse of the Advaita State. Thenceforth I could not deny the conclusion of the Advaita philosophy."

Much private trouble came on Vivekenanda after this. Early in 1884 his father died and his family was faced with dire poverty. The burden of supporting six or seven people fell upon Vivekenanda ; and he was forced to seek employment. Everywhere he met with refusal. This first contact with the realities of life convinced him that unselfish sympathy was a rarity in the world. There was no place in it for the weak, the poor, and the destitute. The words he had once heard—" If God is good and gracious, why then do millions of people die for want of a few morsels of food ? "—rang in his ears. He became exceedingly cross with God. He came to doubt His existence.

Yet this vivid memory of the divine visions he had had since his boyhood, and especially after his contact with Ramakrishna, led him to think that after all God must exist and that there must be some way of experiencing Him. Then came something which must be told in his own words.

" One evening, after a whole day's fast and exposure to rain, I was returning home with tired limbs and jaded mind when, overpowered with exhaustion, I sank down on the outer plinth of a house. I can't say whether I was insensible or not. Suddenly I felt as if, by some divine power, the coverings of my soul were removed one after another. All my former doubts. regarding the co-existence of divine justice and mercy and the presence of misery in creation were automatically solved. By a deep introspection I found the meaning of it all, and was satisfied. As I proceeded homeward I found there was no trace of fatigue in the body, and the mind was refreshed with wonderful strength and peace."

Henceforth he began secretly to prepare himself to renounce the world, and fixed a day for this purpose. He was convinced he was not born like humdrum people to earn money and maintain a family—still less to strive for pleasure. He became deaf to the praise or blame of worldly men. And on the day he had fixed for his renunciation he met Ramakrishna in Calcutta.

Ramakrishna persuaded him to spend the night at Dakshineswar. There Ramakrishna drew him near him, and tenderly touching him, began to sing a song, with tears in his eyes. Vivekenanda says :

"I had repressed my feelings so long that now they overflowed in tears. The meaning of the song was too apparent : he knew I intended to renounce the world. That night he dismissed all others, and calling me to his side, said, ' I know you have come for the Mother's work and will not be able to remain in the world. But for my sake, stay in the world as long as I live.' In saying this he burst into tears. The next day, with his permission I returned home."

Vivekenanda was still, however, assailed by a thousand thoughts regarding the maintenance of his family, and began again to look about for a living. By working in an attorney's office and translating a few books he earned just enough to live from hand to mouth. But this was only temporary and there was no fixed income for the maintenance of his mother and brothers.

One day the idea struck him that God listened to Ramakrishna's prayer, so why should he not ask Ramakrishna to pray for his pecuniary wants ? He hurried to Dakshineswar and insisted on Ramakrishna's making an appeal on behalf of his starving family. Ramakrishna, however, said he could not make any such demands, but told Vivekenanda to go to the Kali temple that night, prostrate himself before the Mother and ask her any boon he liked. Everything was in her power. Vivekenanda went to the temple that night.

" As I went," he says, " I was filled with divine intoxication. My feet were unsteady. My heart was leaping in anticipation of the joy of beholding the Living Goddess and hearing her words. Reaching the temple I cast my eyes on the image and actually found that the Divine Mother was living and conscious. I was caught in a surging wave of devotion. In an ecstasy of joy I prostrated myself again and again before the Mother and prayed, ' Mother, give me discrimination ! Give me renunciation ! Give me knowledge ! Give me devotion ! Grant that I may have an uninterrupted vision of thee ! ' After praying, a serene peace reigned in my soul. I forgot the world. Only the Divine Mother shone within my heart."

When he returned, Ramakrishna asked him whether he had prayed to the Mother for the removal of his worldly troubles. No, he replied : he had forgotten all about them.

Again he went to the temple. But again he forgot his intention, and prayed only for love and devotion.

On his return, Ramakrishna asked him if he could not control himself enough to say those few words, and sent him a third time to the temple, to try once more.

Vivekenanda went for the third time, but on entering the temple was overpowered with a terrible shame. What a trifle to pray to the Mother about! It was like asking a king for a cabbage. In remorse he bowed respectfully to the goddess and said: "Mother, I want nothing but knowledge and devotion."

Coming out of the temple he saw that all this was due to Ramakrishna's will. So he said to Ramakrishna, "Sir, it is you who have cast a charm over my mind and made me forgetful. Now please grant me the boon that my people may no longer suffer from poverty."

Ramakrishna replied: "Such a prayer never comes from my lips. I asked you to pray for yourself but you couldn't do it. Evidently you are not destined to enjoy worldly happiness. Well, I can't help it."

But Vivekenanda would not let him go, and insisted on his granting that prayer. And at last Ramakrishna said, "All right, they will never be in want of plain food and clothing." Vivekenanda then returned to Calcutta.

Afterwards he often said that Ramakrishna was the only person who, ever since they met, had believed in him uniformly—even when his mother and brothers did not. It was his unflinching love and trust that bound him to Ramakrishna for ever. He alone knew how to love another.

But Vivekenanda had not yet had the supreme experience. He had aspired after it and struggled to attain this highest goal. But it had eluded him. Then one evening while he was meditating, it came to him quite unexpectedly. At first he felt as if a light had been placed behind his head. Then he passed beyond all relativity and was lost in the Absolute. He had attained the Nirvikalpa Samadhi.

When he regained a little consciousness of the world he recognized only his head and not his body. He cried out, asking where his body was. A friend said, "Here it is." But Vivekenanda could not recognize it. His friends were terrified, and hastened to inform Ramakrishna who, however, was not in the least alarmed and merely said, "Let him be. He has teased me for it long enough."

After a long time Vivekenanda came to a consciousness of the physical world and found his brother disciples clustered about him. All he knew was that an ineffable peace now bathed his soul.

This was on April 16, 1886 ; and on August 16 of that same year Ramakrishna died. For long he had been suffering agonies from cancer.

But before he died he initiated Vivekenanda with the name of Rama, which he said was his own Ishta Mantra. The effect was miraculous. In the intoxication of his bliss Vivekenanda rushed round and round the house uttering the name of Rama. He was in such an exalted mood that no one dared approach him. And the other disciples grew so alarmed they reported it to Ramakrishna who, however, simply said, "Let him be. He will recover in due time."

A few days before he died Ramakrishna called Vivekenanda to his side when there was no one in the room. He made Vivekenanda sit in front of him and then, gazing at him, he fell into Samadhi. As he did so Vivekenanda felt a subtle force like an electric shock penetrate his body, and gradually he, too, lost consciousness. He did not remember how long he sat there. But when he came to normal consciousness he found Ramakrishna weeping.

Vivekenanda asked him why he wept and he replied : "To-day I have given you my all. Through this power you will do a mighty good in the world. And then only will you go back."

Henceforth Ramakrishna and Vivekenanda were one.

On the death of Ramakrishna the leadership of the little group of disciples fell to Vivekenanda, still only twenty-three years of age. Though busy with his own domestic affairs he set to work to fulfil the sacred task left him by Ramakrishna. Disregarding their vacillations he would spend hours in describing the soul-stirring experiences of the Master. And after a time they set out all over India preaching the message of Ramakrishna. They left their dearest. They suffered the agonies that all saints have to endure. And Vivekenanda went further still. He went to Europe and America. He became famed all over the world. But always he attributed every good he had or did to what his Master, Ramakrishna, had imparted to him.

And the reverence for Ramakrishna has been growing ever since. No Indian of recent years has been so deeply revered. And by some Hindus he is now regarded as a veritable Incarnation of God.

CHAPTER II

MOSLEM MYSTICS

AMONG Moslems it is difficult to find recent examples of the mystical experience. Not that they do not have such experiences: they have them but they shun speaking or writing of them. Centuries ago the Sufis used to write in glorious poetry of the mystic state. And in the present times Inayat Khan undoubtedly based his teaching on some mystical experience he must have had, but of it there is no record. It has, therefore, been necessary to go back nearly a century for an example of mystical experience among Moslems and take the story of the Bab, about whom much now is on record. In a sense he was opposed to mysticism, for he objected to Sufis on account of their doctrine of the Inner Light, their pantheism, and their individualism. Nevertheless, he had undoubtedly enjoyed the mystical experience and his short heroic life—for he suffered martyrdom before he was thirty—gives abundant evidence of that joy and gladness, that serenity and firmness of conviction which are so characteristic of the mystical state.

Among the Shiah sect of the Islamic faith there is a perpetual expectancy—the expectancy of the appearance of the Imam Mahdi. These Shiahs believe that after the ascension into heaven of Mahomed he was succeeded by a line of twelve Imams. The twelfth Imam, who succeeded just a thousand years before the time of the Bab, is said to have only disappeared, and it is believed that he will reappear and fill the Earth with justice. The Shiahs expect the Imam Madhi as eagerly as Jews expected the Messiah.

Among the Shiah Moslems was a sect centred at Kerbela in Mesopotamia who specially concentrated on the expectancy. The leader in the first half of last century was a mulla named Kazim. For some years he had been foretelling the advent of One who would be the bearer of a new and independent revelation. He realized, we are told, how dense were those veils that hinder seekers from apprehending the glory of the hidden Manifestation. He accordingly exerted his utmost endeavour to remove gradually, wisely and cautiously whatever barriers might stand in the way of the full recognition of that hidden Treasure of God. To his disciples he said:

" It is incumbent upon you to renounce all comfort, all earthly possessions, and even your kindred, and seek Him who is the Desire of both your hearts and mine. Never relax in your determination to seek and find Him who is concealed behind the veils of glory. . . . How great, how very great is the cause ! How exalted the station to which I summon you ! How great the mission for which I have trained and prepared you ! "

Kazim died in the year 1843, and among those who were inspired by his words and were seeking the Promised One was a young mulla named Hosain, or Husayn, a native of the Persian Province of Khorasan. He was born in the year 1813, and for nine years he had remained with Kazim, preparing for the advent of the Promised One. This young mulla was described by one of his contemporaries as being the very embodiment of constancy, piety and virtue, and as inspiring others with his rectitude of conduct and passionate loyalty. Such, indeed, was the force of his character and the ardour of his faith that men felt that he, unaided and alone, could achieve the triumph of the Faith of God. Another records of him that no one could question his erudition, his charm, his high integrity, his fairness, his wisdom, or his amazing courage.

And one of his fellow-mullas had paid such a glowing tribute to this character, his high attainments and his ability, that some of those who heard this panegyric suspected Husayn of being the very Promised One whom Kazim had so often declared was living in their midst, though, as yet, unrecognized. So they one day approached him, saying : " Such is our confidence in you that if you claim to be the Promised One we shall all readily and unquestioningly submit ; and we here and now pledge our loyalty and obedience to whatever you bid us perform."

But Husayn replied : " God forbid ! Far be it from His glory that I, who am but dust, should be compared to Him who is the Lord or Lords. . . . Your and my first obligation is to aim at and carry out, both in spirit and in letter, the dying message of our beloved Chief."

He would not admit that he himself was the Promised One ; but he determined to devote his life to the quest of the Messiah ; and after first preparing himself for the holy adventure by spending forty days in retirement and prayer, on vigils and fasting, he set out from Kerbela for Bushire on the Persia Gulf.

And Bushire has interest in this story, for it so

happened that here was born, in the year 1821, one Ali Mahomed, who, as he grew up, attracted much attention on account of his austere practices and pre-occupation with religious matters. He was remarkable for his courtesy and charm, the dignity of his manner and the purity of his character. His father was a merchant, and he himself was engaged in business for a time. But having married and lost the son born of the marriage he decided to make a pilgrimage to the holy city of Kerbela, and there it was that he, like Husayn, had listened to Kazim's prophecies and, also like Husayn, had impressed his fellow-devotees by his piety. Indeed, so wrapt would he be in his devotions that he would seem utterly oblivious of those about him. Tears would rain from his eyes ; and from his lips would fall words of such power and beauty as are not to be surpassed in the noblest passages of Scripture.

" Oh ! God, my God, my beloved, my heart's desire," he would keep repeating with a frequency and an ardour that those near him would interrupt their prayers and marvel at his devotion. And at this time he had a vision which deeply influenced him and which he himself subsequently described.

" In my vision I saw the head of the Imam Husayn hanging upon a tree with drops of blood dropping profusely from his lacerated throat. With feelings of unsurpassed delight I approached that tree, and stretching forth my hand gathered a few drops of that sacred blood and devoutly drank them. When I awoke I found that the Spirit of God had permeated my whole soul and taken possession of it. My heart was thrilled with the joy of the divine presence, and the mysteries of His revelation were unfolded before my eyes in all their glory."

From Kerbela Ali Mahomed had returned to Bushire,

where he had remained until a few months after the death of Kazim, and had then closed his business and gone to Shiraz.

A few months later, Husayn passing through Bushire noted the spiritual atmosphere of the place. But proceeding on his quest he reached Shiraz, and there a little before sunset, as he was walking outside the gate of the city, his eyes suddenly fell on a youth of radiant countenance, who advanced towards him and greeted him with a smile of loving welcome as if he had been his intimate and life-long friend. He invited Husayn to his home, and as Husayn entered the house he was invaded by a feeling of unutterable joy. Oppressed by the mystery of this meeting and by the strain of his search for the Promised One Husayn breathed this prayer : " Oh ! my God. I have striven with all my soul, and until now have failed to find Thy promised Messenger. Yet Thy word faileth not, and Thy promise is sure."

After the evening prayer his youthful host began to question Husayn. " Whom do you regard as Kazim's successor and your leader ? " he asked.

" Our departed teacher exhorted us to forsake our homes in quest of the promised Beloved. I have arisen to accomplish his will, and am still engaged in my quest," replied Husayn.

" Has your teacher indicated any features by which the Promised One might be distinguished ? " inquired Husayn's host.

" Yes," replied Husayn, " he is one of pure lineage, over twenty years of age but less than thirty, endowed with intuitive knowledge and free of bodily defects."

There was a pause : then, with vibrant voice his host exclaimed : " Behold, all these signs are manifest in me ! "

" True," replied Husayn, " but he whose advent we await is a man of unsurpassed holiness, and the Cause he is to reveal to us is a Cause of tremendous power. Many and diverse are the requirements which he who claims to be its visible embodiment must needs fulfil."

When Husayn first started on his quest he had fixed on two standards by which he would test the claims of any to be the Promised One. He had composed a treatise on the hidden teachings propounded by Kazim and to him who could unravel the mysterious allusions he would submit his second test which was to reveal an entirely new commentary on the Surih of Joseph.

This treatise Husayn now presented to his host, in order to test his capacity. To his surprise the young man in a few minutes unravelled all its mysteries and resolved all its problems. In addition he expounded new truths with vividness and power. Then he made a commentary on the Surih of Joseph, without for one moment interrupting the flow of the verses.

Husayn sat enraptured by the magic of his voice and the sweeping force of his revelation. Hour after hour slipped by till suddenly the call of the muadhdhin summoning the faithful to prayer at dawn awakened him from the state of ecstasy into which he had fallen. All the delights, all the ineffable glories which are the priceless possessions of the people of Paradise, he seemed to be experiencing that night ; and he became convinced that his host was none other than the Promised One.

Then his host, who proved to be the Ali Mahomed from Bushire referred to above, addressed Husayn in these words :

" O thou who art the first to believe in me, verily I say unto thee I am The Bab, the Gate of God, and thou art the Bab-ul-Bab, the gate of that Gate. Eighteen souls must, at first, of their own accord, accept me and recognize the truth of my revelation. And when this number is complete, one of them must accompany me on my pilgrimage to Mecca, where I shall deliver the message of God to the Sherif. But it is incumbent upon you not to divulge, either to your companions or to any other soul, that which you have heard. You should continue in prayer until my departure for Hejaz. But, ere I depart, I shall appoint unto each of the eighteen souls his special mission and instruct them to teach the Word of God and quicken the souls of men."

Having spoken these words the Bab dismissed Husayn from his presence.

Little wonder is it that Husayn was dumbfounded at his experiences during that wonderful night. Here was a young man of twenty-four making this startling and tremendous claim that he was the Messiah so long promised, so eagerly expected—one who would be regarded as a divine being, as belonging to a different order of being from common humanity—one who would be the spiritual guide of all Moslems and whose every word must be implicitly obeyed.

This revelation coming suddenly as a thunderbolt upon Husayn fairly numbed his faculties. He was blinded by its dazzling splendour and overwhelmed by its crushing force. Excitement, awe and wonder stirred him to the depths. He was transfigured with a sense of gladness and strength. Hitherto he had been feeble, dejected and timid. Now he felt possessed of such courage and power that, were the whole world with its peoples and potentates to rise against him, he would face them undaunted. The whole universe was but a handful of dust in his hand. He seemed to hear the voice of Gabriel calling unto all mankind, "Awake, for, Lo! the morning light has broken. He who is your Promised One is come."

Faithful to the direction of the Bab he performed his devotions and organized classes. Gradually people gathered about him and marvelled at the spirit which his discourses revealed. On several occasions he would spend the entire night with the Bab and, fascinated by the charm of his utterance, become oblivious of the world. On one such night the Bab foretold that thirteen other followers would arrive and enjoined Husayn : " Pray to God, that He may graciously enable them to walk securely in that path which is finer than a hair and keener than a sword."

The next morning a certain Mulla Ali and twelve companions came to Husayn. They, too, were seeking the Promised One but were surprised at Husayn's lack of agitation and expectancy, till he hinted to Ali that he had already found the object of their quest. Then they all besought God to fulfil His promise. And on the third night there appeared before Ali, while he was wrapt in prayer, a light, and, lo! that light moved before him. Allured by its splendour, he had to follow it, till at last it led him to his promised Beloved. Inspired by the vision he arose and beaming with joy and gladness, he hastened to Husayn. At dawn the two together went to the Bab. Ali was as warmly welcomed as Husayn had been, and a spirit of close and ardent fellowship sprang up between them. The entire chamber seemed to be vitalized by the celestial potency emanating from the Bab. They glowed with intense adoration. New Day had dawned upon them.

Each of Ali's twelve companions in turn found the Bab, and were declared by him to be Letters of the

Living. Others followed. Seventeen were gradually enrolled and appointed as chosen apostles of the Bab, ministers of his faith and diffusers of his light. One only remained to complete the number. Next day, as the Bab, followed by Husayn, was returning to his home there appeared a youth, dishevelled and travel-stained, who approached Husayn and asked him whether he had attained his goal. Then, fixing his gaze upon the Bab who was some steps in advance, he said to Husayn : " Why seek you to hide him from me ? I can recognize him by his gait. None other can manifest the power and majesty that radiate from his holy person." Husayn told the Bab of these words, and the Bab told him to marvel not, for he had been communing with this youth in the spirit. The youth was then accepted. He was only twenty-two, and became known as Quddus. So the eighteen apostles were now complete.

In general the Bab's plan was now this. He himself with one companion would proceed to the holy cities of Mecca and Medina and there, by public proclamation, inaugurate his mission. Having thus done he would return triumphantly from his pilgrimage and establish his Cause in the holy cities of Kerbela and Najaf in Iraq. One of his apostles was to be sent to Turkish territory and another to India. Others were to be sent to different provinces in Persia.

Husayn had hoped that the Bab would have taken him on his contemplated pilgrimage to Mecca, but the Bab had a higher mission for him. Summoning him to his presence the Bab said :

" My covenant with you is now accomplished. Gird up the loins of endeavour and arise to diffuse my Cause. Raise the cry, ' Awake, awake, for, lo ! the Gate of God is open, and the morning light

is shedding its radiance upon all mankind ! The
Promised One is made manifest ; prepare the way for
him, O people of the Earth ! Deprive not yourselves
of its redeeming grace, nor close your eyes to its
glory.' With those whom you find responsive to your
call share the epistles I have revealed to you, that
they may turn from the slough of neglect and soar
into the realm of divine revelation."

The Bab then told Husayn that he had chosen
Quddus as his companion for the pilgrimage to Mecca,
and would leave Husayn behind to face the onslaught
of a fierce and relentless enemy, though he might rest
assured that a bounty unspeakably glorious would be
conferred upon him, as the high mission for which he
had been created would of a surety be accomplished
to the full, and not all the darts of an unbelieving
world could hurt a single hair of his head until his
work was consummated. He was to proceed north
to Teheran, where a secret lay hidden, and thence to
Khorasan, where he was to proclaim the Call anew.
After that he was to return to Kerbela and there await
the Bab's summons.

Ali was then summoned to the Bab's presence and
was directed to proceed to Najaf and Kerbela.

"Your faith," said the Bab, "must be immovable
as the rock, must weather every storm and survive
every calamity. Suffer not denunciations of the
foolish and calumnies of the mullas to afflict you.
If you be slain in the pathway to God, remember
that great will be the reward which will be bestowed
upon you."

The remainder of the apostles were then called to
his presence. To each he gave a special task, and to
each he assigned his own native province as the field

106

of his labours. But all were to refrain from specific reference to the Bab himself. And to all he addressed these parting words :

" You have been chosen as repositories of God's wisdom. It behoves each one of you to manifest the attributes of God, and to exemplify by your deeds and words the signs of His righteousness, His power and His glory. Verily, this is the day spoken of by God in His book : ' On that day will We set a seal upon their mouths ; yet shall their tongues speak unto Us, and their feet shall bear witness to that which they have done.' Ponder also the words of Jesus addressed to His disciples as He sent them forth to propagate the Cause of God : ' Ye are even as the fire which in the darkness of the night has been kindled upon the mountain-top. Let your light shine before the eyes of men. Such must be the purity of your character and the degree of your renunciation, that through you the people of the Earth may recognize and be drawn closer to the Heavenly Father who is the source of purity and grace.' O, my disciples ! Verily I say, immensely exalted is this day above the days of the apostles of old. You are the witnesses of the dawn of the promised Day of God. Purge your hearts of worldly desires and let angelic virtues be your adorning. Strive that by your deeds you may bear witness to the truth. The days when idle worship was deemed sufficient are ended. The time is come when naught but the purest motive, supported by deeds of stainless purity, can ascend to the throne of the Most High. I am preparing you for the advent of a mighty Day, the newly born babe of which will excel the wisest of this present time. Scatter throughout the length and breadth of this land, and with steadfast feet and sanctified hearts, prepare the way for God's coming. Heed not your frailty ; fix your gaze upon the invincible power of your God. Did He not cause Abraham to triumph over the forces of Nimrod ? Did He not enable Moses to vanquish Pharaoh and his hosts ? Has He not established the rule of the poor and lowly Jesus over all the forces of the Jewish people ? Has He not subjected the militant tribes of Arabia to the transforming discipline of His prophet Mahomed ? Arise then in His Name, put your whole trust in Him and victory is surely yours ! "

With such words did the Bab quicken the faith of his disciples and launch them upon their mission. And he well knew the opposition they must expect from the orthodox upholders of ancient tradition, for, besides making the tremendous claim to Messiahship, he was proclaiming drastic innovations. According to him, the Essence of God, the Primal Divine Unity, transcends all human comprehension. All we can know is Its manifestations. In essence all Prophets are one. One Universal Intelligence speaks to mankind through successive agents according to the capacity and needs of the time—through Abraham, Moses, Christ, Mahomed, and now through the latest manifestation, himself. But he would not be the last of all. There never would be a last. For the world is eternal and progress unending. Another would follow him. And to each a boundless devotion must be given. This was the Bab's teaching.

The first to leave and the first to suffer was Ali. Immediately on receiving his commission from the Bab he set out for Najaf. Arrived in this holy city he proceeded to carry out the Bab's intention of introducing the new Faith into Turkish territory. Accordingly, in the presence of the leading men of Shiah Islam, he fearlessly announced the manifestation of

the Bab, the Gate, whose advent they were eagerly
awaiting. In proof of this claim Ali recounted the
number of verses, prayers, homilies and scientific
treatises which streamed from the pen of the Bab.
But instead of welcoming these life-giving evidences
of a new-born revelation the mullas pronounced Ali a
heretic and expelled him from the assembly. Eventually he was bound and delivered into the hands of
the Turkish Government, arraigned as a wrecker of
Islam, a disgrace to the Faith and worthy of the
penalty of death. He was taken to Baghdad, where
he was publicly accused of being an infidel, an abro-
gator of the laws of Islam, and a repudiator of its
rituals and standards. He was again thrown into
prison. Then he was deported to Constantinople.
And after that nothing more was ever heard of him.

Husayn remained with the Bab some days after
Ali's departure, and then proceeded to Isphahan,
where he fearlessly and unreservedly delivered the
message with which he had been entrusted. He was
immediately denounced as claiming that he whose
cause he was now championing was the revealer of a
divinely inspired book whose tone and language resembled the Koran. Thus was he disrupting the holy
Faith of Islam. His denouncers appealed to the
Governor, but he refused to interfere in such a matter,
and Husayn was able to remain in peace and make a
few converts before proceeding to Teheran. At the
Persian capital he was told of one Baha-ullah, the
noble son of a noble father of high standing. This
young man of eight-and-twenty had high intellectual
attainments and was devoted to religious pursuits.
Husayn entrusted to one of his adherents a scroll to

be handed personally to Baha-ullah. The latter read the scroll and sent back the messenger to Husayn with a small present and an expression of his appreciation and love. Husayn, on receipt of the present and message, fervently kissed the present and then took the messenger in his arms and kissed his eyes. The messenger was amazed, and wondered what kind of a bond it was that could unite these two souls and kindle so fervent a fellowship in their hearts.

A few days later Husayn left Teheran for Khorasan. In that province he exhibited in an astounding manner the effects of that regenerating power with which the Bab had invested him. In whatever gathering he appeared, no matter how great the number, or how representative the character of the divines who were present, he alone came to the front as the chief speaker. His fine character, as well as his extreme devoutness, ennobled his already high reputation. He made many converts among the mullas, the most notable of whom was Mirza Mahomed Baquir, who became a devoted follower of the Bab. Love of the Bab, indeed, inflamed the new convert's soul with such a consuming passion that no one could resist its force. He became the terror of his enemies and the inspiration of his friends.

As soon as Husayn had won such able and devoted supporters to the Cause he reported the result to the Bab, who, on receipt of the good news, kept repeating, " How marvellous, how exceedingly marvellous ! " What especially pleased the Bab in Husayn's letter was his reference to Baha-ullah's immediate response to the divine message and the news that Baha-ullah had boldly initiated a campaign in his native province. The Bab was gladdened at the marvellous success. Now he was assured that, if he himself fell a victim to the tyranny of his foes, his Cause would live: the master-hand of Baha-ullah would direct it, and under his direction it would flourish and eventually yield its choicest fruits.

His mind thus eased, the Bab, accompanied by Quddus, now joined a company of pilgrims leaving for Mecca. They proceeded in the month of October 1844, first to Bushire, and from there by sailing boat to Jeddah on the Red Sea.

High seas and the complete absence of comfort could neither interfere with the regularity of the Bab's devotions nor perturb the peacefulness of his meditations and prayers. "Whenever, by day or night, I chanced to meet them," says a fellow-pilgrim, " I invariably found the Bab and Quddus together, both absorbed in their work—the Bab in dictating, and Quddus in taking down his words."

Upon his arrival at Jeddah the Bab donned the pilgrim's garb, and mounting a camel, set out for Mecca. One day a roving Bedouin snatched the Bab's saddle-bag, which was lying on the ground, and vanished into the desert. The bag contained the Bab's writings, and his servant wished to pursue the thief. But the Bab restrained him, saying:

" Had I allowed you, you would surely have overtaken and punished him. But this was not to be. The writings which that bag contained are destined to reach, through the instrumentality of this Arab, such places as we could never have succeeded in attaining. Grieve not, therefore, at this action, for this was decreed by God, the Ordainer, the Almighty."

Many a time afterwards did the Bab, on similar occasions, seek to comfort his friends by such reflections. By words such as these he turned the bitterness of regret and resentment into radiant acquiescence in the Divine purpose and into joyous submission to God's will.

Arrived at Mecca, he performed all the prescribed rites of worship. With the utmost dignity and calm, and with extreme simplicity and reverence he compassed the Kabba. On the last day of his pilgrimage he met a noted member of the Shayki community to which Kazim had belonged, and in those hallowed precincts he fearlessly appealed to him. Holding his hand the Bab said :

" Verily, I declare, none beside me in this day, whether in the East or in the West, can claim to be the Gate that leadeth men to the knowledge of God. My proof is none other than that same proof whereby the truth of the Prophet Mahomed was established. Ask me whatsoever thou pleasest and now, at this very moment, I pledge myself to reveal such verses as can demonstrate the truth of my mission.

" Thou must choose either to submit thyself unreservedly to my Cause or entirely to repudiate it. No other alternative is thine. But if thou choose to reject my message I will not let thine hand go until thou pledge thy word to declare thy repudiation publicly.

" Thus shall he who speaketh the truth be made known, and he that speaketh falsely be condemned to eternal misery and everlasting shame."

This peremptory challenge thrust so suddenly upon Mirza Muhit distressed him profoundly. He excused himself from giving any immediate reply, and the two parted.

The Bab also addressed an epistle to the Sherif

of the holy city, wherein he set forth in clear and unmistakable language, the distinguishing features of his mission and called upon him to arise and embrace the Cause. But this epistle the Sherif mislaid in the press of business, and it was not for some time after that he read it. Under these two rebuffs the Bab's mission to Mecca had little present result. The powers of orthodoxy were too strong.

From Mecca the Bab proceeded to Medina. As he approached that holy city he called to mind the stirring events that had immortalized the name of Him who had lived and died within its walls. Those scenes which bore testimony to the creative power of that undying Genius seemed to be re-enacted before his eyes. He also remembered, as he trod that holy ground, that shining Herald of his own Dispensation, Shayk Ahmad-i-Aksai. There came to him, too, the vision of those holy men, pioneers and martyrs of the Faith who had fallen gloriously on the field of battle. Their sacred dust was reanimated by the gentle tread of his feet. Their shades were stirred by the reviving breath of his presence. They seemed to be addressing to him this fervent plea :

" Return not unto thy native land, we beseech thee, O thou beloved of our hearts ! Abide thou in our midst, for here, far from the tumult of thine enemies who are lying in wait for thee, thou shalt be safe and secure. We are fearful for thee. We dread the plottings and machinations of thy foes."

"Fear not," the indomitable Spirit of the Bab replied, " I am come into the world to bear witness to the glory of sacrifice. You are aware of the intensity of my longing. You realize the degree of my renunciation. Rather, therefore, beseech the Lord your God to hasten the hour of my martyrdom and to accept my sacrifice. Grieve not if I depart from this land, for I am hastening to fulfil my destiny."

He returned to Jeddah, embarked on a ship and reached Bushire nine months after his departure on the pilgrimage. He had not effected the object with which he had gone to Mecca. This youth from Shiraz had been received with icy contempt by the powers that be in the holy city. But his spirit was undaunted.

While still at Bushire the Bab bade Quddus, his faithful companion during his pilgrimage, to depart for Shiraz.

"The hour of separation," said the Bab, "hath struck—a separation to which no reunion will follow except in the Kingdom of God, in the presence of the King of Glory. The hand of destiny will ere long plunge you into an ocean of tribulation for His sake. I, too, will follow you. I, too, will be immersed beneath its depths. Rejoice with exceeding gladness, for you have been chosen as the standard-bearer of the host of the afflicted. You are in the vanguard of that noble army who will suffer martyrdom in His name. But you will attain the presence of Him, who is the one object of our adoration and love. In His presence you will forget the harm that shall have befallen you. The hosts of the Unseen will hasten forth to assist you and will proclaim to all the world your heroism and glory. And yours will be the ineffable joy of quaffing the cup of martyrdom for His sake."

Having thus spoken, the Bab delivered into his hands a copy of " The Seven Qualifications," a treatise in which he had set forth the essential requirements of those who had attained to a knowledge of the new Revelation and had recognized its claim.

Quddus was affectionately welcomed at Shiraz by
the Bab's maternal uncle, Siyyid Ali, and succeeded
in persuading him to embrace the Cause. And so
steadfast became Siyyid Ali's faith, and so profound
grew his love for the Bab that he consecrated his whole
life to his service. With unrelaxing vigilance he arose
to defend the Cause. He scorned fatigue, and per-
severed in his task until the hour when, in company
with the Seven Martyrs, he laid down his life for Him.

Quddus also gave the Bab's treatise to a mulla
named Sadik, and stressed the necessity of immediately putting its provisions into effect. And so enraptured was Sadik by the treatise that he unhesi-
tatingly resolved to carry out all the observances it
contained. Driven by the impelling force inherent in
the Bab's treatise he one day, while leading the congregation in prayer, suddenly proclaimed the message
of the Bab.

Consternation seized the entire congregation. The
distinguished divines who occupied the front seats
loudly protested.

" Woe betide us, the guardians and protectors of the
Faith of God ! Behold, this man has hoisted the
standard of heresy. Down with this infamous
traitor ! "

The populace echoed these protestations. The
whole city was aroused. Public order was seriously
threatened and the Governor had to intervene and
inquire into the cause of this sudden commotion.

He was informed that a disciple of the young man
called the Bab had arrived in Shiraz and was propagating the teachings of his Master. " This disciple,"
the Governor was further informed, " claims that his
teacher is the author of a new revelation contained in
a book which he asserts is divinely inspired. Mulla

Sadik has embraced that faith and is fearlessly summoning the multitude to the acceptance of that message. He declares its recognition to be the first obligation of every loyal and pious follower of Shiah Islam."

Hearing this, the Governor promptly ordered the arrest of both Quddus and Sadik, and the copy of the Bab's treatise was seized by the police.

" Tell us," angrily asked the Governor as he turned to Sadik, " if you are aware of the opening passages of the treatise wherein the Bab addresses the rulers and kings of the Earth in these terms : ' Divest yourselves of the robe of sovereignty, for He who is the King in truth, hath been made manifest! The Kingdom is God's.' If this be true it must necessarily apply to my sovereign. Must Mahomed Shah lay down his crown and abandon his sovereignty ? Must I, too, abdicate my power and relinquish my position ? "

" When once the truth of the Revelation announced by the Author of these words," replied Sadik, " shall have been definitely established, the truth of whatever has fallen from His lips will likewise be vindicated. If these words be the word of God, the abdication of Mahomed Shah and his like can matter but little. It can in no wise turn aside the Divine purpose nor alter the sovereignty of the Almighty and eternal King."

The Governor was sorely displeased with such an answer. He reviled and cursed Sadik, and ordered his attendants to scourge him with a thousand lashes, to burn the beards of both Quddus and Sadik, to pierce their noses and pass a cord through the incision and lead them by it through the city.

With magnificent fortitude both resigned themselves to their fate, and a joyous exultation invaded their souls. Subsequently, they were expelled from Shiraz and warned that if they ever returned to the city they would be crucified.

The Governor then sought out the Bab and sent a guard to Bushire to bring him in chains to Shiraz. On the way they met the Bab himself, who, approaching the leader, delivered himself into his hands. On his arrival in Shiraz the Governor himself hastily summoned him to his presence.

" Do you realise," he angrily protested, " what a great mischief you have kindled ? Are you aware what a disgrace you have become to the holy Faith of Islam and to the august person of our sovereign ? Are you not the man who claims to be the author of a new revelation annulling the sacred precepts of the Koran ? "

" If any bad man come unto you," replied the Bab in the words of the Koran, " clear up the matter at once, lest through ignorance ye harm others, and be speedily constrained to repent of what ye have done."

" What," exclaimed the Governor, " Dare you ascribe evil, and ignorance, and folly to us ? "

Then turning to his attendant, he bade him strike the Bab in the face. And so violent was the blow that the Bab's turban fell to the ground. But the leading Mulla of Shiraz, highly disapproving of the conduct of the Governor, ordered the turban to be replaced upon the Bab's head, and explained to the Governor the circumstances in which the verse quoted by the Bab had been revealed. By this means he sought to calm the Governor's fury.

" The wise course," argued the Mulla, " is to inquire into this matter with great care, and judge according to the precepts of the Holy Book."

The Governor readily consented and, after giving sureties, the Bab was allowed to go to the house of his

117

maternal uncle, where he remained in strict seclusion
for some time.

And there he was secretly joined by Husayn, his
first disciple, who had made his way thither from
Khorasan. Several times at night did the two meet
and converse till the break of day. But Husayn's
intercourse with the Bab became known. The populace feared his contemplating a still fiercer onslaught
upon their time-honoured institutions. So the Bab
instructed him to return to his native province of
Khorasan. The Bab likewise dismissed his companions. And these, spreading through the length
and breadth of the country, fearlessly proclaimed
to their countrymen the regenerating power of the
new-born Revelation. A wave of passionate inquiry
swayed the minds and hearts of both the leaders and
the masses of the people. Amazement and wonder
seized those who had heard from the lips of the
messengers of the Bab the tale of those signs and
testimonies which had heralded the birth of his manifestation. The Shah himself was moved to inquire
into the matter, and despatched Sayad Yahya, the
most learned of his subjects, to interview the Bab.

For about two hours this envoy directed the attention of the Bab to the most abstruse themes in the
teachings of Islam. But the conciseness and lucidity
of the Bab's answers so excited his wonder and admiration that he, too, became a convert. And such
was the state of certitude to which he attained that
he affirmed that if all the powers of the Earth were to
be leagued against him, they would be powerless to
shake his confidence in the greatness of the Bab's Cause.

So the Bab enjoyed comparative tranquillity for a
time. But meanwhile the Governor was bending
every effort to involve the Bab in fresh embarrass-

ments. And being informed that every night eager crowds gathered to visit the Bab, he forthwith ordered his arrest. The chief constable broke into the house where the Bab was staying, arrested him, and carried off all documents. On hearing of this, however, the Shah dismissed the Governor from office. And on obtaining his freedom the Bab proceeded to Isphahan, where he was most hospitably received by the chief Mulla.

There, for a time, things went well.

An unceasing stream of visitors flowed to his residence. A few indeed came merely to satisfy their curiosity, but others came to obtain a deeper understanding of his Faith, and still others to seek a remedy for their ills and sufferings, and his popularity grew. But his growing popularity soon aroused the resentment of the ecclesiastical authorities. They viewed with envy the ascendancy which he was slowly acquiring over the thoughts and consciences of their followers. With feelings of dismay they beheld on every side evidences of his all-pervasive influence invading the stronghold of orthodoxy and subverting their foundations. They accordingly summoned a gathering, and at it signed and sealed a document which condemned him as a heretic and declared him to be deserving of the penalty of death. They sent him to Tabriz and thence to Mah Ku, a place so remote that they hoped that by sending him there the tide of his rising influence would be stemmed and every tie that bound him to the body of his disciples throughout the country be severed.

Confined within the walls of the castle the Bab was indeed separated from his disciples, but he was able to devote his time the more to the composition of the Persian Bayan, in which he laid down the laws and precepts of his dispensation, plainly and emphatically announced the advent of a subsequent Revelation, and

persistently urged his followers to seek and find
" Him whom God would make manifest."

Meanwhile, Husayn, who had been endeavouring to
spread the knowledge of the new Revelation in Meshed,
when he heard of the Bab's incarceration, determined
to walk the whole way from the eastern side of Persia
to the western to see him. The Bab affectionately
embraced him on his arrival, and at the end of nine
days dismissed him with these words : " On foot you
have walked from your native province to this place,
and on foot you must return. . . . You should visit
on your way the believers of Tabriz, Teheran and other
places. To each you will convey the expression of
my love and tender affection. . . . You will strive
to inflame their hearts anew with the fire of the love
of God and will endeavour to fortify their faith in
His Revelation."

Husayn proceeded first to Teheran and thence to
Barfurush, the home of Quddus ; and there his keen
insight swiftly apprehended the magnitude of the power
latent in Quddus and the nobility of his character.

Husayn then continued his journey to Meshed,
where he built a house, in which he was soon joined by
Quddus. A steady stream of visitors poured to see
Quddus, acknowledging the claim of the Cause and
willingly enlisting under its banner. In time such a
conflagration was lighted in the hearts of men that its
quickening power was felt to the most outlying parts.
And while the Almighty, through Quddus, had in
Khorasan in the East lit a fire that glowed in hottest
flame, He had in Kerbela, beyond the western confines of Persia, kindled the light of Tahirih,[1] who had

[1] Also known as Qurral-i-Ayni.

120

been converted to the Cause of the Bab by reading his writings at Kerbela. Unwarned and uninvited, she had perceived the dawning light of the promised Revelation breaking upon the city of Shiraz, and was prompted to pen her message and plead her fidelity to him who was the revealer of that light. She vehemently denounced the corruption and perversity of her generation, and fearlessly advocated a fundamental revolution in the habits and manners of her people. Her indomitable spirit was quickened by the fire of her love for the Bab. All who met her were ensnared by her bewitching eloquence. None could resist her charm ; and few could escape the contagion of her belief. She was able to fire the imagination of a considerable number of both the Persian and the Arab inhabitants of Iraq and lead them to join forces with those in Persia. Eventually she herself came to Persia, and was sent by Baha-ullah to Khorasan with a company of believers.

In the meanwhile, disturbances had occurred in Meshed. The number of seekers had swelled to such proportions as to excite the apprehension of the authorities. And the chief constable, determining to assert his rights, ordered the arrest of Husayn's special attendant, named Hasan. They pierced his nose, passed a cord through the incision, and with this halter led him through the streets. Husayn tried to appease the anger of his companions. But their hearts burned with impatience to redress that bitter injury. A number of them banded themselves together and loudly raised through the streets of Meshed the cry of " Ya Sahibaz-Zaman " [1] as a protest against this sudden affront to the dignity of their faith. The city

---

[1] " O Lord of the Age ! "—one of the titles of the promised Messiah.

re-echoed with the sound of their voices. And the reverberation of their shouts reached even the outlying regions of the province and raised a tumult in the hearts of men.

That very night Quddus bade farewell to his companions, departed from Meshed and journeyed to Badasht, where he was joined by Baha-ullah and also by Tahirih. Here a memorable and decisive conference took place. Every day witnessed the abrogation of a new law or the repudiation of a long-established tradition. The veils that guarded the sanctity of the ordinances of Islam were sternly rent asunder, and the idols that had so long claimed the adoration of their blind worshippers were rudely demolished. At one meeting, suddenly, the figure of Tahirih, adorned and unveiled, appeared before the eyes of the assembled companions. Consternation seized the gathering. To behold her face unveiled was to them inconceivable. To gaze even at her shadow they deemed improper. Yet quietly, and with perfect dignity, she advanced towards Quddus, and seated herself on his right-hand side. Her unruffled serenity contrasted sharply with the affrighted countenances of those who gazed upon her. The face of Quddus betrayed a feeling of inexpressible anger. His attitude failed, however, to move her. A feeling of joy and triumph illumined her face. Undeterred by the tumult she had raised, she rose from her seat without the least premeditation, and in language like the words of the Koran, delivered an appeal, at the end of which she declared :

" I am the Word which the Messiah is to utter, the Word which will put to flight the chiefs and nobles of the Earth. This day is the day of rejoicing— the day on which the fetters of the past are burst asunder. Let those who have shared in the great achievement arise and embrace each other."

That memorable day witnessed the most revolutionary changes in the life and habits of the assembled followers of the Bab. Their manner of worship underwent a sudden and fundamental transformation. The prayers and ceremonials by which those devout worshippers had been disciplined were irrevocably discarded. The clarion-call of the new Order had been sounded. And mountain and valley re-echoed the shouts with which that enthusiastic band hailed the extinction of the old and the birth of the new Day.

Husayn had now, July 1848, decided to proceed on a pilgrimage to Kerbela. Before he had departed, however, a messenger arrived bearing for him the Bab's turban. "Adorn your head," was the message he bore from the Bab, "with my green turban ; and unfurling the Black Standard before you, hasten to assist my beloved Quddus." As soon as he received the message Husayn left Meshed. Outside the city he hoisted the Black Standard, placed the turban of the Bab upon his head and gave the signal for the march, and wherever he and his fellow-disciples tarried on the way he would fearlessly proclaim the message of the New Day.

Arriving near Damghan he pointed in the direction of Mazindaran and said :

"This is the way that leads to our Kerbela. I, together with seventy-two of my companions, shall suffer death for the sake of the Well-Beloved. Whoso is unable to renounce the world, let him now depart, for later he will be unable to escape."

The news of their approach alarmed Saidul-Ulama. The widespread and growing popularity of Husayn, the Black Standard which waved before him, above all, the number, the discipline, and the enthusiasm of his companions, combined to arouse the implacable hatred of that cruel and overbearing doctor of the law. He bade the crier summon the people of Barfurush to the masjid and announce that a sermon of such momentous consequence was to be delivered by him that no loyal adherent of Islam could afford to ignore it. As a result, an immense crowd of men, women and children thronged the masjid, saw him ascend the pulpit, fling his turban to the ground, tear open the neck of his shirt, and bewail the plight into which the Faith had fallen.

" Awake," he thundered from the pulpit, " for our enemies stand at our very doors ready to wipe out all that we cherish as pure and holy in Islam. Should we fail to resist them, none will be left to survive their onslaught. It is the duty of all the inhabitants of Barfurush, both young and old, both men and women, to arm themselves against these contemptible wreckers of Islam, and by every means resist their onset. To-morrow, at the hour of dawn, let all of you arise and march out to exterminate their forces."

The entire congregation rose in response. His passionate eloquence, the undisputed authority he exercised over them, and the dread of losing their own lives and property combined to induce them to make every preparation for the coming encounter. They armed themselves with every available weapon and set out at break of day to face and slay the enemies of their Faith.

Three miles from Barfurush Husayn and his companions encountered their enemies. A fierce expression of savagery rested upon their countenances. The foulest imprecations fell unceasingly from their lips. And Husayn's companions, in the face of this angry populace, made as if to unsheathe their swords.

" Not yet," commanded their leader, " not until the aggressor forces us to protect ourselves must our swords leave their scabbards."

Scarcely had he uttered these words than the enemy opened fire and six of the companions were immediately hurled to the ground.

" Beloved leader," exclaimed one of them, " we have followed you with no other desire than to sacrifice ourselves in the path of the Cause. Allow us, we pray you, to defend ourselves."

" The time is not yet," replied Husayn, " the number is not yet complete."

A bullet immediately afterwards pierced the heart of one of his companions who had walked all the way from Meshed. And at the sight of that devoted companion fallen dead at his feet, Husayn raised his eyes to heaven and prayed :

" Behold, O God, my God, the plight of Thy chosen companions, and witness the welcome which these people have accorded Thy loved ones. Thou knowest we cherish no other desire than to guide them to the way of Truth and to confer upon them the knowledge of Thy Revelation. Thou hast commanded us to defend our lives against the assaults of the enemy. Faithful to Thy command, I now arise with my companions to resist the attack which they have launched against us."

Unsheathing his sword and spurring his charger into the midst of the enemy, Husayn then pursued the assailant of his fallen companion. Unmindful of the bullets that rained upon him, he forced his way through the ranks of the enemy, rode straight to the

125

residence of the Saidul-Ulama, and thrice making the circuit of his house, cried out :

"Let that contemptible coward who has incited the inhabitants of this town to wage holy war against us emerge from his inglorious retreat. Has he forgotten that he who preaches a holy war must needs himself march at the head of his followers, and by his own deeds sustain their enthusiasm ? "

To the crowd which had gathered about him Husayn addressed these words :

" O, followers of the Prophet of God, and shiahs of the Imams of His Faith ! Why have ye risen against us ? Why deem the shedding of our blood meritorious in the sight of God ? Did we ever repudiate the truth of your Faith ? Is this the hospitality which the Apostle of God has enjoined His followers to accord to both the faithful and the infidel ? Consider : I alone, with no other weapon than my sword, have emerged unscathed from the midst of the fire with which ye have besieged me. God has protected me and will establish the ascendancy of His Faith in your eyes."

Husayn then proceeded to the caravanserai, closed the gates, assembled his companions, and as evening approached, asked whether anyone would arise, and, renouncing his life for the sake of his Faith, ascend to the roof of the caravanserai and sound the call to prayer. A youth gladly responded. No sooner had the opening words of " Allah-a-Akbar " dropped from his lips than a bullet struck, and killed him.

" Let another among you arise," urged Husayn, " and with the self-same renunciation, proceed with the prayer which that youth was unable to finish."

Another youth started to his feet and had no sooner uttered the words, " I bear witness that Mahomed is the Apostle of God " than he, too, was struck down. A third youth, at the bidding of his Chief, attempted to complete the prayer, and was uttering the words, " There is no God, but God," when he, in his turn, fell dead. The fall of the third companion decided Husayn to throw open the gate of the caravanserai. Leaping on horseback and followed by his companions, he charged his assailants and decimated the forces that had been arrayed against him.

A few days later he proceeded to the shrine of Shaykh Tabarsi, and on reaching it he commenced to build a fort, where he was soon to be joined by Quddus.

The arrival of Quddus was enthusiastically welcomed, and he now took over the leadership. Every morning and every afternoon Quddus would summon Husayn and the most distinguished of his companions and ask them to chant the writings of the Bab. Despising all danger and oblivious of his own needs Quddus continued his daily communion with his Beloved, writing His praises, and rousing the defenders of the fort to fresh exertions.

" My soul is wedded to the telling of Thee," he was wont to exclaim ; " remembrance of Thee is the stay and solace of my life ! I glory in that I was the first to suffer ignominiously for Thy sake in Shiraz. I long to be the first to suffer a death that shall be worthy of Thy Cause."

On the other hand, the imperious Saidul-Ulama addressed a burning appeal to Nasirudin, the Shah who had recently ascended the throne.

" The standard of revolt," he pleaded, " has been raised by the contemptible sect of the Babis. This wretched band of irresponsible agitators has dared to strike at the very foundations of Your Majesty's authority. They have built themselves a fort and are directing a campaign against you. With unswerving obstinacy they have proclaimed their independent sovereignty—a sovereignty that would abase to the dust the imperial diadem of your illustrious ancestors. You stand at the threshold of your reign. What greater triumph could signalise the commencement of your rule than the extirpation of this hateful creed ? But should you vacillate in your policy I feel it my duty to warn you, that not only this Province, but the whole of Persia will repudiate your authority and surrender to their cause."

The Shah referred the matter to the military authorities and instructed them to take whatever measures they might deem fit to eradicate these disturbers of his realm. An army was raised. The bread and even the water for the defenders were intercepted. But, ere the commander launched his attack, he sent a messenger to Husayn to ascertain the purpose of his activities.

"Tell your master," replied Husayn, "that we utterly repudiate any intention of subverting the foundation of the monarchy. Our Cause concerns the revelation of the Promised One and is a matter for the spiritual authorities. Let the prince who commands the army direct the ulamas of Sari and Barfurush to betake themselves to this place, and ask us to demonstrate the validity of the Revelation proclaimed by the Bab. Let the Koran decide as to who speaks the truth. Let the prince himself decide as to who speaks the truth. And let him also decide how he would treat us if we fail to establish the truth of our Cause."

The appeal had no effect on the prince. Three days later he launched an attack upon the fort. Quartering his hosts upon a height he gave the signal to open fire.

" Mount your steeds, O heroes of God ! " Quddus exclaimed as he ordered the gates of the fort to be thrown open. And Husayn, with two hundred and two of his companions, ran to their horses and followed Quddus as he rode out to the enemy's stronghold. At a given moment the enemy discharged a thousand bullets, one of which struck Quddus in the mouth. Husayn and others hastened to the rescue of his friend and with pain and sorrow conducted their wounded leader to the shelter of the stronghold, where Quddus thus exhorted them :

" We should submit to whatever is the will of God. Though my body be afflicted, my soul is immersed in gladness. My gratitude to God knows no bounds. If you love me, suffer not that this joy be obscured by the sight of your lamentations."

This memorable engagement took place in December 1848. In that same month Beha-ullah set out from Nur for the fort of Tabarsi. But on the way he and his companions were seized and brought before the Governor of Amul, and a Sayad urged in vehement language that these followers of the Bab be put to death.

" These obscure sectarians," he cried, " are the sworn enemies both of the State and of the Faith of Islam. We must at all cost extirpate the heresy."

The Governor, in order to check the passions which had been aroused, ordered his attendants to prepare the rods to bastinado the captives. They were commencing to bind the servants when Baha-ullah intervened, saying :

" None of these men is guilty of any crime. I offer myself as a willing victim of your chastisement."

The Governor was reluctantly compelled to give

orders that the Baha-ullah alone should be beaten. The same treatment (beating by the bastinado) that had been meted out to the Bab five months previously at Tabriz, Baha-ullah now suffered in the presence of the assembled ulamas of Amul. And he had the additional mortification of not being able to throw in his lot with the defenders of fort Tabarsi.

Meanwhile, a renewed attack was made upon the fort, and to meet it Husayn prepared himself. He performed his ablutions, clothed himself in new garments, attired his head with the Bab's turban, and prepared for the approaching encounter. An indefinable joy illumined his face. Alone with Quddus, he poured forth all that his enraptured soul could no longer restrain. Then, as soon as the morning-star had risen, he started to his feet, mounted his charger, gave the signal to open the gates of the fort, rode out at the head of three hundred and thirteen companions and, dashing forward, overcame the resistance of barricade after barricade. Alas! he was soon struck in the breast by a bullet. Bleeding profusely, he dismounted, staggered a few steps, and fell exhausted to the ground, where he lay till two of his companions came to the rescue and bore him to the fort, into the presence of Quddus.

"You have hastened the hour of your departure," said Quddus, "and have abandoned me to the mercy of my foes. Please God, I will ere long join you and taste the sweetness of heaven's ineffable delight."

"May my life be a ransom to you," was Husayn's reply.

A long time elapsed before Quddus would admit his companions to the room. When they entered it they found that Husayn had already expired. But a faint smile still lingered on his face; and such was the

peacefulness of his countenance that he seemed only
to have fallen asleep. Quddus himself attended to
his burial, clothed him in his own shirt, and gave instructions for him to be laid to rest near the shrine of
Shaykh Tabarsi.

" Well is it with you to have remained to your last
hour faithful to the Covenant of God," said Quddus,
as he laid a parting kiss upon his eyes and forehead,
and began speaking with such poignancy that the
seven companions who were standing beside him
wept profusely and wished that they had been sacrificed in his stead. Then with his own hands he laid
the body in the tomb, and cautioned those who were
standing near to conceal even from their companions
the spot which served as his resting-place.

It was at the hour of dawn on February 2, 1849,
that the burial of Husayn took place. He was but
six and thirty years of age when he quaffed the cup
of martyrdom. The traits of mind and of character
which from his very youth he displayed, the pro-
fundity of his learning, the tenacity of his faith, his
intrepid courage, his singleness of purpose, his high
sense of justice and unswerving devotion, marked him
as an outstanding figure among those who, by their lives,
have borne witness to the glory of the new Revelation.
And such was his devotion to the Bab that, says one
who knew him, if anyone did so much as mention his
name he could not restrain his tears; often when engaged in perusing his writings he would be almost beside himself with rapture, and nearly faint with joy.

For many weeks longer the siege of Tabarsi continued. The food of the besieged was reduced to the
flesh of horses. Even the leather of their saddles was

consumed by these hard-pressed companions. And they boiled the grass and devoured it with avidity. But as their strength declined Quddus multiplied his visits to them, and endeavoured by his words of cheer and hope to lighten the load of their agony.

" A glimpse of his face and the magic of his words, would transmute our despondency into golden joy," said one of his followers. " We were reinforced with a strength of such intensity, that had the hosts of our enemies suddenly appeared before us we felt ourselves able to vanquish any foe."

The enemy were surprised to find that the booming of their guns had failed to silence the voice of prayer and the acclamations of joy which the besieged raised in answer to their threats. Instead of the surrender which they expected, the call to prayer, the chanting of the Koran, and the chorus of gladsome voices intoning hymns of thanksgiving unceasingly reached their ears.

In the month of May, accompanied by the roar of cannons, several regiments of infantry and cavalry rushed to storm the fort. And the sound of their approach impelled Quddus to send out his companions to repulse their attack.

" Never since our occupation of this fort," said he, " have we under any circumstances attempted to direct an offensive against our opponents. Not until they unchained their attack upon us did we arise to defend our lives. Our sole, our unalterable purpose has been to vindicate by our deeds, and by our readiness to shed our blood in the path of our Faith, the exalted character of our mission. But the hour is fast approaching when we shall have to consummate this task.'

The Commander of the enemy forces now sent an

emissary requesting that two representatives be delegated by the beseiged to conduct confidential negotiations with him in the hope of arriving at a peaceful settlement. Accordingly, Quddus instructed two of his companions to act as his representatives. They were courteously received and the Commander wrote in the margin of a Koran :

" I swear by this most holy Book, by the righteousness of God who has revealed it, and the Mission of Him who was inspired with its verses, that I cherish no other purpose than to promote peace and friendliness between us. Come forth from your stronghold and rest assured that no hand will be stretched forth against you."

Quddus received the Koran from the hand of his messenger, reverently kissed it and said : " O, our Lord, decide between us and between our people with truth ; for the best to decide art Thou." Then he bade his companions prepare to leave the fort. " By our response to their invitation," he told them, " we shall demonstrate the sincerity of our intentions."

Attired with the green turban the Bab had sent him, Quddus mounted the favourite steed of the Commander, which had been sent for him. His chief companions, sayads and learned divines rose before him, the remainder followed on foot, two hundred and two in all.

Then followed an act of grossest treachery. Fire was opened upon them. Any who escaped the bullets were killed by the swords of the officers and spears of the men. Of the captives a few were cut to pieces with the sword, others were torn asunder, a number was bound to trees and riddled with bullets, and still others were blown from the mouths of cannon and

133

consigned to the flames. Yet in the very throes of death these unconquerable heroes were still heard to utter the words, " Holy, holy, O Lord our God, Lord of the angels and the spirit."

Quddus himself was not killed with the others : he was detained as a prisoner and taken to Barfurush. There the Commander was reluctant to ill-treat his captive. But the hatred with which Quddus and his Cause inspired the Saidul-Ulama blazed into furious rage as he witnessed the increasing evidence that the Commander was inclined to allow so formidable an opponent to slip from his grasp. Day and night he remonstrated with him. In the fury of his despair he appealed to the mob. And the whole of Barfurush were aroused by the persistency of his call, till, fearing that his own life might be endangered, the Commander summoned to his presence the leading ulamas, to consult with them as to the measures that should be taken to allay the popular excitement ; and Quddus also was brought before him.

" For what reason," the Saidul-Ulama impertinently inquired of Quddus, " have you, by wearing a green turban, arrogated to yourself a right which only he who is a true descendant of the Prophet can claim ? Do you not know that whoso defies this sacred tradition is accursed of God ? "

Intimidated by the imprecations of the ulamas, and forgetful of his oath, the Commander abjectly surrendered Quddus to the hands of his unrelenting foes. And the people arose to perpetrate upon their victim acts of such atrocious cruelty as no pen can describe. He was stripped of his clothes, his turban bestowed upon him by the Bab was befouled. Barefooted, bareheaded, and loaded with chains, he was paraded through the streets, followed and scorned by the entire population of the town. Assailed with knives and axes by the scum of the women, his body was pierced and mutilated and eventually delivered to the flames.

Yet, amidst all his torments Quddus was heard whispering forgiveness to his foes. " Forgive, O my God, the trespasses of these people. Deal with them in thy mercy, for they know not what we have already discovered and cherish. Show them, O God, the Way of Truth, and turn their ignorance into faith."

These things happened in May 1849. And all this time tales of the signs and wonders which the Bab's unnumbered admirers had witnessed were being transmitted from mouth to mouth, and had given rise to a wave of unprecedented enthusiasm which rapidly spread over the whole country. It swept over Teheran itself and roused the ecclesiastical dignitaries to fresh exertions against him. For they trembled at the progress of a Movement which, if allowed to run its course, would soon engulf the institutions upon which their authority and their very existence depended. They saw on every side increasing evidence of a faith and devotion such as they themselves had been powerless to evoke, of a loyalty which struck at the very roots of the fabric which their own hands had reared, and which all the resources at their command had as yet failed to undermine. The Shah's minister accordingly issued orders for the immediate convocation of the ecclesiastical dignitaries of Tabriz for the express purpose of arraigning the Bab and of seeking means for the extinction of his influence. And the Bab was brought to Tabriz for this investigation.

This convocation was held in the official residence

of the Governor, and a number of the most distinguished Shaykhis and doctors of divinity were amongst the convened. The heir to the throne himself attended. Nizamul-Ulama presided. A multitude of people besieged the entrance to the hall, and were pressing forward in such large numbers that a passage had to be forced for the Bab.

As he entered the assembly the expression of confidence which sat upon his brow and the spirit of power which shone from his whole being deeply impressed those who saw him, and a mysterious silence fell upon men, till it was broken by the Nizamul-Ulama :

" Who do you claim to be," he asked the Bab, " and what is the message which you have brought ? "

" I am, I am, I am the Promised One ! " exclaimed the Bab, " I am the One whose name you have for a thousand years invoked, at whose mention you have risen, whose advent you have longed to witness, and the hour of whose Revelation you have prayed to God to hasten. Verily I say, it behoves the people, both of the East and of the West, to obey my Word and to pledge allegiance to my Person."

Immediately after he had declared himself to be the Promised One a feeling of awe seized those who were present. They dropped their hands in silent confusion. The pallor of their faces betrayed the agitation of their hearts. But not all were thus awed. A certain Mulla Mahomed who had himself, like the Bab, been a disciple of Kazim at Kerbela, sternly reprimanded him, saying :

" You wretched and immature lad of Shiraz ! You have already subverted Iraq : would you now raise a like turmoil in Adhirbayjan ? "

" Your Honour," replied the Bab, " I have not

come hither of my own accord. I have been summoned to this place."

" The claim which you have advanced," said the Nizamul-Ulama, " is a stupendous one : it must needs be supported by incontrovertible evidence."

" The most convincing evidence of the truth of the Mission of the Prophet of God is admittedly his own word," replied the Bab. " He himself testifies to this truth : ' Is it not enough for them that We have sent down to Thee the Book ? ' The power to produce such evidence has been given to me by God. Within the space of two days and two nights I declare myself able to reveal verses of such number as will equal the whole of the Koran."

A systematic course of browbeating and mockery was now pursued by a hostile set in the assembly. The Nizamul-Ulama was sorely displeased at their attitude ; and a few others were, likewise, inclined to denounce the disgraceful treatment being meted out to the Bab. But the Mulla persisted in his vehement denunciation :

" I warn you," he loudly protested. " if you allow this man to pursue his activities, the day will come when the entire population of Tabriz will have flocked to his standard. When that day comes, if he signify his wish that all the ulamas of Tabriz, that the heir-apparent himself, should be expelled from the city and that he alone should assume the reins of civil and ecclesiastical authority, no one of you will be able to oppose him. The entire city, nay, the whole province, will on that day with one voice support him."

These persistent denunciations excited the apprehension of the authorities, and they took counsel together how the progress of his Faith might be resisted. Finally, it was decided that the Bab should receive, at the hands of the Governor's bodyguard, the chastisement which he deserved. The guard, however, refused to accede to the request, perferring not to interfere in a matter which they considered the sole concern of the ulamas. Thereupon the Shaykul-Islam decided to inflict the punishment himself, and summoning the Bab to his home he, with his own hand, bastinadoed him.

From Tabriz the Bab was taken back to Chihrig, where he remained for some months. Meanwhile, in other parts of Persia than in that part in which Husayn and Quddus had lost their lives disturbances had occurred. And by now the authorities in Teheran were alarmed at the recurrent manifestations of an indomitable will and a fierce and inflexible tenacity of faith. Though the Imperial army had everywhere triumphed, yet it was clear that the spirit responsible for such rare heroism was by no means vanquished. The loyalty which the remnants of that scattered band bore to their captive leader remained unimpaired. Far from being extinguished it had blazed up more intense and devastating than ever. Above all, he who had kindled that flame and nourished the spirit was still alive ; and, despite his isolation, he was able to exercise his influence to the full. Extinguish that light, choke the stream at its very source, and the torrent that had brought so much devastation in its wake would run dry. Such was the thought in the mind of the Grand Vazir, who, summoning his counsellors, communicated to them his fears and acquainted them with his plans.

" Behold the storm," he exclaimed, " which the Faith of the Bab has provoked in the hearts of my fellow countrymen ! Nothing short of his public execution can enable the distracted country to recover its tranquillity. If you are able to advise a better remedy acquaint me with it, for my sole purpose is to ensure the peace of my countrymen."

Not a single voice dared venture a reply, except that of the Minister of War, who urged that to put to death a banished Sayad for the deeds of a band of irresponsible agitators would manifestly be an act of cruelty.

Disregarding the advice of his counsellor the Vazir despatched orders for the Bab to be brought again to Tabriz. And three days after the Bab's arrival, a further order was received from Vazir commanding the Governor to execute his prisoner on the very day the order should reach him. The Governor, however, objected. He expressed to the bearer of the order his consternation. " The task I am called upon to do," he said, " is a task that only ignoble persons would accept."

This refusal being communicated to the Vazir, he thereupon ordered the bearer himself to carry out without delay and in its entirety the instructions previously given.

Deprived of his turban and sash, twin emblems of his noble lineage, the Bab, together with Siyyid Husayn, his amanuensis, was taken to the barracks. As he approached the courtyard a youth suddenly leaped forward, forcing his way through the crowd and utterly ignoring the perils which such an attempt might involve. His face was haggard, his feet were bare, his hair dishevelled. Breathless with excitement and exhausted with fatigue he flung himself at the feet of the Bab and, seizing the hem of his garment, passionately implored him :

" Send me not from thee, O Master. Wherever thou goest, suffer me to follow thee."

" Mahomed Ali," answered the Bab, " arise and rest

139

assured that you will be with me. To-morrow you shall witness what God hath decreed."

Siyyid Husayn bore witness to the following :

" That night the face of the Bab was aglow with a joy such as had never before shone from his countenance. Indifferent to the storm that raged about him he conversed with us in gay and cheerful mood. The sorrows that had weighed so heavily on him seemed to have completely vanished. Their weight appeared to have dissolved away in the consciousness of coming victory."

Early in the morning the Governor ordered his head lictor to conduct the Bab into the presence of the leading mullas and obtain from them the authorization required for his execution. No sooner had the lictor secured the necessary documents than he delivered his captive into the hands of Sam Khan, Colonel of the Christian regiment of Urumiyya, assuring him that he could proceed with his task now that he had received the sanction of the civil and ecclesiastical authorities of the realm. The youth Mahomed Ali, bursting into tears, entreated to be allowed to remain with his master. So he also was delivered into the hands of Sam Khan.

Sam Khan then ordered his men to drive a nail into the pillar separating two rooms and to make fast two ropes to that nail, from which the Bab and his companion were to be separately suspended. Mahomed Ali begged Sam Khan to have his body placed in such a position that it would shield the body of the Bab. And he was eventually placed so that his head reposed on the breast of his master.

As soon as they were fastened a regiment of soldiers ranged itself in three files, each of which was ordered to open its fire in turn. The smoke of the firing was such as to turn the light of the noonday sun into darkness. And as soon as the cloud of smoke had cleared away an astounded multitude, who had crowded on to the roof of the barracks as well as the tops of adjoining houses, beheld a scene which their eyes could scarcely believe. There, standing before them alive and unhurt, was the companion of the Bab, whilst the Bab himself had vanished uninjured from their sight. Though the cords with which they had been suspended were cut in pieces by the bullets, yet their bodies had miraculously escaped.

" The Bab has gone from our sight," rang out the voices of the bewildered multitude. They set out in search for him, and eventually found him in a room engaged in conversation with Siyyid Husayn.

Stunned by the force of this tremendous revelation. Sam Khan ordered his men to leave the barracks at once, and he refused ever again to associate his regiment with any act injurious to the Bab.

No sooner had Sam Khan departed than the Colonel of the bodyguard volunteered to carry out the execution. On the same wall, and in the same manner, the Bab and his companion were again suspended, while the regiment was formed in line to fire on them.

" Had you believed in me, O wayward generation," were the last words of the Bab to the gazing multitude, as the regiment was preparing to fire, " every one of you would have followed the example of this youth and willingly would have sacrificed himself in my path. The day will come when you will recognize me. But in that day I shall have ceased to be with you."

The regiment fired, and this time the bodies of the Bab and his companion were shattered and blended into one mass of mingled flesh and bone.

141

That very moment a gale arose and swept over the city. A whirlwind of dust of incredible density obscured the light of the sun and blinded the eyes of the people. The entire city remained enveloped in darkness from noon till night.

This martyrdom of the Bab took place on July 9, 1850, thirty-one years from the date of his birth.

His body was dead. His spirit lived on. Husayn had been slain in battle. Quddus had been done to death in captivity. But Baha-ullah lived. The One who shall be made manifest was alive. And in him and in others had been engendered such love for the Bab and what he stood for as, in the words of the chronicler, no eye had ever beheld nor mortal heart conceived : if branches of every tree were turned into pens, and all the seas into ink, and Earth and Heaven rolled into one parchment, the immensity of that love would still remain untold. This love for the Cause still survived. And it was sufficient. Baha-ullah was, indeed, despoiled of his possessions, deserted by his friends, driven into exile from his native land and, even in exile, confined to his house. But in him the Cause was still alive—and more than alive, purified and ennobled by the fiery trials through which it had passed.

Under the wise control and direction of Baha-ullah from his prison-house, first at Baghdad and then at Acre in Syria, there grew what is now known as the Bahai Movement which, silently propagating itself, has now spread to Europe and America as well as to India and Egypt, while the bodily remains of the Bab, long secretly guarded, now find a resting-place on Mount Carmel in a Tomb-shrine, which is a place of pilgrimage to visitors from all over the world.

CHAPTER III

A ROMAN CATHOLIC MYSTIC

STE THÉRÈSE DE LISIEUX

THE Tomb-shrine of the Bab has been erected on Mount Carmel. And to Mount Carmel have resorted hermits and pilgrims for at least two thousand years. In the time of Samuel there lived on Carmel hermits known as " Sons of the Prophets." In the fourth century A.D. Carmel was a place of pilgrimage. And in about A.D. 1155 an Order of such vigour was founded that it spread similar foundations in many parts of Europe. It was known as the Order of Mount Carmel. And among its branches was that founded in 1582 at Avila in Spain by that great mystic Ste Teresa. The old Order had become lax, but in this new foundation the practices of poverty, penance and the contemplative life were carried out in a truly austere fashion. In the early part of the nineteenth century a convent of this Order was established at the little town of Lisieux in Normandy. And among the nuns of the convent was one now known as Ste Thérèse de Lisieux, and also as " The Little Flower."

Though she lived for only twenty-four years, from 1873 to 1897, and only in a secluded convent in a remote provincial town, yet in this short space she had made such an impression that a quarter of a

143

century later she was, with tremendous pomp and ceremony and after protracted examination, declared by the Pope to be a saint.   In the presence of twenty-three crimson-robed Cardinals, of some two hundred other prelates, and of thousands of people inside St. Peter's at Rome, Pope Pius XI pronounced these words : " We declare the blessed Thérèse of the Child Jesus to be a Saint of God's Church ; and we inscribe her name in the catalogue of Saints."   And so popular was this canonization that for the first time in the history of such ceremonies there came a thunder-clap of applause.   The multitude could not contain its joy.   The silver trumpets sounded, the great bells of St. Peter rang out, and for an hour were answered by all the bells in Rome.   Further, she is known and reverenced and beloved throughout the world.   Her autobiography has been translated into every European language, and into many other non-European.   Over a million copies of it have been sold.   Thousands of pilgrims every year visit her grave and the convent wherein she lived.   People look for miracles.   And thousands believe that to this day she works them.   But surely the greatest miracle of all is that one so young and tender, and so secluded from the general life of the world, should in this short time have been able to make so deep an impression upon the human race.

What was the secret of that power, and whence she derived it, I would now inquire.

The Little Flower, as Ste Thérèse de Lisieux is everywhere known, is often portrayed in pictures wearing an insipid, sentimental expression without any vigour or spirit in it.   But delicate, gentle and loving as she was, she had the unflinching courage of a hero, and her nerve was of steel.   She would

144

bite her lip through rather than show the pain she suffered. She was French of the French, with all the brightness, the ardency and the vigour characteristic of her country-women, and all their grace of expression. She was born of parents both of whom were deeply religious, so that she inherited a religious disposition. And in her this disposition was vehemently religious. Through life she retained a childlike simplicity, but with that simplicity went also that pertinacity of a child which will not be denied what it has set itself on : her will was imperious ; she would not be thwarted. Gentle as she might be she could be as impetuous as a mountain torrent, and unbelievably stubborn. And humble as she was she had Everestian ambitions ; nothing short of the highest would satisfy her. But most characteristic of all was her joyousness and lovability. Even reading about her one cannot help falling in love with her. An inexhaustible fountain of love seemed to be perpetually welling up within her. A touch, and it would gush forth. And this capacity for love meant extreme, abnormal sensitivity—extreme capacity for feeling pain as well as joy.

This was her innate disposition, the foundation on which she started and the fountain of her life. And from outside she early received an idea which profoundly affected her thought for the rest of her life, and which even at the age of three years she applied to circumstances with all the ruthless logic of a child —and of a French child at that. She was brought up to believe that the joys of heaven would only be reached when this earthly life was over. She was devoted to her mother and, wishing her to be happy as quickly as possible, she hoped her mother would soon die. To that extreme did she apply this idea which had so early been implanted by those around her.

She was born in 1873, the ninth child of Louis and Zélie Martin, lower middle-class provincials of France. And from the first she was enveloped in love. She was the youngest child, and both father and mother poured all their affection on her, while her sisters also were devoted to her. Moreover her home was a hot-house of religion. With her wilfulness and headstrong impetuosity she might, she thinks, have become very wicked. But she was checked from erring and shown the way to perfection. And even as a child she possessed great self-control. She could keep herself in as well as let herself go.

And from quite early days she had a remarkable love of nature. Much of her life appears to us as forced. But through all this constraint, love of nature persisted. Her childish heart was touched " by the vision of the cornfields, studded with cornflowers, poppies and marguerites " ; and she loved " far-stretching views, sunlit spaces, and stately trees." All the beauties of nature cast their spell upon her and raised her soul to Heaven. The stars she would look up at " with untold delight." Orion's belt had a peculiar fascination for her and looked to her like a cluster of diamonds. With her head thrown back she would gaze untiringly at the starry skies.

The sea she saw for the first time when she was between six and seven.

" I could not turn away my eyes ; its majesty, the roaring of the waves, the whole vast spectacle deeply impressed me and spoke to my soul of God's power and greatness. . . . That same evening, at the hour when the sun seems to sink into the broad expanse of waters, leaving behind it a trail of light, I sat on a lonely rock and let my gaze linger on this path of splendour."

Snow, too, had a great attraction for her. She loved its purity and radiance. But it was flowers that she chiefly adored. And among flowers in especial the rose. It is because of her love of flowers that she is known as The Little Flower.

When she was still only four her first great sorrow came. Her mother died. And for some years her naturally happy disposition deserted her. From being lively and demonstrative she became timid and shy, and so sensitive that a look was often sufficient to make her burst into tears. She could not bear to be noticed by or to meet strangers. She was only at ease with her dear ones at home. She had made her sister, Pauline, her " mother " ; and her father's affectionate heart gave her its loving care.

Her spiritual development soon commenced. As a little child her religious instinct spontaneously showed itself in her making tiny altars in a recess in the garden-wall and decorating them with flowers. And in her bedroom she arranged a little altar in her own way, with minute candlesticks, vases and flowers.

Both her father and her sisters set themselves to train her spiritually. She was taught to pray when quite small, and prayer became very natural and necessary to her. But entirely of herself she early learned to meditate—meditate, that is, in the un-premeditated European way, not in the concentrated intense fashion of the Indians. When out fishing with her father she would sit on the grass at a little distance from him and, without knowing she was meditating, deep reflections would own her mind. Far-off sounds wafted towards her on the murmuring breeze, and faint notes of music from the neighbouring town tinged her thoughts with melancholy, she writes, and she understood more fully that only in Heaven would there be unclouded joy.

Her first impression of the nearness of God came to her, as it comes to many children, from a thunderstorm. Angry clouds had darkened the blue sky. A storm burst overhead. Vivid lightning flashed. And a thunderbolt fell in a field close by. Not a bit frightened, she looked round her on every side to lose nothing of the splendid scene. She was overjoyed—in a rapture. God seemed so near.

Joy also came to her from confession. When she made her first confession and received absolution, the priest exhorting her to be devout to Our Lady, she came away feeling more light-hearted and happy than ever before. The influence she had received remained for a long time with her. She afterwards went to confession for all the great Feasts, and they filled her with transports of joy. The Feasts themselves also she loved. They were to her a foretaste of Heaven.

Yet with all her capacity for enjoyment, and with all her happy nature, she had also great suffering. Naturally timid and sensitive and indisposed to play like other children, she suffered much from her elder companions at the school to which she was sent at the age of eight and a half. She was not spoilt at home ; she was corrected for any faults. And this was necessary, for she had an imperious temper and could stamp her foot in a fury. But the little kindnesses of home were a real necessity for her. Without them she might not, in spite of her courage, have been able to endure the bruises on her delicate nature. And soon her second " mother " was to be removed from her to a convent. " I beheld life as it really is," she said, " full of suffering and constant partings, and I shed most bitter tears." As she entered the church she was crying bitterly, and she even wondered how the sun could go on shining.

But already she began to feel her vocation. She felt that the Carmelite Convent to which her sister had gone was where God wished her also to go. And she felt it so strongly there was no possible room for doubt. It was not the dream of an impressionable child, she averred, but " the certainty of a divine call." And it brought with it a wonderful peace.

She carried her resolution into execution and managed to obtain an interview alone with the Mother Prioress. The kindly Mother expressed her belief in Thérèse's vocation but told her that postulants— seekers for admission to a religious order—were not received at the age of nine ; she must wait till she was sixteen.

Under the strain of disappointment and waiting her health gave way. She became dangerously ill. She had acute headaches. She uttered terrifying cries, spoke horrible nonsense, and had shocking hallucinations. It was feared that her mind was becoming deranged. She seemed to be at death's door. But in her room was a statue of the Virgin Mary, and this was to bring her relief. Utterly exhausted, and finding no help on earth, she sought her heavenly Mother's aid and entreated her with all her heart to have pity on her. In the event followed one of those visions which so influenced her life, and which will be described in her own words.

" Suddenly the statue became animated and radiantly beautiful—with a divine beauty that no words of mine can ever convey. The look upon Our Lady's face was unspeakably kind and compassionate, but what penetrated to the very depths of my soul was her gracious smile. Instantly all my pain vanished, my eyes filled, and big tears fell silently—tears of purest heavenly joy."

She decided she would tell no one, for if she did her happiness would leave her. But her Cousin Marie, who was in the room at the time and had been earnestly praying to the Virgin Mary, had seen Thérèse gazing fixedly on the statue, had seen how her face had become transfigured, and had been filled with wonder and admiration at her supernatural expression and said to herself : " Thérèse is cured." Further, Marie was convinced that the Blessed Virgin, while restoring Thérèse's bodily health, had granted her some hidden grace. So when she was alone with Thérèse she pressed her with inquiries. And Thérèse, unable to resist her tender solicitations and astonished at finding her secret already known, told her everything. The result was, as she had foreseen. Her happiness was turned into sorrow. For four years the remembrance of the vision caused her real pain. Marie had begged to be allowed to tell the nuns at Carmel and Thérèse had not liked to refuse. Consequently, when she next visited the convent the nuns kept asking her questions. These questions troubled and grieved her. Had she only kept her secret her happiness would have been secure, she said.

As to the statue which had been the indirect means of bringing this vision to Ste Thérèse, it is a copy nearly three feet high of the Madonna carved by Bouchardon in the eighteenth century for the Church of St. Sulpice in Paris. It was afterwards taken to the infirmary of the convent. And in her last illness, when Ste Thérèse was taken to the infirmary she said to her Cousin Marie who was also there, as on the former occasion : " Never has She seemed to me more beautiful, but to-day it is the statue, whereas that other day you know well it was not."

Ste Thérèse was now fast emerging from childhood and was developing into a girl. We have already seen how fond she was of nature. She had also the Frenchwoman's love of art. Her sister Pauline used to show her pictures. The sight of " The Little Flower of the Divine Prisoner " suggested to her so many thoughts that it cast her into a kind of ecstasy. From her earliest days she had had in her heart the desire to paint. She had watched her sister Pauline painting, and she had heard her sister Céline offered painting lessons, and she had always wished to paint herself, but she had kept in silence about it. To express her thoughts in verse was another of her desires. And this to some extent she was able to satisfy later, and her little poems have been added to her autobiography.

In reading also she took delight and preferred books to games. She loved tales of chivalry and of the patriotic deeds of the heroines of France. She longed to do as they had done. Especially would she emulate Ste Joan of Arc.

She was now thirteen and the time for her first Communion was approaching. During three months she was prepared for it. Her sister Pauline had written a little book for her help ; and another sister spoke to her every evening, arousing her ardour and telling of the imperishable riches which are within our reach and of the folly of seeking the perishable riches of this world. The last days of the preparation were spent in retreat in the Abbey School. Days of joy they were to her—such joy as could not, she believed, be experienced outside a religious house. The

number of children was small. Each could receive
individual care. Motherly affection was shown them
by the mistresses. And every night the first mistress
tenderly kissed her.

"At last there dawned the most beautiful day
of all the days of my life," she writes, "How perfectly I remember even the smallest detail of those
sacred hours! The joyful awakening, the reverent
and tender embraces of my mistresses and older companions . . . above all, our entrance into the chapel
and the melody of the morning hymn . . . ' How
sweet was the first embrace of Jesus!' It was indeed an embrace of love. I felt that I was loved,
and I said: 'I love Thee and I give myself to Thee
for ever.' Jesus asked nothing of me, and claimed
no sacrifice; for a long time He and little Thérèse
had known and understood each other. That day our
meeting was more than simple recognition; it was a
perfect union. We were no longer two. Thérèse had
disappeared like a drop of water lost in the immensity
of the ocean. Jesus alone remained. He was the
Master and King. Had not Thérèse asked Him to
take away the liberty which frightened her? She
felt herself so weak and frail that she wished to be
for ever united to the Divine Strength.

"And then my joy became so intense, so deep,
that it could not be restrained: tears of happiness
welled up and overflowed. My companions were astonished. No one knew that all the joy of Heaven
had come down into one heart, and that that heart
—exiled, weak and mortal—could not contain it without tears. . . . Joy alone, a joy too deep for words,
overflowed within me."

The next morning seemed veiled in melancholy,
and she longed for the day when she could receive
Jesus again.

At her second Communion her tears flowed once more with inexpressible sweetness, while she recalled and repeated again and again the words of St. Paul: "I live. Yet not I, but Christ liveth in me."

Soon now she went into retreat again to prepare for Confirmation, and made ready with the greatest care for the coming of the Holy Ghost. Like the Apostles, she looked with joy for the promised Comforter. But at the time of Confirmation she did not feel the mighty wind of the First Pentecost; only the gentle breeze which the prophet Elias heard on Mount Horeb.

The crucial stage of her life was now approaching. Within was the imperative urge—the ambition—the aspiration. From without was the insistent call which to her sensitive ears came clear and commanding. And before her were obstacles and trials and disappointments which only her not-to-be-denied, impetuous will could overcome, and suffering which only her indomitable courage could endure.

Her supreme ambition had from childhood been " to love God as He had never been loved before." She was born with an inexhaustible capacity for love. She was always yearning to be loved. And all her great love she would wish to lavish upon God and accomplish to perfection His designs on her soul. This was her heart's desire. Holiness which was truly holy she desired. She would love Jesus—even madly. Love alone drew her. Under love's sweet rule she would not merely march: she would fly. She knew she was born for great things. And at twenty-two she wrote that she still had " the same daring confidence " that one day she would " become a *great saint*." She longed for the beauties of

Heaven, and it was to win these for her soul that she pined to be trained.

Such were her ambitions and aspirations. And while still very young—only fourteen—the clear call came. "The divine call was becoming so insistent," she wrote, "that had it been necessary for me to go through fire to follow Our Lord I would have cast myself into the flames." The call was to Carmel, that austere convent which two of her sisters had already entered.

She longed to enter Carmel. But how could she persuade her father to let his youngest—and perhaps dearest—girl go where he would only be able to see her occasionally and then only under severe restrictions ? And she was still only fourteen and a half. Terrible struggles she went through before she could decide to make the request. She chose the Feast of Pentecost, and prayed for light from the Holy Ghost. In the afternoon, seeing her father sitting in the garden, she silently went and sat by his side, her eyes already wet with tears. He looked at her tenderly, and pressing her to his heart, said : "What is it, little Queen ? Tell me." Through her tears she spoke of her great desire to enter Carmel. He too wept but said not one word to turn her : he merely pointed out that she was still very young, and then, yielding to her entreaties, gave his consent.

Having obtained this, she thought she could straightway enter the convent. To her dismay she was told that the Superior of the convent, a priest, would not allow her to enter till she was twenty-one. She went with her father to him, but no urging from them both would make him change his mind.

She could only get over this obstacle by going to the Bishop of Bayeux. She went to him with her father, and to make herself look older, put her hair up ! Her father left her to make her own petition. It was a trial to her to do this, but she spoke with all the eloquence she could command. The Bishop was kindly but non-committal. He must refer, he said, to the Superior of the convent. And this, of course, was fatal to her desire, for the Superior had already refused. Her only resource now was to appeal to the Pope himself, and this she determined to make.

A pilgrimage was starting for Rome, and she and her father joined it. They arrived there in November 1887, and with the other pilgrims obtained an audience of the Pope. To obtain the permission to enter Carmel she would have to ask the Holy Father ; and she trembled at the mere thought of addressing the Pope himself in the presence of Bishops, Archbishops and Cardinals.

" Leo XIII, wearing a cassock and cape of white, was seated on a dais, while round him were grouped various dignitaries of the Church. According to custom, each visitor, kneeling in turn and kissing first the foot and then the hand of Sovereign Pontiff, finally received his blessing. At this moment two of the Noble Guard would place their hands on the pilgrim's shoulder as a sign to rise and pass on to the adjoining hall, thus leaving the way clear for the next.

" No one uttered a word, but I was firmly determined to speak, when suddenly the Vicar-General of Bayeux, who was standing to the right of His Holiness, announced in a loud voice that he absolutely forbade anyone to address the Holy Father. On hearing this my heart beat wildly, as if it would break. I looked for counsel to Céline [her sister], and she whispered : ' Speak.'

" The next moment I was on my knees before the

Pope. After I had kissed his foot he extended his hand. Then raising my eyes, which were blinded with tears, I said imploringly : ' Holy Father, I have a great favour to ask of you.'   At once he bent down towards me until his head almost touched my own, while his piercing black eyes seemed to read my very soul. ' Holy Father,' I repeated, ' in honour of your jubilee, allow me to enter Carmel at the age of fifteen.'

" Surprised and displeased, the Vicar-General said quickly : ' Holy Father, this is a child who desires to become a Carmelite, and the Superiors of the Carmel are looking into the matter.' ' Well, my child,' said His Holiness, ' do what the Superiors may decide.'

" Clasping my hands and resting them on his knee, I made one last effort : ' Holy Father, if only you were to say " Yes " everyone else would be willing.' He looked fixedly at me, and said clearly, each syllable strongly emphasised : ' Well, child ! well. You will enter if it be God's will.'

" Once again I was going to plead when two of the Noble Guard bade me rise. Seeing, however, that the request was of no avail and that my hands remained resting on the knees of His Holiness, they took me by the arms, and with the help of the Vicar-General, lifted me to my feet. But just as I was thus being forced to move, the dear Holy Father placed his hand gently on my lips, then, raising it, blessed me, while his eyes followed me as I turned away. . . .

" My sorrow was indeed crushing. Nevertheless my soul remained in peace, inasmuch as I had done all that lay in my power to respond to my Divine Master's call."

Courage and indomitable spirit could scarcely have gone further. And they had their reward. On

December 28 a letter was received from the Bishop by the Prioress, saying that Thérèse might enter the Convent immediately.

II

What was this convent which she was to enter ? What kind of life was it upon which she had so set her heart ? The convent was one established by the Carmelite Order, in the quiet little town of Lisieux in Normandy. It is built of brick and roofed with slate—plain and gloomy. Round it are high walls. Inside are straight white-washed passages and cold cells, each nine feet square, bare of ornament and furnished with a straw mattress on a bed of boards, a jug and basin, a stool, a table, and a plain wooden Cross. And the convent was run on lines of almost ferocious austerity. In it would be about twenty-nine. All liberty of speech, action and use of time has to be surrendered, all work done in silence. Conversation would be allowed only during recreation and then only under direction. They would rise at 5 a.m. and retire at 10.30 p.m. Most of the day would be spent in services, study of the Bible, meditation and private prayer. Some time would be occupied in manual work. But only twice a day would intervals of an hour each be given to recreation. In this convent, those ties so peculiarly dear to her would be almost completely severed. Never again would she be able to go outside the convent walls. Never again would she be able to see the home in which she had been brought up and which had for her so many of the tenderest associations. Only occasionally would her father and sisters be able to come to see her, and then only under restricted conditions. The old daily intimacy of intercourse would be gone for ever. Gone, too, would be any hope of enjoying the love of a man for her, or of ever bearing a little one. Those deep instincts and cravings with which every woman is by nature endowed would have to be for ever stifled. And never again would she be able to enjoy the beauties of nature—to wander in the meadows and the woods or gather the wild flowers she had loved so well. She had just passed through the Alps on the way to Rome. The mountains had impressed her with the greatness and majesty of God. Enclosed in Carmel she would be able to see " but a little space of sky." The beauties of nature which had raised her soul to heaven would be for ever shut out from her.

All these deep—and one might truthfully say divine —enjoyments of life ; all these enjoyments of home, of love, and of nature she would have to forgo for ever.

And what would she get in return ? Certainly, no material comforts. Everything material that belonged to her she would have to give up. Even her cell she would not be able to call her own : it would be common property, it would be " our " cell. In that cell would not be even the comfort of a fire. She would have to pray, and meditate, and read and work in the chill and damp of a northern winter. The bed would be hard ; the bed-clothing insufficient. And the number of deaths among the poor nuns was evidence enough of the little regard which was given in the Convent to the care of bodily health. And the convent itself was not attractive. The building was plain, and even the chapel dreary. There was nothing that would satisfy her artistic instincts.

Seeing that she would have to give up the perfectly legitimate and natural enjoyments of life and to expect every kind of physical discomfort, the life before her must have held the prospects of some higher enjoyment or she could not have been so irresistibly attracted to it. What was it that so powerfully drew her to this seclusion? In her formal declaration of her reasons for entering the convent she stated that she was going there " to save souls and especially to pray for priests." And we may suppose that in fulfilling this deepest desire of her nature she would expect to find that joy which only the satisfaction of her whole soul could ever give. Neither the joys of home nor of nature could equal the joy of bringing souls to heaven, was evidently what she thought.

After a last look at the dear home of her childhood she set out for the convent with her father and sisters. And there they all together attended Mass.

" At the Communion, when our Divine Lord entered our hearts, I heard sobs on every side. I did not shed a tear, but as I led the way to the cloister door the beating of my heart became so violent I wondered if I was going to die. Oh! the agony of that moment! One must go through it to understand it.

" I embraced all my loved ones. Then I knelt for Papa's blessing, and he too knelt as he blessed me through his tears. To see this old man giving his child to God while she was still in the springtime of life was a sight to gladden the Angels.

" At length the door closed upon me, and I found a loving welcome in the arms of those dear sisters who, each in turn, had been to me a mother, and likewise from the family of my adoption, whose tender devotedness is not dreamed of by the outside world. My desire was now accomplished, and my soul was filled with so deep a peace that it baffles all attempt at description.

" Everything in the convent delighted me, especially our (my) little cell. I repeat, however, that my happiness was calm and peaceful. . . . I was, indeed, amply rewarded for all I had gone through, and it was with untold joy that I kept repeating : ' Now I am here for ever.' "

But all was not to be easy with her—even spiritually. No sooner was she in the convent than she experienced " great spiritual aridity "—doubtless the reaction from the emotional strain of entering. Then the Mother-Superior treated her with much severity. She seemed to Ste Thérèse to be perpetually finding fault with her. And when occasionally Ste Thérèse went to her for spiritual direction she seemed to be scolding her all the time. Then the Novice Mistress would send her out every afternoon to weed the garden, in addition to her regular work of looking after the linen, cleaning a staircase and dormitory, and gathering the vegetables.

And from the confessional and spiritual direction she obtained no comfort in these first days. She found extreme difficulty in opening her heart at Confessional. And kind though the Sub-Prioress was in her spiritual guidance, words failed poor little Thérèse when she tried to speak of what passed in her soul. Thus the time of her spiritual direction became " a torture and a real martyrdom."

Her spiritual aridity increased, and she found no comfort in Heaven or on Earth And at the end of her year of novitiate when she had expected she might make her Profession—that is, take the vows of poverty, chastity and obedience—she was told by the Mother-Superior that she must not think of it for another eight months. She fell into a state of utter spiritual desolation. And she often slept during meditation. She felt assured that she was wholly unsuited for the Carmelite life. The darkness became so intense that one thing only was clear : she had no vocation and must return to the world. On the very eve of the day appointed for her Profession the most furious storm of her whole spiritual life raged within her. In her despair she took her courage in her hands, and told first the Novice Mistress, and then the Mother-Superior what was going on in her soul. The former laughed at her fears and the Mother-Superior's consoling words dispelled the last shadow of doubt.

Next morning her soul was flooded with heavenly joy, and in great peace she made her vows. Jesus was now her Spouse, and she could ask Him any favour. She longed that every sinner on earth might be converted and all captive souls in purgatory set free. For herself she desired that her baptismal robe might never be sullied. She would seek naught but Jesus. Above all, she asked for love—for love without limit. She felt that time could never take away her happiness. And that night, as she gazed upon the glorious starlit sky, she was filled with peace and joy, and thought that before long she would take flight to heaven and there be united to her Divine Spouse in eternal bliss.

It must have been about this time that she had what she called a " transport of love," when she remained for a whole week far removed from the world.

" It is," she writes, " impossible for me to explain it, but it seemed as if I went about my work with a body other than my own ; and that a veil had been cast over all earthly things. But I was not then consumed by a real flame ; I was able to bear it all, without expectation of seeing the ties that

161

bound me to life give way under the weight of joy; whilst on the occasion of which I speak, one minute, one second longer, and my soul must have left my body."

Again in the year 1891, when the Foundress of the convent died in her eighty-seventh year, Ste Thérèse had another spiritual experience. She was watching at the bedside of the dying Foundress when a kind of torpor came over her. But she says:

" At the moment her soul passed to God an extra-ordinary change was wrought in my whole being. In an instant I was filled with an indescribable joy and fervour, as if the soul of our blessed Foundress had made me a sharer in the happiness she already possessed."

Ste Thérèse had had this spiritual experience and several other " transports of love " while she was in the convent, besides the vision of the Virgin Mary during her childhood. But the supreme experience came to her. in June 1895—that is when she was twenty-two years of age—a few days after her Act of Oblation.

" I was in the choir," she says, " beginning the Way of the Cross, when suddenly I felt myself wounded by a dart of fire so ardent that I thought I should die. I cannot describe the transport, and no comparison would convey an idea of the intensity of the flame. It seemed as though an invisible force plunged me wholly into fire. But what fire!—what sweetness. . . . Flames of love, or rather, oceans of grace filled my soul."

This is as far as she could describe her experiences in words. But she always protested against being asked to describe them. " I would not and I could not tell all," she would say. " Some things lose their fragrance when exposed to the air ; and one's innermost thoughts cannot be translated into earthly words without instantly losing their deep and heavenly meaning." We can, however, learn some little more about her experiences from the way in which they outwardly affected her.

On one occasion a novice coming unexpectedly upon her in her cell, found her industriously sewing but lost in contemplation, and she was struck by the heavenly expression on her countenance. Her sister also records that, speaking to her once of the manner in which the Holy Ghost takes possession of the soul, her words were so inflamed and her look became suddenly so ardent that, unable to endure the ardency, she covered her eyes and withdrew, filled with a sense of the supernatural she never forgot.

These were the sublime heights of spiritual enjoyment and the most truly real things in her life. But life had also for her many trials, pains and disappointments. Secluded as she might be in the convent and sheltered from the roughs and temptations of the world, she was in no haven of rest. She had to lead a life of intense spiritual activity, with many of the joys of the spirit, it is true, but with many also of its sufferings. She was to learn by hard experience, what she already knew, that she had to expect that the heights of the spirit are only attained through much suffering as well as sacrifice.

Even after her Profession there were times when the darkness within her soul was so thick that she no longer knew if God loved her. These thoughts tortured her. And one night when she was lost in darkness there came out of it an accursed voice which said : "Are you certain God loves you ? " She was still tormented by distractions and drowsiness during prayer and meditation. Her great desire was to become a saint, but she felt as much below a saint as a grain of sand is below a mountain. And what hid God from her was not merely a veil which she was on the point of rending asunder but " a wall which reached to the very heavens, shutting out the starry night." She still had meditations passed in utter dryness.

Then there were the ordinary irritations and annoyances of communal life. The devil would bring before her the defects of a Sister. Another Sister would get on her nerves and she would be tempted to go a long way round to avoid meeting her. Again, when she was allowed to speak on spiritual subjects with some other Sister she found that, after all, the conversation did not attain the desired end of inciting them to an ardent love of their Divine Spouse. Then another Sister fidgeted incessantly with her rosary, and she was bathed in perspiration in the effort to prevent herself from turning round and with one glance silence the offender. Yet another Sister kept splashing her with dirty water while they were washing linen at the laundry, and she was tempted to draw back and ostentatiously wipe her face to show the delinquent that she ought to be more careful.

She had two of her own sisters in the convent, and it might be thought that the companionship of these would be a compensation to her for separation from home and for all these petty irritations. The contrary was the case. The rules of solitude and silence were strictly observed in the convent. There was no sitting and chatting familiarly in each other's rooms. They only met at recreation. And she keenly

felt having to repress her affection towards them.
Then she fell ill through having worn for too long
a small penitential cross, the sharp iron points of
which had entered into her flesh.

It was a matter of honour with her—and indeed it
was the Carmelite rule—to do nothing to alleviate
suffering or make the religious life comfortable and
agreeable. And the Mother-Superior acted strictly
on this principle. Ste Thérèse's companions in the
Novitiate, seeing how pale she looked, tried to obtain
a dispensation for her from early rising. But the
Mother Prioress would yield to no such request. "A
soul of such mettle," she would say, "ought not to
be dealt with as a child : dispensations are not meant
for her. Let her be, for God will sustain her."

The Mother Prioress was right about the mettle.
Ste Thérèse had the courage to face the bitterest
irritations. The nun who was her pet aversion she
treated with such special attention that she asked
what it was Thérèse saw in her to make her love
her so much. And impetuous as she was by nature,
she yet schooled herself to submit to the authority
of the Mother Prioress, even when she believed her
orders were not right.

And her ambitions were still with her. She would
love till she died of love. She would love Jesus to
madness. She prayed Jesus to draw her into the
fire of His love and to unite her so closely to Him
that He might live and act in her. She would fix
her gaze on Him and long to be *fascinated* by His
divine eyes and to become Love's prey. And she
hoped that one day He would, like a Divine Eagle,
swoop down and bear her away to the source of all
love and plunge her into a glowing abyss that she
might become for ever its happy victim. So she

would feel at one time. At another time she would feel—little unfledged bird though she was—that the eagle's spirit was hers. So, notwithstanding her littleness, she would dare to gaze upon the Divine Sun of Love and would burn to dart upward into its fires. She could only flutter her wings, but she would fain fly as the eagle. And when inflamed with this soaring ambition she would wield the sword, she would be a priest, an apostle, a martyr, a doctor of the Church. She would do the most heroic deeds. She would burn with the spirit of the Crusader. She would gladly die on the battlefield in defence of the Church. She would be a light unto souls. She would travel the world over to raise on heathen soil the standard of the Cross. And one mission would not satisfy her : she would spread the Gospel in all parts of the Earth, even to the farthest isles. But her greatest desire of all was to win the martyr's palm. She would be scourged. She would be crucified. She would be flayed alive. She would be plunged into boiling oil. She would be ground by the teeth of wild beasts. Martyrdom had been the dream of her youth. It had only grown more vivid in Carmel's narrow cell.

Then she read the twelfth and thirteenth chapters of the first Epistle of St. Paul to the Corinthians, and saw that all cannot be apostles, nor all prophets, nor all teachers, nor all healers. She read that though there was the same Spirit there were " diversities of gifts."

" The same Spirit of God worketh all in all," but there are " diversities of operations. . . . To one is given the word of wisdom ; to another the word of knowledge by the same Spirit ; to another the working of miracles ; to another prophecy. The body is one but hath many members. If the whole body were an eye, where were the hearing ? If the whole were hearing, where were the smelling ? And whether one member suffer, all the members suffer with it ; or one member be honoured, all the members rejoice with it."

This she read and understood from the twelfth chapter. She could not be anything. She might not be either an apostle or a prophet or a martyr. She might not be one of these. Yet she was determined to reach God. And as the chapter closed she read how St. Paul would show "a more excellent way." And she read in a new light what she must have often and often read and heard before, the famous thirteenth chapter. Charity—Love—was the more excellent way to God. Charity gave her the clue. She might have the gift of prophecy, she might understand all mysteries, she might have all knowledge, she might have faith enough to remove mountains, she might give all she had to feed the poor, she might suffer a martyr's death, but all would be of no avail if she had not charity. Charity—Love—was the one essential.

Things now became clear to her. She might not be the eye of the body—of the Church. She might not be the ear. But the body must have a heart ; and she would be that heart—that heart on fire with love. Only love imparts life to all the members. Should it fail, apostles would no longer preach, martyrs no longer sacrifice their lives. Love was the one thing needful.

Beside herself with joy she cried out : " O Jesus, my vocation is found at last—my vocation is love." She had found her place in the Church. She would be the love in the heart of Mother-Church.

But love proves itself by deeds. What should she do ? She, the little one, would strew flowers by the way. And the flowers would be the smallest actions done for Love. Each word, each look, each little daily sacrifice—all would be done for Love's dear sake. He that ruleth his spirit is greater than he that taketh cities. Through little acts of charity, practised in the dark, missionaries would be helped, plentiful alms would be obtained, and churches would be built. Love was to be the mainspring of every action. She would have everyone enter whole-heartedly into her little way. These would be the flowers which she would strew by the way to the Throne of God. And she would sing Love's canticle in silvery tones. Not in loud organ peals but in gentlest tones would she sing as she scattered her flowers. And should any of her roses be gathered from amid thorns, she would still sing. The longer and sharper the thorns the sweeter would grow her song.

This was the new way she found to God. This was the path to Perfection. The little way. The way of little sacrifices, little kindnesses. And it was an ordinary way which everyone might follow.

Nor was it from any littleness of soul that she chose the little way. Only the greatest soul could see the greatness of this little way. She was great enough to see that to do to perfection the little things of everyday life, and do them with the glow of love in the heart and a smile on the lips, is the sure and certain way of reaching heaven. But she knew well that it would require of her a concentration, a persistency and inflexibility of purpose which even the greatest heroes might lack, and she steadied her soul for the effort.

She became a Mistress of Novices, and through

guiding others she learned much. Nothing escaped
her. She was often surprised at her clear-sightedness.
She would have preferred to suffer a thousand re-
proofs rather than inflict one, yet she felt it necessary
to cause pain at times, and her novices thought her
severe. All souls have much the same battle to fight,
but as each soul is different from the others, each
must be dealt with according to her own needs.
With some she had to humble herself and not be
afraid of confessing her own struggles and defeats.
In dealing with others this would never do : self-
abasement would be mistaken for weakness. With
them her only hope of success lay in being firm, and
in never going back on what she had said. And
she had to be careful not to be too kind. She must
not go too far in the direction her heart would lead
her. A single word too much might bring to the
ground an edifice which had taken years to build.
The novices themselves soon recognized that a dose
of bitterness is worth a surfeit of sweetness.

What her ambitions and ideals were has already
been noted. Some of her governing ideas might also
here be described. One of the most deeply rooted
was that this Earth is a place of misery and we
must look for happiness in a life after death. She
always expected to die young, and it almost seems as
if she wanted to. If life here was so miserable and
life there was so blissful the only logical conclusion
would be that the sooner she left this earthly life the
better. She believed in the presence of guardian
angels about her. But also in the Devil. One night,
when ill, she begged that her bed might be sprinkled
with holy water, saying : " The Devil is beside me.
I do not see him but I feel him ; he torments me,
holding me with a grip of iron that I may not find

one crumb of comfort and adding to my sufferings that I may be driven to despair."

How far she distinguished between Jesus and God is not always clear. She, of course, regarded Jesus as the ideal of perfection and as her Spouse. She constantly felt His spirit in her and believed that at Holy Communion He entered into her. She also regarded Him as the Divine Artist and herself as His little brush by means of which He would paint the most beautiful colours. And she looked forward to that glorious day when, with His retinue of virgins, she would follow Him through His boundless realm singing His new canticle—the Canticle of Love.

God she regarded as pure Spirit. No human eye could see Him. But one day, as she was watching in the garden with one of her own sisters, she stood still to watch a little white hen sheltering her chickens under her wing. Her eyes filled with tears. Even when she reached her cell it was some time before she could speak through her tears. She had realized the tenderness of God—the mercy of God. She could not tell all that had stirred her heart. And she realized that only on rare occasions could what she saw be disclosed. Otherwise, no one could survive the sweetness of it. But may we surmise that in that moment she had sensed the Motherhood of God? That in that tender, self-sacrificing, sheltering mother-love, common to animals and birds as well as to women, she had divined in a flash an essential characteristic of God?

Of the efficacy and power of prayer she was deeply convinced. For her it was an uplifting of the heart, a glance towards Heaven, a cry of gratitude and of love in times of sorrow as well as of joy. It was through prayer, she wrote, that St. Paul, St. Augus-

tine, St. Thomas Aquinas, St. John of the Cross and
Ste Teresa had acquired the wonderful knowledge
that had enthralled men's minds. It was with prayer
as a lever that they had uplifted the world.

Seven years had gone by since Ste Thérèse entered
Carmel when a great joy came. For years she had
felt a longing to have had a brother who would be a
priest. Now the Mother Prioress called her aside
while she was at work washing and read a letter
from a young seminarist in which he said he had
been inspired by Ste Thérèse to ask for a Sister who
would devote herself especially to his salvation, together with that of the souls one day to be entrusted
to him. And she was then chosen to have this future
missionary for her brother. Such an unlooked-for
fulfilment of her great wish filled her heart with the
joy of a child. She had not tasted such happiness
for years.

Now and again she would write to her new brother.
But letters were dangerous. Correspondence might
preoccupy and injure the soul. Too often fair words
written and fair words received might be merely
an exchange of false coin. It was by prayer and
sacrifice that missionaries could best be helped, she
considered.

The next year a second brother was given to her.
She represented that having given all her slender
merits to one future apostle, she feared they could not
be given to another. But she was told that obedience
would double those merits. In the depth of her
heart she agreed. The zeal of a Carmelite ought to
embrace the whole world.

Ste Thérèse had also had as her " spiritual hero " a

171

French missionary, Thèophane Vènard, who, at the age of thirty-two, in the year 1861 had been martyred in Tongking. In the beauty of his soul, the romance and holiness of his nature, and his love of home there was a deep affinity between her and him. And she once explained the reason for her admiration of him in particular. It was because he was a *little* saint whose life was quite ordinary ; because he had an ardent love for the Immaculate Mother and likewise a great love for those at home.

So the years went by in the convent. But all the time the austerity of the Rule was telling on her. She had entered it with a delicate constitution ; and, though she never complained, the food was most unpalatable to her digestion, and the want of a fire in winter caused her the greatest physical suffering. And already in the convent she had known at close quarters what death was. In 1891 an epidemic of influenza had broken out in it. She herself had had a slight attack. The worst sufferers were nursed by those who could hardly stand. Death was all round them. No sooner had one died than they had to leave her and attend to another. On her nineteenth birthday the Sub-Prioress had died and Ste Thérèse had assisted at her last agony. One morning she had a presentiment that one Sister named Magdalen was dead. She went to her cell and found her lying dead, fully dressed. So Ste Thérèse knew well what death was. Yet it did not daunt her. She had always believed that she would die young. And in April 1896, when she was still only twenty-three, she had the first warning of the end. She had a hæmorrhage in the night. The next day was Good Friday when severe penances have to be practised and a novice, seeing her face livid, begged permission from her to tell the Mother Prioress and get her some reprieve from the penance ; but Ste Thérèse strictly forbade it, saying that what she was suffering was nothing in comparison with what Jesus had suffered on that day. She kept her sufferings to herself, and it was only in May, 1897, that even her own sisters knew of this first warning. Then they gently reproached her for not having told them ; and a more strengthening diet was given her.

For some months the cough ceased. Then she took a serious turn for the worse—and, as it proved, for the worst. She would continue to take the community exercises, but at night she would ascend the steps to her cell with the greatest difficulty, pausing for breath after each step. Utterly exhausted she would take a full hour to undress. Even then she had only a hard pallet on which to lie. The night was full of pain. But when asked if she would not like some help during those lonely hours, she said she was delighted to suffer alone : " The moment I receive sympathy and am loaded with attentions I am no longer happy." She had always accustomed herself to suffering. And once—before this illness—she had said : " When painful and disagreeable things come my way, instead of looking gloomy I greet them with a smile. At first I did not always succeed. Now it has become a habit."

For several days during August she seemed beside herself and implored that prayers might be offered for her, and until the end she remained in a state of extreme anguish. After the middle of August she was unable, because of her continual sickness, to receive Holy Communion. Then she became so weak that she was unable to make the slightest movement without assistance. Even whispers near caused her pain. And it was only with the greatest difficulty that she could articulate a word. Yet a sweet smile was always on her lips. Her one fear was lest she should give the Sisters any extra trouble. And up till two days before her death she would not allow anyone to remain with her through the night.

On September 30 came the end. She gazed with inexpressible tenderness on the statue of the Madonna which had been in her home and which had been brought into the infirmary. Then looking on her crucifix she said : "Oh ! . . . I love Him . . . My God, I . . . love . . . Thee."

These were her last words (and previously to her sister Céline, as a last word of adieu, she had said : "It is love alone that counts "). And a little later she suddenly raised herself as though called by a mysterious voice. Her eyes shone with unutterable joy as she fixed them a little above the statue. And so she passed away with the joy of that last rapture imprinted on her face.

She had always thought she would die young. She had almost *wished* to die young. From her childhood she had regarded earth as a place of exile : heaven as her home ; earth as all misery : heaven as full of joy. To leave earth and ascend to heaven was naturally, therefore, her desire. The thought of entering heaven transported her with joy. And when near the end the chaplain asked her if she were resigned to die, she told him that she needed more resignation to live and that the thought of death brought her nothing but joy.

Yet at this very time a profound change was taking place within her. She was no longer desiring to spend eternity enjoying herself in heaven ; she was already wanting to return and work on earth.

When a Sister was speaking to her of the happiness of heaven, she replied : " It is not that which attracts me ; it is Love. To love, to be loved, and to return to earth to win love for our Love. . . . I know well that everyone will love me."

One evening when her Sister, Mother Agnes of Jesus, went to the infirmary—and that must have been not more than two days before the end—Ste Thérèse welcomed her with an extraordinary expression of joy and said :

" Mother, some notes from a distant concert have just reached my ears, and the thought came to me that soon I shall be listening to the music of Paradise. Yet this thought gave me only a moment's joy. For one hope only fills my heart—the hope of the love I shall receive and the love I shall be able to give. I feel my mission is soon to begin—my mission to make others love God as I love Him—to teach souls my *little* way. *I will spend my heaven in doing good upon earth.*"

" You will look down on us from heaven," the Sisters said to her.

" No," she replied, " I will *come* down. Would God have given me this ever-increasing desire to do good on earth after my death unless He had meant me to fulfil it ? "

She died then with an ever-dwindling desire for the happiness of heaven and an ever-increasing desire to work for good on this earth.

And it has been in actual experience that she still, as it were, lives and moves among men. Since she entered the convent at the age of fifteen no one outside her family had seen her. Yet only a few years after her death, from all parts of the civilized world petitions poured in on the Vatican urging her Beatification and afterwards her Canonization. During the Great War soldiers of every rank joined in the appeal. A steadily increasing stream of pilgrims came to kneel before the simple cross under which what was mortal of her lay. In 1923, the year of her Beatification, three hundred thousand pilgrims visited Lisieux. Cardinals came from Rome, from England and from America. The town was gaily decorated. Thirty prelates and eight hundred priests formed the escort of the precious remains. Officers and soldiers whom she had helped during the war formed a guard of honour. While between sixty and eighty thousand pilgrims lined the route.

Whether she had gained her ambition of following Jesus with His retinue of virgins we know not. But one thing we do know as an established fact ; that her spirit is now inspiring hundreds of thousands of persons here on earth. And we may be sure it will work on here for ages to come. If she had lived she would still be only just over sixty. And her highest aspirations could scarcely have expected that in so short a time—even in the lifetime of her elder sisters —so amazing a result should have been achieved. She had tried to love God as He had never been loved before. Through God's embodiment in Jesus she must have loved Him as none has exceeded. She had entered into the Spirit of Jesus and therefore into the Spirit of God. He had been' imbued with that Spirit and she had imbibed It to overflowing. And now, through her life and her death, she had been the means of imbuing thousands of others with the Spirit of God. It is a miracle far surpassing the miraculous cure of bodily ailments. And it was because of the very ordinariness of her life ; because she did all the little trivialities of everyday life in the Spirit of God that she is so widely popular. She had spirit enough to do things on the grandest scale. But her life lay in the little way. And in the little way what she did she did to perfection. That is why her appeal is so wide. She would spend her heaven in doing good upon earth. Along the little way she had followed—the way of childlikeness—she would help others to go. And such a lead others have gladly followed. This is the precious result of her short heroic life.

CHAPTER IV

A PROTESTANT MYSTIC

THE GOLDEN FOUNTAIN

IN two little books named *The Golden Fountain* and *The Prodigal's Return* there are described the spiritual experiences of an English Christian woman which bear such remarkable resemblances to the experiences of Hindu mystics that they are now included in this survey for comparison with others. And they are the more remarkable because the experient had read nothing of Hindu or even Christian mysticism and had made her way by her own unaided efforts—even without the aid of the Church to which she belonged. That is to say she came naturally to her experiences. There was no question of her experiences being suggested to her, or of her following any particular tradition.

In spiritual matters she was so reserved that she could not bear the publicity of her name upon the books, and they were therefore published anonymously. And as even after her death, which occurred about six years ago, she wished to remain anonymous we can only gather from occasional sentences and references in her three little books [1] what her story

---

[1] *The Golden Fountain, The Prodigal's Return,* and *The Romance of the Soul*—all published by J. M. Watkins.

was. But we infer from them that she was outwardly an ordinary "society woman" such as are
met by thousands in every European country, brought
up and living in neither specially religious nor specially
irreligious surroundings.

She was English but of French Huguenot descent
on both her father's and her mother's side. She
writes of "being dressed in the latest fashion" and
of "balls and parties," of winters at Rome "in continuous gaiety amongst a brilliant cosmopolitan world
of men and women who lived in palaces, surrounded
with art and luxury." At her first ball—and often
afterwards—she knew "the surging exultation and
intoxicating joy of life." Love of the world and of
social life was a strong feeling with her for many
years. And "in social life, in brilliant scenes of light
and laughter, music and love, I seemed to ride on
the crest of a wave in the marvellous glamour of
youth."

When she was a little over thirty she was married
to an officer in the British Army, who soon after the
marriage was called to serve in the South African
War and who afterwards served in the Great War.
With him she travelled to many parts of the world :
and when in England they lived in the country among
the hunting set, though while he was hunting or
shooting she would be walking on the downs or tending flowers in the walled garden of an old country
house.

This was her social setting : nothing out of the
ordinary, one way or the other. And the same with
her religious surroundings. Her family went to church
once on Sundays—"if it was fine." And she says
of herself that she was never pious and never read a
religious book.

How then came it about that apparently so ordinary a woman living so ordinary a life should have enjoyed so extraordinary a religious experience ? The answer is, that deep within her was something very, very different from what she ever allowed to appear upon the surface. Her inner disposition differed greatly from her outward seeming. She held herself in hand and had a strong sense of discipline and self-control. Outwardly she conformed to the society in which she was immersed. Inwardly her whole soul rebelled against the conventionality around her. Though she may have had little of what she calls " piety," she acknowledges having " a deep thirst for the perfect and the holy and the pure." And in the quiet solemnity of a church, or under the blue skies she would detach herself from her surroundings and " wistfully reach up and out towards the ineffable holiness and purity of God—unattainable though He seemed." Society did not satisfy that something living within her " which knew a terrible necessity for God."

This vehement Godward urge—this urge to all that is holy and perfect—was evidently the focusing to a single direction of an exceptionally loving disposition, of an admiration of all beauty, and of an ardent curiosity to know the truth of things.

Withal she had a quite extraordinary capacity for suffering, due perhaps to her peculiarly sensitive nature—though doubtless also her sensitivity was enhanced by this very suffering, the sensitivity heightening the suffering and the suffering intensifying the sensitivity. For a sufferer must necessarily be sensitive, and a sensitive person a sufferer.

We may sum her up, then, as being of an exceedingly impressionable and responsive nature, quick to register and respond to the most delicate impressions

180

and eagerly reaching after the most perfect things in life.

The impetuous urge within her was strong enough not to be baulked till it had broken through the narrow surroundings of a woman of society. And she herself was sensitive enough and active enough to respond to those intimations from the kingdom of Spirit which we sometimes term the Grace of God, without which she herself acknowledged she could never have experienced what she did.

Let us now examine in more detail, first her own innate disposition and then the circumstances under which she was able to force her way through the tough integument which encased her, and under the influence of the enveloping sunshine blossom forth in such rare and exquisite beauty.

Of her innate disposition the dominating feature was this passionate love to which reference has already been made. Her first memory was of the face and neck and bosom of the nurse upon whose heart she lay, of her voice telling her that she must leave, and immediately after, of the anguish and the *pain* of love.

Next we are told of her " darling brothers," from whom she had often to part when they went back to school.

" When they came home I overflowed with happiness and sang all day long in my heart. But the last night of the holidays was a time of anguish. Oh, the pain of love at parting ! There never was a pain so terrible as suffering love. The last meal : the last hour : the last look ! "

Of her mother we hear little. But to her father she was devoted. She believed he guided her char-

181

acter with the greatest judgment, above all things teaching her the need of self-control. He was a man of leisure, we are told, and acquainted with many of the celebrated people of the day, both in England and on the Continent. On no subject was he unread, and he would engage in wonderful and brilliant discussions. And though naturally of a somewhat violent temper, he had so brought himself under control that towards high and low alike he had become all that was most sweet and patient, gentle and sympathetic.

To this talented and kindly father she gave her obedience, though his call upon her was on one critical occasion certainly not wise. And in his last years, when he was overtaken with heart disease, she tended him to the length of losing her health.

Love of nurse, love of brothers, love of father she had in abundance. Stronger, deeper, more passionate was the love of the woman in her for man. She was a woman through and through, with the great natural, healthy passions of a woman. What she describes as " the first faint breath of the mystery of sex " she felt when she was only five. She was a bridesmaid, and she recalls the church, the altar, and great awe, and afterwards a long white table, white flowers, and a white bride, and grown men smilingly delightful, tempting her with sweets and cakes, and a new, strange interest arising in her like a flood of exultation.

At sixteen, tall and healthy, she received her first offer of marriage and with it her first vision of the love and passion of men. She recoiled from it with a great shyness and aversion. She felt the pull of strong forces within her and was fearful of herself. For interests and instincts within her corresponded to

182

this dangerous capacity of her. The world, she felt, held many strange fires : some holy and beautiful : some far otherwise.

Yet, though she recoiled she was also attracted. She knew she had great powers over the emotions of men. She became deeply interested in them. And from that time till her marriage she was never without a lover.

Finally, she fell in love. She came to the consciousness of it not gradually but all in an instant. She had no chance of drawing back, for it was already fully completed before she was aware of it. When the time came to speak of it to her parents her mother would not hear of the marriage : there was no money. Two brilliant opportunities offered themselves—money, position. She could bring herself to neither. Love was everything. A prolonged secret engagement therefore had to follow.

In all this love of society, love of brothers, love of father, love of lovers she was an ordinary, natural woman. But beneath this ordinary family and social life, from the deep, inmost centre of her, was that which she never revealed to anyone about her—not even to her husband. " I was always reserved," she writes, " and never admitted anyone into the deep things of my life."

In those deeps she " sighed and moaned for God." As a little girl she " believed in God with the complete and peaceful faith of childhood." When she shut her eyes she saw God very plainly. " He was a White Figure, in white robes, on a white throne, amongst the clouds." At eighteen, in the midst of her social gaiety her mind and her heart imperatively demanded solitude. And in this solitude and in silence she sought the beautiful in nature. In contemplating the sky or a distant scene, she would in some mysterious way inhale the very essence of the Beautiful. At this time it did not occur to her that this was a way of the spirit's struggle towards the Eternal. But later on she came to regard the Beautiful as with Love one of the twin golden paths that lead us to the God from whom all beauty proceeds.

Her way was this. She would first seat herself in such a position that her body would not fall, so that she could completely forget it. Then she would look about her and drink in the beauty of the scene till her eyes came to rest upon the spot which for her was most beautiful, and there they would remain fixed. All thoughts would then be folded up so that her mind flowing in a single direction would concentrate upon the selected beauty. This would soon vanish and she would see nothing whatever. But borne away into a place of complete silence and emptiness, she would there assimilate and inwardly enjoy the soaring essence of the beauty which she had previously drawn into her mind through her eyes. No longer conscious of seeing outwardly she would live entirely from the inward.

This, which she called her " beautiful pastime," she would resort to almost daily. For it she had to seek solitude. And solitude is not easy to find. But she would seek it even in a churchyard. And there she would see no graves—only the sky, or a marvellous cloud, pink with the kisses of the sun.

Yet in this " pastime " all was not joy. There was also " a strange, inexpressible sadness." The beauty of nature was not enough. The more beauty she saw, the more she longed for something to which she could not put a name. And at times the ache of this pain became terrible, almost agonizing.

And all this time, while she was seething with love, and pursuing beauty, she was devoured with a curiosity to know the truth about every single thing she saw. In astronomy, biology and geology she found a new and marvellous interest. Her young and healthy intelligence had a voracious appetite—but only for science, and not for either philosophy or religion. And science, and her clever but sceptical brother, turned her to atheism. While her father, perceiving the way she was tending, made matters worse by begging her, out of love and obedience to himself, to give up reading all science.

A wise Hindu sage, when a young Indian told him that he had become an atheist, congratulated him. And on the youth expressing his astonishment that a man of God should congratulate him on becoming an atheist, the sage replied : " Your becoming an atheist shows that you have begun to think. Go on thinking." If her father had advised her to follow science through to its foundations and further on to philosophy and pursue truth to the very furthest extreme, she would have found satisfaction for her soul. As it was, tragedy followed. She dutifully and lovingly obeyed her revered father, and in consequence suffered tortures. Being thwarted in her search for truth, her pursuit of beauty atrophied in sympathy. She became afraid to turn to the love of nature. She had to abandon her " beautiful pastime." The pain of it had become unendurable.

There ensued a terrible conflict. Her intelligence said : " Give yourself up to the world. Console yourself with material achievements." Fortunately, her heart said : " Abandonment to the world is impossible. There is no consolation to the heart without God." In that darkest and driest time of all she

still felt " the same piercing desire and need for God."
To a woman atheism is intolerable, she afterwards
wrote. Her very nature, loving, tender, sensitive, and
clinging, demands belief in God. Without God, she
knew herself incapable of overcoming the evil of the
world or even her own petty nature. The high moral
standard demanded of woman was impossible of
achievement for mere reasons of race-welfare. The
personal reason, the Personal God was essential to
high virtue.

So she listened to her heart and not to the voice
of worldly wisdom. But for two terrible years she
had to fight for her faith. And it was only then
that she began to find a reward. Little by little a
faint hope—fragile, often hardly perceptible—began
to creep into her mind. What else but his thoughts
and aspirations raised man above the beasts ; and
if even a grain of dust is imperishable, were these
thoughts and aspirations alone to end in nothing ?
It was but a reasonable inference to say No. And
in the realm of ideal thought she might again find
her faith. This was the faint ray of hope which came
to her after those two ghastly years of atheism.

And in Rome she was further drawn away from
atheism. The continuous gaiety of her life did not
really satisfy her. Nor did the works of art. She
did not pretend that sculptures and pictures affected
her at all—that is, we may presume, her soul. She
was interested in them. She greatly admired them.
They were part of her education. But that was
all. What really did affect her—and that most
deeply—were the temples, those silent emblems of
man's worship of an unknown God. They strangely
appealed to her. Could she but find God ! Could
she but truly believe and be at peace ! Even that

would be welcome. Even that, without actually finding God.

Then came a further step forward. She attended one of the great ceremonies at the Vatican. Lifted high in his chair on the shoulders of his bearers the Pope—it must have been Leo XIII—was approaching. He came slowly along, his hand raised in a general blessing on the whole multitude. As he came nearer she saw distinctly the delicate ivory face, the great dark eyes shining with a fire she had never seen before. She was moved to the depth of her being. For the first time in her life she saw holiness. Something in her gaze arrested the Pope's attention. He had his chair stopped immediately above her, and leaning over, blessed her individually. No longer had she a body. No longer was there anything in the world but holiness. Holiness, and her enraptured soul. Till she had seen it living before her she had not realized it; but now she knew. Holiness was far beyond the beautiful.

Faith was now coming to the aid of hope. But faith in a very different form from what she had known before—wider, purer, infinitely more powerful. The pain of those struggling years of doubt and negation had after all been worth while. She now saw that without them she could never have found so strong a faith as she now possessed. God was, indeed, still at an indefinite and infinite distance. But of His existence she was now completely certain. He was still far away, but He was there. She had outgrown her atheism. And if she had not yet had full experience of the Spirit of God she no longer doubted His existence.

It was soon after this that she married. But only four months later her husband had to leave her to take part in the war in South Africa. And now doubts began to assail her about the goodness of God. He might exist. But was He always good? With her almost infinite capacity for suffering she was deeply pained by this separation from her husband. As in the days of parting with her schoolboy brothers and as on the death of her beloved father, there was what she described as " this terrible pain of love that must part." Love had always seemed to her the most beautiful thing in life. Yet always it was love that hurt her most.

Wherefore this suffering? she asked herself. Harsh, rebellious thoughts frequently invaded her. The whole scheme of nature appeared to her unreasonably cruel. The joy of festivities, even of human love, did not equal the anguish of grief over others, or of the sufferings of physical ill-health. Sorrow was more weighty than joy—and far more durable. Ready to hand were the means to console herself with the here and now; and again she was tempted to throw herself once more into worldly interests and enjoyment. She felt betrayed in her love and hurt towards God. If He was not the actual Author of pain, at any rate He was the Permitter. A tremendous fear of God now grew up in her, and all her actions were governed by this weighty and immediate fear of Him.

Her husband was away for fifteen months, and all that time she made no spiritual advance whatever. But when he at last returned and they again took up their married life in a happy world of their own her spirit seemed to revive. In the winter, while he was hunting, she would spend much time by herself and again be feeling her way towards God. She would once more indulge in her " pastime " of contemplating the beauties of nature. And she would work in the garden and observe and admire everything that lived close at hand in the hedgerows and the fields. And when she thought of these and beheld the beauties of nature and the glories of the endless sky her heart melted with tenderness and admiration for the marvellous Maker of it all.

She would engage in this contemplation of nature, but she does not appear to have sought God through prayer. She says indeed that at this time she seldom said any prayers at all. She had convinced herself by some odd train of reasoning that women were not acceptable to God. She did, however, pay public respect to God by attending church ; and she then worshipped Him with profound reverence though with great sadness. And it is noticeable that with all her harsh feelings towards God on account of the suffering in the world and with all her strange ideas as to His attitude towards women, she did still feel the urgent *need* of God. Even the strong human love which she was now enjoying was insufficient to give to life any sense of adequacy. God Himself she required. And not mere knowledge that He existed. To know Him to be was no consolation. Nothing would suffice her but some form of personal contact.

And before she could obtain that contact she had to go through still further suffering. Her husband was ordered again to South Africa and this time she was able to go with him. But while there, a terrible misfortune befell her. She was struck by lightning. Every nerve seemed electrocuted. Her sufferings were almost unendurable. And her suffering was not merely physical : it was spiritual as well. She convinced herself that her loved one had changed—that he was indifferent to her sufferings. It is permissible

189

to suggest that he also may have suffered from her highly strained state of nerves. Be that as it may, as far as she was concerned she was deeply pained at what seemed to her this revelation of the natural imperfection of human love ; and in her illness she was tremendously alone.

Arrived at this pass she took an entirely new turn. Hitherto, she had sought God direct. Now she turned to Jesus. Profoundly saddened as she was, she thought more and more of Jesus' love. And she commenced to meditate upon his life and character and love till gradually she made of him " a sweet Mind-Companion."

That Jesus Christ was God she knew to be the faith of the Church. But that he actually was God she felt no conviction whatever. Indeed, such a belief was to her incomprehensible. She thought of him as a perfect man with divine powers. He was her Jesus. She denied nothing and kept a perfectly open mind. But she loved him for himself as the Man Jesus.

We do not gather from her writings that she had at this time read any " lives " of Jesus or made any definite study of his teachings. Probably she caught her impressions of him directly from the Bible and from what she would hear in church.

And here it is necessary to notice one of her most remarkable characteristics—her power of dramatization. As a little girl she had pictured to herself a great angel who stood with pen and book in hand and wrote down all her sins. This terrible angel was a great reality to her. And God was a White Figure in white robes on a white throne, to whom the angel every evening read out her faults.

At the age of thirteen or fourteen she evolved in

her dreams a companion who was at the same time herself and yet also a marvellous creature of unlimited possibilities and virtues. This dream-companion even had wings and flew with such ease from the tops of the highest buildings, and floated so delightfully over her favourite fields or brooks that she found it hard to believe that she herself did not actually fly. Glorious things they did together. Nothing daunted them. Little now she cared for books of adventure. She and her dream-companion had adventures infinitely more wonderful than any read of in books.

Moreover, her companion not only had wings but was extremely good. The angel with the book had nothing to record against her. As they both grew older the actual wings were folded up and put away. But the virtues remained ; and a certain high standard of life was evolved which was afterwards extremely useful to her. And when she grew up and became exceedingly gay she still retained the habit of this double existence. It remained with her even after marriage and kept her out of mischief. Clothed in the body of her double she would wander where she listed. She need never be dull. She would go to balls and parties, or with great ease visit the mountains and watch the sunsets or the incomparable beauty of dawn. Delicate excursions, too, she would make into the strange, the wonderful, and the sublime, and in these invisible worlds gather crystal flowers whose scent was Romance.

Such was her habit of dramatization and she evidently carried it with her in her meditations on Jesus.

She was thirty-six years of age when she began these meditations. Her spiritual advancement had been incredibly slow, she believed. And now again her meditations went on without any apparent result. Then one day, on returning from a walk she had commenced thinking with great nearness and intimacy of Jesus when suddenly, with the most intense vividness, he presented himself before her consciousness so that she inwardly perceived him.

At once she was overcome by a great agony of remorse for her unworthiness. It was as though her heart and mind had broken in pieces and melted in the stress of a fearful pain. This lasted for an hour, increasing till it became wholly unendurable. Her wonderful Lord had come to pay her a visit and she was not fit to receive him.

Up till now she had publicly confessed herself a sinner. And privately also she had thought of herself as a sinner, but without being much perturbed by the thought. Now, by this presentment of himself she suddenly, and with terrible clearness, came to see the " whole insufferable offensiveness " of herself.

For some weeks she remained half stunned with astonishment. Then she determined to become less selfish, less irritable, less impatient, to be more considerate with others and more rigidly truthful. And whatever her difficulties might be she now had the immense incentive to please her Jesus—her tender and wonderful and perfect friend.

This was what she afterwards called her first conversion.

Two years went by and then, on an Easter morning, as she knelt in prayer at the close of the Church Service, he suddenly presented himself again. And again she saw herself, and went down and down into fearful abysses of spiritual pain, suffering even more than she had on his first presentment to her.

This was her second conversion.

After this her soul knew Jesus as Christ, the Son of God. And her mind and heart accepted this without any further wonder or question. A great repose began to fall upon her. The world and all its interests seemed to be softly blown out of her heart by the wings of a great new love—her love for the Risen Christ. Though outwardly her friends saw no change, yet inwardly she was changing month by month. She was distressed as she thought that the great love for her husband was beginning to fade. Yet it was rather that her heart was grown so large that no man could fill it. She felt within her immense, incomprehensible capacity for love which the whole world seemed even absurdly inadequate to satisfy.

She had a garden full of old-fashioned flowers and surrounded by a high wall. In this garden she would love to work. And there, far away from the world she would think about God—about God so hidden, yet so near her heart. And whilst she worked a robin would seek her out and sing to her all to herself a tiny, gentle song of which she never grew tired. And if she stayed quite still he would come so close to her as almost to touch her. Was not she like that robin ? she asked herself. Did she not want to come closer and closer to the feet of God ? So every day, just as the robin sang to her she would sing out of her own heart a little, gentle song to the hidden God Who called her, but Who, when she answered Him, would not let her find Him, or make any sign.

While she was left dumb with pain and wonder at this mystery there suddenly came the tremendous shock of the Great War. Her husband was among the first who went to it. And all her love for him, which she had thought to be fading, now rose up again to its full strength. But again her capacity for suffering showed itself. The very strength and perfection of her love made it a greater instrument for torture. She thought of Christ in the Garden of Gethsemane. He understood and knew all pain and she had his companionship. But he afforded her no cessation of pain. And she shrank appalled from the suffering she was already enduring and the suffering she knew lay before her.

And now she was possessed by what she calls a " horrible kind of second sight." So that she became aware of much that was happening to her husband—of his being perpetually pressed backward, fighting for his life, and lying out exhausted in open fields at night. And this was not the only instance in her life of such experience. As a little girl she had suffered agonies when in a train crossing a railway bridge and had become acutely aware that the bridge was about to give way—which it did when the following train passed over. She had also possessed an aptitude for fortune-telling, but after practising it for a couple of years, had pushed it from her as an intolerable nuisance.

Months and years dragged by. Sometimes the pain of it all was eased. Sometimes it was increased. Her soul reached down into great and fearful depths. She envied the soldiers dying upon the battlefields. Life became more terrible to her than death. A painful illness came and lasted for months. Having no home, she was obliged to endure the misery of it as best she could amongst strangers. She touched the very lowest depths. She loathed her life and often longed that she might never awake in the morning.

But during her illness some light did come. She became exceedingly near to Christ—more vividly near than she could possibly describe. And out of this time of suffering she learned submission. Perhaps a too great submission. For later she was to see that an onward-driving resolution to win through—a powerful determination to seek and obtain the immediate protection and assistance of God—was required of the soul. But for the time she was bewildered and mystified by her own unhappiness and by the unhappiness of those around, and she sank, in her submission, into a too lethargic state of resignation.

A great battle was now raging in France and her husband was in the very foremost part of it. At last the day came when the shadow of these two fearful years rose up and overwhelmed her altogether. So she went up to the wild lonely hill where she had so often contended with God for His help. And then, for the first time in her life, she found nothing between God and herself.

Like a man standing in a very dark place, seeing nothing, but knowing himself near to another she knew herself to be in very great nearness to God. She had no need for eyes to see outwardly, because of the immense magnetism of this inward awareness. At one moment her heart and mind ran like water before Him, praying and beseeching Him for help. At another her soul stood straight up before Him, contending and claiming help because she could bear no more. And it felt to her as though the Spirit of God stood over against her spirit, and for more than an hour her spirit wrestled with God's Spirit.

But He gave her no answer, no sign, no help. He

gave her nothing but that awful silence which seemed to hang for ever between God and man. And she became exhausted and turned away in despair from God, from supplication, from striving. And very quiet, and profoundly sad, she stood looking out across the hills to the distant view.

Then, mutely wondering at the meaning of it all—this lovely peace of the evening sky, and nearly all the nations of the earth fighting together in blood and fury and pain—she was commencing to walk away, when suddenly she was surrounded by a great whiteness which blotted out all her surroundings, though she stood there with her eyes wide open. And the cloud pricked so that she said to herself, "It is an electric cloud." And it pricked her from her head down to her elbows, but no further. And she stood there quite placid and quiet, and feeling no fear—only a very great wonder.

Then there began to be poured into her an indescribably great vitality so that she said to herself, "I am being filled with some marvellous elixir." And it filled her from the feet up, gently and slowly, so that she could notice every advance. As it rose higher in her she grew to feel freed of the law of gravitation and possessed of the capacity to pass where and how she would. She was like a free spirit.

For some moments she tasted a new form of living. Words were unable to describe the splendour of it—the glory, the liberty, the boundless joy.

And this incomprehensible Power rose and rose in her until it reached the very crown of her head. And immediately it had quite filled her a marvellous thing happened. The wall which had been a dreadful barrier between God and her came down entirely. Immediately she loved Him. And so filled with love

196

was she, and so great was the force, and wonder, and delight of it, that she had to cry her love aloud.

Then slowly the vivid whiteness melted away so that once more she saw everything around her just as before.

For a little while she continued to stand there very still and thoughtful—for she was filled with wonder and great peace. Then slowly she turned to walk home. But now she walked as a new creature in a new world. Her heart felt like the heart of an angel—glowing white-hot with the love of God. And all her sorrows had fled away in a vast joy.

This was God's answer. This was His help. After years and years of wrestling and struggling, in one moment He had let her find Him : He had poured His paradise into her soul. Never was such inconceivable joy—never such gladness ! The whole of space was scarce large enough to hold her. She needed it all. And she welcomed its immensity as once it had oppressed her. God and her soul, and love, and light, and space !

After this for some weeks she went through extraordinary spiritual experiences, the like of which had never previously so much as entered into her heart to imagine. And she came to these experiences with great innocence as she had never read any religious or psychological book. For a period of some months she was in such a state of exaltation and enhancement of all her faculties that she did not know herself. Without any intention or endeavour on her own part she was suddenly become like a veritable house of art ! The most beautiful music flowed through her mind—a music without a trace of sadness in it. And it swayed her so that she would go into a white-heat of emotion over it. Colour and form, imagery of all kinds would pass through her, till she cried out with regret that she had not the training of an artist to bring them to material expression. An object of quite ordinary charm would seem, because of this something which now filled her, to expand into prodigious beauty. The very pavements and houses, mean and hideous as they were, would overflow with some inexplicable glamour. The world was turned into paradise.

But this wonderful state of things gradually passed away. And again she was tasting sadness. At one time of day she would be in an ecstasy of delight, and an hour later in some altogether unreasonable depth of depression. Her love for God was as great as ever, but it had become a love all made of tears. Most certainly she had not found the peace of God. On the contrary, her life had become an indescribable turmoil.

Her fellow-beings gave her no help. Men could no longer please her and she could not please God! Spiritually she was alone. And physically also she would have liked to be alone. And she ached and longed, and dreamed of solitude till it was like a sickness.

Then, believing herself to be a sensible and practical person she would say to herself that, her condition being so unreasonable, must be got out of, and she must make every effort to do it.

She prayed for two things—that she might love God with a cheerful countenance, and that He would teach her quickly what to pray for. In answer He gave her the impulse to pray for more and greater love.

Next she banished her own feelings as much as

possible and returned to the thought of Jesus and
to loving inward conversation with him. And with
all her will and strength she strove to climb out of
her miserable condition.

Then one night, as she composed herself as usual
for sleep, she lay for a time neither asleep nor yet
quite awake, for the wakefulness was not the usual
wakefulness. Then her consciousness became alight
with a new fiery energy of life and seemed to extend
to an infinite distance beyond her body and yet remain connected with her body. She lived in a manner
totally new and totally incomprehensible—a life in
which none of her senses was used and which was
yet a thousand times as vivid as ordinary life. It
was living at white heat—without forms, without
sound, without sight, without anything which she
had ever been aware of in this world. And it was
living at terrible speed.

For six weeks every night she entered this condition. And the duration and power and intensity
of it increased by degrees. It felt as if her soul
was projected or travelled for incalculable distances
beyond her body. And she learned to comprehend
and to know a new manner of living, as a swimmer
learns a new mode of progression by means of his
swimming.

By the end of three weeks she was able to remain
nightly for many hours in this condition. And it
was always acco mpanied by an intense and vivid consciousness of God. But as this consciousness of God
became more and more vivid, so did her body suffer
more and more. She could hardly eat the smallest
morsels of food, and even they almost choked her.
She had scarcely any sleep, and she suffered at night

from her breathing and heart. Yet she was perfectly healthy. Her love of God gave her supreme confidence. She was glad that He should do as He pleased with her ; and she had no anxiety whatever.

As she came out of this intense abstraction—this strange valley of humiliation, poverty, solitude—it seemed a necessary prelude to the great, the supreme experience of her life. For now the joyousness of her spiritual experience increased. The nights were not at all a time of sleep or repose, but of rapturous living.

The sixth week came, and she began to fear the nights and their tremendous living. The happiness, the light, the poignancy and the rapture of it were becoming more than she could bear. Secretly she began to wonder whether God did not intend to draw her soul so near to Him that she would die of the splendour of this living.

Then came a night when she passed beyond ideas, beyond melody, beyond beauty, into vast lost spaces, and depths of untellable bliss, into a Light. And the Light was an ecstasy of delight. And the Light was an ocean of bliss. And the Light was Life and Love. And the Light was too deep contact with God And the Light was unbearable joy.

Her soul, her whole being, was terrified of God, and of joy. She dared not think of Him or pray. Like some pitiful, wounded child she crept to the feet of Jesus. And when on the following evening she composed herself for the night, she wondered tremblingly to what God would again expose her. But for the first time in six weeks she fell into a natural sleep and knew no more until the morning.

Then she knew that the lesson was over. "Mighty and Terrible God it was enough!" she exclaimed. And that night—that Night of Terror, that Night of Too Great Happiness, as she called it—was for her soul the turning point of her destiny. That night altered her soul for ever more. That night she knew God as deeply as He can be known whilst the soul is in the flesh.

Wonderful, beautiful weeks went by, filled with divine, indescribable peace. The Presence of God was with her day and night. And the world was no longer the world she had known it—a place where men and women fought and sinned and toiled and anguished. It had become a paradise. And the glamour of life in unity with God became past all comprehension and all words. Life was one long essence of delight—a harmony of flowing out and back again to God.

A wonderful change had crept all through her. If God could come at any moment of the day or night and turn over every secret page of heart and mind He would not have found one thought or glimmer of any sort or kind of lust. And all at once she realized the miracle that Christ had worked in her, and the words came over her mind, "Though thy sins be as scarlet, they shall be white as snow." Tears of joy that was an agony of gratitude poured like rain down her face. And very quietly she took her heart and her mind and her soul and laid them for ever at the feet of Jesus.

Then one evening as she knelt, as was her custom, for a few moments of intense prayer, her heart and mind with great power bent wholly and singly upon God, He drew her powerfully to Him. And He en-

compassed her with so much glamour that this singleness and concentration of thought continued longer
than usual. And because of the magnetism the concentration became an intensity of penetration. And
God turned on to her and her mind became faint
and died and she could no longer think of or on
God. For she was one with Him. One with Him
though still her own self.

She was become Ineffable Joy. She had been in
contact with God in an unutterable bliss and repose.
And this time He had given her the bliss tenderly and
not as on that Night of Terror. And this most blessed
happening happened to her every day for a short time,
usually lasting for a few moments—God in this way
enabling her to contemplate and know Him. And she
saw that this experience was in some ways at one with
her " beautiful pastime " (of meditating on the beauties
of nature), but with this tremendous difference—that
whereas her mind had formerly concentrated itself
upon the beautiful, and remaining mind had soared
away above all forms into its nebulous essence in a
strange, seductive anguish, it was now drawn and
magnetized beyond the beautiful directly to the maker
of Beauty. In this living was no note of pain, but a
marvellous joy. And the soaring was like a death or
swooning of the mind : she was living with that which
was above mind.

This is her experience, extended over several months,
of what is sometimes called union with God, or Realization of God, but which she preferred to call contact
with God and which might perhaps be simply described as awareness or consciousness of the Spirit
which animates the universe. As a thoughtful cell
in her brain might become aware of the spirit which

animated her, so did she in these experiences become aware of the Spirit which animates the universe. That is possibly how her experience of contact with God might be described. And we may be helped to understand the better by studying her own reflections on them.

First, we may note that she kept on insisting that they were indescribable. In the same breath as she described them she would say that they were past all description. What she had found was " impossible to pass on to others." " In this celestial living," she says, " are happenings which cannot be communicated, or even indicated to others, because they reach beyond words, beyond all other experiences, beyond all particularization, beyond any possible previous imagination. . . ." But what the ravishment of happiness was cannot be known or guessed till we ourselves have experienced it. It can be known but not named.

And besides this impossibility of describing her experiences she had a natural shyness in communicating these intimate things of the soul to any other. Though here also was the counter-desire of wanting to tell everybody. She was filled with the beauty of her experiences as lovers are filled with the beauty of their love. And she longed to speak about it. But she was frightened. Something held her back.

What she could not speak about to her friends she could, under the cloak of anonymity, tell to the world at large. And she could at least try to describe the indescribable. And these subsequent reflections of hers upon her descriptions may perhaps aid us still better to understand her experiences.

She had sought God. She had spent years of striving. She had known the stress, the sweat of climbing to God's footstool—the sweat that at times was like drops of blood wrung out of her soul, out of her heart, out of her mind. And now that she had found God, all this had been forgotten on the instant. But what was God like when she had found Him? How far different was He from the White Figure sitting on a white throne of her childhood?

Evidently He was no Figure at all. No concrete Object. No Form. " It cannot possibly be said," she writes, " that in ecstasy we see God : it is a question of ' knowing ' Him through the higher part of the soul in lesser or in deeper degrees." She did not see God but she experienced Him. The Divine radiations and penetration were the fulfilment of all her desires and needs—and fulfilment in over-abounding measure.

This finding God is " encounter with the Supreme Spirit. It is life at its perfection point—a stupendous felicity, and that repose in bliss for which all souls secretly long. It is the meeting of the Wisher and the Wished ; of Desire with the Desired. And yet being unthinkable fulfilment it is above all, or any wishes, and beyond desire. . . . In this Spirit-life we meet the ideas of God uncrystallized into any form. They penetrate the soul. She flashes to them, she becomes them, she reaches unimaginable heights of bliss. . . .

" God is life itself to us—the air, the bread, and the blood of the soul. No one can live without, at every moment, drawing upon Him, however unconscious they may be that they are."

The tremendousness of God is one of her chief impressions. " To find God is to live tremendously," she writes. And she speaks of the " immensity of God's attraction," of " the terrible might of the activity of celestial joy."

Answering the question whether God does not feel to be a fire, she says :

" Yes, and no, for we feel we shall be consumed, and yet it is not a burning which is experienced, but a blissful energy of the most inexpressible and unbearable intensity, which seems to disintegrate or disperse the flesh. So long as this is given with certain limits the experience is blissful to heart and mind. Beyond that limit it is bliss-agony. Beyond this again it would soon be death to the body—a very terrible feeling which does not bear remembering or thinking about."

And this bliss—this ecstasy of delight—is the essential feature of union with God. And the value of ecstasy to him to whom it is granted is that " it raises him above faith into certitude ; and the strength and peace given by certitude are such that joy is neither here nor there : the soul can wait for it. In these experiences

" the soul stood steadied before God in an unutterable happiness which she perceived had no limit but God's will and her own capacity to endure the rapture. . . . There is nothing in life," she adds, " so wonderful, so rapturous as the swift reunion of the soul with God. And the joy is not only the joy of the soul, because the heart and the mind have their full of it too : they too have ached, and thirsted and longed, and now are satisfied."

And the joy begets a love in comparison with which every love on earth is a poor, pale counterfeit.

Union with God is all one same joy ; it is the joy of angels reduced to such a degree as makes it bearable to the flesh. It is a mode of heavenly living.

This indeed is the main conclusion—that in finding God she had discovered a new mode of living—a higher state of being—which she calls " the angelic state."

"Ecstasies inspire and awaken the soul : they convince the mind absolutely of the existence of another form of living." And this form of living is the true love-state brought to completion by beholding God. And "when God communicates Himself to the soul she lives in a manner never previously conceived of, reaching an experience of living in which every perfection is present to her as being there in such unlimited abundance that the soul is overwhelmed by it and must fall back to the less because of the insupportable excess of perfections."

And it is to be noted that "this perfection of living is given and withdrawn outside of her own will." Her experience indicated that it did not depend *only* on her whether she found this new and joyous mode of living. Doubtless, it would not have come to her unless she had sought and striven and sweated drops of blood from the soul. Yet with all this agony of striving she might never have attained this celestial living by herself. Something more was needed. Something from outside her—something from above.

She speaks of grace coming and departing—and coming in lesser and greater intensity—of the presence of God, love and comfort enveloping the soul.

There is penetration by radiation from outside, and she is overpowered by the might and the excess of joy. Yet we note that in this new state

"we are not lost in God—that is to say we do not disappear as a living individual consciousness : our consciousness is increased to a prodigious degree, and we are one with God. . . . We become by the love of Him so large that we seem to embrace the whole universe within our own self ! In some mysterious way we become in sympathy with all things in the bond of His making."

And in the same deep, mysterious fashion marriage-love in all its aspects is included in this love of God. To the lover of God all affections go up and are enclosed in one affection, so that we have no love for anyone or anything apart from God. And marriage-love is included in this. In every way it can become a sacrament, she says. There is nothing in it which is not holy. In no way does the marriage bond of the body separate the spirit from acceptableness to God. Marriage is the physical prototype in this physical world of the spiritual union with God in the spiritual world. This relationship between men and women is His thought, His plan, not ours. Our responsibility is only to keep the bond of it pure and clean and sweet, and submit ourselves in all things as completely and orderly as possible to His plans, whatever they may be. He has no wish to impose distress and suffering on us. His will towards us is pure joy, pure love, pure peace, pure sweetness. This bond of earthly marriage is of the flesh and can be kept by the body, and yet the heart, mind and soul remain in lovely, perfect charity. This was the exquisite freedom she found.

What was the effect upon her—the immediate effect of the moment and the deep-down ultimate effect upon her whole life ? We might well suppose that at least the momentary effect of such a terrific experience would be the shattering of her nerves. She was always of a tense, sensitive, highly strung nature ; and on the face of it we would conjecture that the impact on her of such tremendous spiritual forces would have smashed her delicate nervous system to shreds. The result was precisely the opposite. The inrush of the spirit actually steadied her. She says

of herself that she was " never so sane, so capable—
never so perfectly poised."

And she was a great deal more than sane, and
capable and perfectly poised : her whole life was
altered. She felt an " immense and altogether indescribable enhancement of life and of all her faculties."
In great amazement she would say to herself that she
had never until then known what life was.

The more she saw of other people the more she
realized how greatly changed she was. They were
bound. She was free. They were bound by anxieties,
worries, apprehension of evil things, sadness, fears of
death for their loved ones or for themselves. She was
freed of all these troubles. She seemed to herself to
have been lifted into the way of Love. True, she had
to struggle, suffer and endure in order to keep herself
in this way of Love. But her sufferings, struggles and
endurances were for love, and in love, and because of
love. They were in themselves beautiful. And in
recollection they left nothing inharmonious. They
were the difficult prelude to a glorious melody.

She does acknowledge, however, that it took much
time and much pain to learn how to combine this inward life of blessed intercourse with God with the
outward life of intercourse with her fellow-beings. In
the early stages she had innumerable difficulties and
was terrified of losing God. She did not understand
how to leave God and return to earthly duties. At
times when, while she was altogether wrapped up in
God, the voice of some fellow-being would recall her
to the world the pain would be so great as to be
nothing less than anguish. This return, however, she
learned in time to accomplish without a shock. What
remained and grew was the difficulty of carrying on
a conversation with anyone unless it was about God,

or about some work for Him. She could not converse for more than an hour on any other subject without the most deadly exhaustion, both bodily and spiritual. Her face and lips would lose all colour and her eyes their vitality. And so dreadful was the distress of her whole being that she was obliged, upon any kind of pretext, to withdraw from all companions, and, if it were only for five minutes, be alone with God. Then, once she was again united with Him her whole being would be revivified. For nothing else in life was so wonderful, so rapturous as this swift reunion of her soul with God.

The result upon her of these spiritual experiences was that the efforts of her entire being were now bent on trying to perfect herself. The feeling for God which before ecstasy was a deep and often very painful longing now increased to a burning, never-ceasing desire for Him. And whereas before union God's Presence had been near—though how near she knew not, or whether she could be sure of finding it—now, after union, she was certain of finding God's Presence everywhere and at any time.

God would, indeed, withdraw Himself at times. And then she would suffer renewed agonies. But she would know whereabouts He was. He would merely disappear from her consciousness but not so entirely that she could not partly find Him.

Amongst the most noticeable changes in her mind, she remarked that it had become very simple in its requirements and very restful. It no longer darted here and there gathering in this and that fancied treasure, as a bird darts at flies. It had dropped out-side objects in order to hover round the thoughts of God. And these thoughts were not particularized; they floated quietly and contentedly in a general peaceful fragrance of beauty. It was the same contentment as a mother has beside her babe, neither talking to it nor touching it but happy in knowing that it was near—or as two lovers sitting near together and happy without any need of speech.

Yet it is remarkable that she did not consider herself rendered permanently incapable of sin. She expressly says that, even after all the blessings God had showered upon her she did not trust herself : she still remained fundamentally the sinner. Love and grace might surround her, might save her from herself, might beautify her, and make her shine. But potentially at every step she remained the sinner, she said.

There were, of course, times of waning after waxing to such heights. There were joyless, flat, ungracious times when a kind of paralysis of the soul, and dreary torpor set in. This was terrible. And she would feel that this withered state must endure to the end. She became convinced that God had nothing more to give and had withdrawn His graciousness from her comprehension, leaving her as a tiny, unwanted speck in the vast universe. But these sufferings she came to see were just what was required to develop courage, humility, endurance, love, and generosity.

Another very remarkable effect upon her was that the poignancy and distress of pain disappeared. Trouble of several kinds came to her—the death of one very dear, the severe illness of another, a serious operation on her brother, and a slight but very painful operation on herself. She felt terribly nervous and fearful of the pain of her own and her brother's operation. But she hung on to God, and by means and because of love, she passed out of herself and was able to hand over everything which she was, or had, or thought, or did to God ; and in exchange she received His peace. Thus-wise she handed over her brother and her dead and her anxieties for herself into His hands and went to her operation with the same serenity that she would go to meet a friend. She was calm, and less nervous than anyone else. The anæsthetic failed before the operation was completed and she was aware of atrocious pain. Yet by the grace of God her mind and soul were able immediately to raise and to maintain themselves in high consciousness of God so that the operation could be finished without a cry or movement of the body. And this grace continued for days afterwards, and though the pain of wounds continued severe enough to interfere with sleep, her mind remained calm as a lake. Pain had no sting or fear or fret.

The main effect, however, was to create a piercing need in her to share her joy with others. To all her fellow-souls she cried, " Why fret and toil, why sweat and anguish for the things of earth, when our own God has in His hand such bliss and peace and happiness to give to every man ? Oh, come and receive it : every man his share."

She had this great longing to share the knowledge and the exquisite balm with her fellows. She longed to speak about it ; to know how they felt about it. But she was frightened to speak. Something held her back. Perhaps her native reticence. But also the difficulty of making people understand. To illustrate a mere fraction of this difficulty she takes the case of a man born blind.

" You put a blade of grass and a leaf of a tree in his hand and you say to him ' This is grass, and this is a leaf, and both are green.' ' And what,' he asks, ' is green ? ' And to save your life you cannot make him know what it is. How then shall God, who can be neither seen, nor heard, nor touched, be made known by one to the other ? He must be experienced to be known."

There was the further difficulty that through being misunderstood more harm than good might be done.

But this much she did do. Constantly the words, " Visit the sick," came to her. She was weary of sick people, having seen so much of them. But the words came again with the gentleness of Christ. And the gentleness pierced. So that day she went to the village to visit the sick again, and she looked at them lovingly and tenderly, and tenderly and lovingly they looked at her. And some say, " It is as if God came into the house with you." And tears come into her eyes, and she says, " It may be so, because He sent me." And they gaze at her lovingly, and lovingly she gazes at them. And it seems to her that she can no longer tell where " they " cease and where " she " begins. And the peculiar sweetness of Christ pierces her through from her heart to her feet. And so she comprehends that Holy Love is not alone just God and her, but is also God and her and the others, and God and the others and her.

Also for total strangers, passers-by in the street, fellow-passengers by road and rail, here and there, this one and that, she would pray, joyously, lovingly holding them up before God for His help and blessing.

It rapidly became the only sorrow of her life that people did not all come to share this life in which she lived. " How that parable knocks at the heart, ' Go out into the highways and hedges and compel them to come in.' To know all the fullness of life and not to be able to bring even my nearest and dearest into it— what a terrible mystery is this !—it is an agony."

So she wrote ; and others besides her have felt the same restraining reticence.   Yet she did not die without having enshrined her spirit in her little anonymous books ; and through them that spirit may penetrate deeper and spread further, perhaps, than she had ever supposed to be possible.

CHAPTER V

MASS MYSTICISM

THE WELSH REVIVAL

SO far we have considered individuals only. Now we shall consider a mass movement. From time to time in history there occur spiritual upheavals. The placid, set face of mankind is stirred, and men's souls begin to seethe. Such revivals, whether in art or religion, become associated with the name of some one individual—as, for example, in the case of the Franciscan revival. But they do not necessarily originate with that individual. He may be only the one round whom the movement centres, as he may be the one above all others who may best be able to represent and express the essence of the movement, which itself must ultimately originate in the Creative Spirit of the universe, while his part is in a unique degree to manifest and express that Spirit.

The Welsh Revival of 1904–5 was one of such spiritual upheavals in recent times. It became associated with the name of Evan Roberts. He did not actually originate the movement. But he was its chief embodiment ; and he more fully and effectively than any other manifested its spirit.

Evan Roberts had none of what are ordinarily considered the advantages of life. He was not born of rich, or even well-to-do parents. He had no public

214

school or university education. He was first a miner and then a blacksmith, and his parents were just simple working-class folk.

Outwardly and seemingly he possessed no advantages in the struggle of life. Inwardly he had an incalculably great advantage over his fellows. He was endowed with an inordinate love of all high and pure and holy things, and with a sweet, loving and most sincere and genuine disposition. And he was brought up in a home where spiritual things counted. While there was little money there was much affection.

His father was a pump-man and miner ; and his mother was the daughter of a blacksmith. Both parents were of a strongly religious disposition, but it was to the firmness and love of his mother that he probably owed most. He was one of fourteen children of these simple-minded poor, industrious parents, and was born in 1878.

Between four and five years of age he went to school, but owing to the necessity of having to earn something towards his living he had to leave school three months before he reached his twelfth year. And at this early start in life he is said to have had a strong affection for his parents, to have been willingly obedient to them, orderly in his habits, and clean in dress, word and conduct.

At twelve he became a door-boy, looking after doors in the pit of a colliery and earning his first salary. Wishing to improve his position he began cutting coal with another man, and at sixteen he and a friend undertook the working of a heading and earned five-shillings a day each.

Even when mining, though, he had his Bible by him and used to read it in snatches. And away from his work he would read much and attend Chapel meetings where he attracted so much attention by his faithful attendance and earnestness of demeanour that at twenty-one he was appointed to speak on " Practical Atheism " at a church meeting. And young though he was at the time he was not unfitted for such a task, as he had six years before been made teacher in a Sunday school and proved such a success in winning the confidence of children that he had later been appointed superintendent of the children's school.

At the age of twenty-four he gave up coal-mining and began to learn the trade of blacksmith. And at this period the intensity of his longing to spend his life in the service of Christ began to deepen. He would spend hours in prayer and reading the Bible ; and a friend who lived with him says of him that he was the most real and truest friend he had ever met. He was seldom seen to take his meals without having his Bible on the table. And, as he became more and more possessed of the idea of devoting his whole life to God, it became less and less possible to continue his work as a blacksmith. So after fifteen months he abandoned the work and took steps to qualify himself for the Ministry.

At this time he read much—in addition to the Bible. Especially was he influenced by Sheldon's *In His Steps ; or, What Would Jesus Do?* He learned music and could play on the piano, harmonium and organ, and could understand the spirit and quality of singing. Also, he wrote verses. And in both music and poetry he was much influenced by the Calvinist Methodist hymn-book. And the more he read and prayed and taught the more his spiritual appetite grew. He could not have enough. His spirit was ever reaching out in prayer for more—and of the very holiest.

But now came most terrible spiritual conflicts.

Spiritual heights are not climbed without struggle and endurance. The more he strove to purify his thoughts and life the more conscious he became both of his own shortcomings and of the evils in the world about him, and the more he yearned to better it. His mind dwelling constantly on the purity and holiness of Christ became intensely aware how far short of that standard he himself was ; and he struggled and strained to be more like Him. Then his attachment to his fellows made him yearn to get them also to be more like Christ : and he would have liked to have given up all his time and all his energies to this twin task of bettering himself and bettering his fellows. But between him and the fulfilment of his task were many obstacles. He had to earn a living ; and while earning a living it was hard to find the time and the opportunity for training himself. Home ties also bound him. It was a difficult thing for a young, half-trained blacksmith to break away from home and from his trade to set out and reform the world. Who was he ? men would say, and his own family would say, to set himself above them.

Throughout 1903 his desire to become a preacher grew in strength, and in November he wrote to a friend in the ministry saying he had definitely decided to give up his trade of blacksmith and qualify for the ministry. " I have had enough of bodily labour, as my soul thirsts for knowledge and a wider sphere of usefulness." His friend encouraged him, and in December 1903 he decided, once for all, to abandon his trade and train himself for the ministry. But he had still to face his family, and the uncle who had put up the money for his training as blacksmith. It was a situation from which he shrank, and his mother had to act as intermediary.

His first sermon was preached on December 18, 1903, in the chapel of his native place, Loughor, his text being, " And He said to them all, if any man will come after Me, let him deny himself, and take up his cross daily and follow Me." It well exemplified the ruling passion of his life—to get the world to follow Jesus.

Subsequently he was allowed to go through the Swansea district on probation, attending each of twelve churches. He commenced in January 1904 ; and in April he was accepted as a candidate for the ministry and urged to prepare for the provincial examination which was to be held in August.

These were the outward circumstances. Inwardly he was all the time preparing himself by prayer. Hours every day he would spend in prayer. And prayer had always been the distinguishing feature of his religious life. From childhood it was as natural to him as breathing. He would completely lose himself in prayer, and constantly feel himself drawn into communion with God. And not in audible words would he pray but in the silence of his heart. And when he prayed in public his prayers were of extra-ordinary intensity. His supplications to Heaven showed a yearning of spirit and an agony of soul that profoundly moved his hearers. They came from the depth of his soul with such feeling as to melt the hearts of the congregations. With such fervency and such earnestness would he pray as to shake his whole con-stitution and leave him in a weakened condition. Men were awestruck with his strange intensity. Every word seemed the product of his whole being, body and soul ; and his sighs appeared to rise from the deep and pass along every nerve.

As a result of this long and persistent yearning after

218

God he had in the spring of 1904, while he was preparing himself for the ministry, the supreme experience of his life :

" One Friday night last spring (1904), when praying by my bedside before retiring, I was taken up into a great expanse. without time or space—it was communion with God. Before this it was a far-off God that I had. I was frightened that night, but never since. So great was my shivering that I rocked the bed and my brother awakened, took hold of me, thinking I was ill. After that I was awakened every night a little after one. This was most strange, for through the years I slept like a rock and no disturbance in my room would arouse me. From that hour I was taken up into divine fellowship for about four hours. What it was I cannot tell you, except that it was divine. About five I was allowed to sleep until nine."

In an interview with Mr. W. T. Stead he described the same experience :

" At one o'clock in the morning suddenly I was wakened up out of my sleep, and I found myself, with unspeakable joy and awe, in the very presence of Almighty God. And for the space of four hours I was privileged to speak face to face with Him as a man speaks face to face with a friend. At four o'clock it seemed to me as if I again returned to earth."

In answer to Mr. Stead's question whether he was not dreaming he replied :

" No, I was wide awake. And it was not only that morning, but every morning for three or four months. Always I enjoyed four hours of that wonderful communion with God. I cannot describe it. I felt it, and it changed all my nature. I saw things in a different light. And I knew that God was going to work in the land, and not this land only but all the world."

In his home they would question him about being so late, but " it was too divine," he said later, " to say anything about." " It was the most divine, light and happy communion "—the most divine thing he ever experienced.

In another description of this experience to the Rev. D. M. Phillips, he said that God used to be in the distance to him till then, but then He came so near as to fill him with divine awe. Every member in his body trembled until the bed was shaking and Dan, his brother, awoke and shouted, " Are you ill, Evan ? " " Oh ! no," he answered, " beginning to get well I am."

This experience continued unceasingly for three months, and it was so sweet he feared to lose it if he went, as he had intended, to the Grammar School at Newcastle-Emlyn to train for the ministry. Again a terrible struggle took place within him—the struggle between the desire to go off there and then on his mission to save men's souls and the desire to educate himself further for his task. If he went to the school he might lose his precious daily communion with God and lose the opportunity of working for God. If he did not go he might embark half-trained on his career. He sought light in prayer and decided to go to the school ; and he entered it on September 13, 1904.

But it happened as he had feared. For a whole month God came to him no more. He was in darkness. His heart became as a stone. Even the sight of the Cross brought no tears to his eyes. At the same time he was quite unable to remain with any book except the Bible. He could not get his mind on to grammar and algebra and Latin and other subjects required for the examination. When engaged in his school books he was possessed with some strange, unaccountable feeling and suffered most terribly in body and mind. His only relief was to throw away the school book and seize the Bible. Then only did peace come. He conferred with able men and when they advised him to cling to his studies he summoned all his powers to adopt their advice and prayed earnestly for strength of purpose. But nothing availed. He must proceed at once on his life's work.

The deciding moment came when the Rev. Seth Joshua commenced a series of meetings in the Methodist chapel at Newcastle-Emlyn, on Sunday, September 25, 1904. Evan Roberts was confined to his bed with a severe cold. But his friend Sydney Evans attended the Monday meeting and reported that it was full of God and that it was attended by a number of young ladies from New Quay in Cardiganshire, amongst whom the revival spirit had broken out in February. On Tuesday, Sydney Evans and some other students came to Evan Roberts to persuade him to come to the meeting.

" The minute they asked me," said Evan Roberts, " I felt the Spirit descending on me. The irresistible possessed me, and I rushed to the chapel without my overcoat. The divine influence began to bear on me heavily. I had been praying on Monday evening in the house for strength for the girls from New Quay. But the Spirit would not allow me to pray in chapel on Tuesday night. I felt hard, and wept bitterly because of my hardness of heart."

On Wednesday they were to go to Blaenanerch for a meeting. But he felt like a flint—as if every feeling

221

had been swept from his bosom. In the evening they returned to Newcastle-Emlyn. On that evening he attended a meeting conducted by the Rev. Seth Joshua. And in response to the latter's request for all who possessed full assurance of faith to stand, he was one of the first of the very few who stood up.

The following day, September 29, was another of the crucial days in his career. With Mr. Joshua and about twenty others they again started for Blaenan-erch. On the way his feelings varied up and down—now gloomy, hard and cold, now joyous. But at the evening meeting all was definite and decisive.

"My bosom," he said, "was full to overflowing. On our way to the nine o'clock service the Rev. Seth Joshua said : ' We are going to have a wonderful meeting to-day.' I answered, ' I am just bursting.' I felt in going to the meeting that I was compelled to pray.

"When the meeting commenced many prayed, and I asked the Holy Spirit, ' Shall I pray now ? ' ' No,' said the Spirit. Shortly, some wonderful influence came over me. I felt some living energy or force entering my bosom. It held my breath. My legs trembled terribly. This living energy increased and increased as one after the other prayed, until it nearly burst me. And as each finished I asked, ' Shall I pray now ? '

"When someone finished, I prayed. My bosom boiled all through, and if I had not prayed I would have burst. What boiled my bosom ? It was the verse, ' For God commendeth His love.' I fell on my knees with my arms stretched out on the seat before me. The perspiration poured down my face. And my tears streamed so quickly I thought that the blood came out. It was awful on me for about ten minutes. I cried, ' Bend me, bend me. Oh ! Oh !

Oh ! ' It was God commending His love that bent me, and I not seeing anything in Him to commend.

" After I was bent, a wave of peace filled my bosom. When I was in this feeling the audience sang heartily :

> ' I am coming, Lord !
> Coming now to Thee ! '

" What came to my mind after this was the bending in the day of judgment. Then I was filled with sympathy for the people who will have to bend in the judgment day, and I wept. Afterwards, the salvation of souls weighed heavily on me. I felt on fire to go through all Wales to tell about the Saviour."

Evan Roberts had at last found himself. The call from without had met the urge from within and he had found his " vocation." It was, in his own words, " the most awful and most pleasant day " of his life.

The next day he planned out a scheme for going through all Wales to offer Christ to sinners. He and Sydney Evans and seven women, including some of those from New Quay, were to undertake the task. As to the cost, he intended to defray all expenses himself. He had £200 in the bank, and he would use the whole.

On the Saturday—October 1—he went over to New Quay, fifteen miles distant, to talk over the plan. There he received a warm welcome from his friends, and they prayed for light, but none was forthcoming, and he returned to Newcastle-Emlyn the same evening. For some days more he remained there discussing with Sydney Evans his next steps and scheming to save one hundred thousand souls in Wales.

To his brother Dan he writes at this time that he was " healthy and joyful," that he had lost all nervousness and was "courageous for Christ and joyful in Christ." He wonders whether Dan is in possession of the joy of the Gospel.

"I know that you have peace," he writes, "but ask for joy, though if you wish to possess it you must be ready to do what the Spirit will say : you must be ready to give yourself absolutely into the hands of the Holy Spirit."

In a similar gladsome strain he writes on October 11 to Mr. Davies, a member of Moriah Chapel at Loughor : "I was having great pleasure with the work before, but now I am having the most pure joy on earth." And in addition to reiterating that he had "lost all nervousness" he also mentions that he had lost some physical impediment which had prevented him singing and he could now "sing all day long."

In a letter to his sister Mary, dated October 28, he again refers to the sense of joy which possessed him.

"The old fashion was to draw a long face when speaking of religious things. But it was most part of it based on hypocrisy and based on the thought that God is a solemn and just God, forgetting that God is a happy God and a joyful God. Now, however, when we speak of religion we are full of joy. Our faces are lit up with joy."

At this very time, though, he had much to test his capacity for happiness. In the same letter to his sister he tells of obstacles he is encountering. "Downright lies" are being told about him. "Some say we go to see the young girls, and not for the cause. . . . Others say we are only shamming. . . . Others scoff and make light of these spiritual things." And besides these minor obstructions there was the more serious trial that many were thinking his mind was becoming deranged. His late hours, his deep praying, disturbed his landlady and made her think there was something " strange " about him. And when in the daytime he would incessantly gaze at the sun and during the night at the moon and stars he caused no little anxiety to his acquaintances. But though he well knew the opinion of many as to his mental derangement, that would not make him swerve : he meant to have a revival.

On October 28 he attended a revival meeting conducted by the Rev. Joseph Jenkins and assisted by many from New Quay. It was full of religious enthusiasm, and he found himself in his element. Thinking that Jesus was not sufficiently glorified, he prayed in such a manner as no one in the audience had heard before. The fervour created was intense. And, though the meeting began at six, it was not till eleven that they could close, and it was not till 3 a.m. that he and Sydney Evans could get to bed. Even then they did not sleep, and Evan Roberts began to weep bitterly and sigh deeply in thinking of Christ's humiliation and the greatness of His love. He said next morning that he did not sleep all night, and the divine outpouring had been so heavy he had to shut it out and beg God to withhold His hand.

Events were now moving to a crisis. A decision to go home to Loughor and work among the young people there was come to during the evening service on Sunday, October 30, at Newcastle-Emlyn. It was made under the impelling influence of the Holy Spirit. In the morning service, at an afternoon meeting, and at tea he had felt himself under some wonderful influence, and his prayers and manner had been so strange that his friends were burdened with care for his mental condition. At the evening service he seemed to them to be unconscious of all that was going on and to be absorbed in communion with God. He himself, in a letter written the next morning, says that the Spirit brought the care of the young people (at Loughor) before him so powerfully that it was impossible for him to keep his mind from them. " I had to pray three times for quietness. From that time until the end of the service the place was filled with the Divine Presence and at times I would lose the minister, seeing only his form." In another letter, also written the next day, he says there seemed to be a voice, as if it said, " You must go, you must go." And he had a vision of a meeting of young people at Loughor.

The spiritual impulse and the voice and the vision determined him, and that same night he told his friends that the next morning he was going home to Loughor. And what that decision must have meant we may realize when we recall that it was only a few months previously that he had given up his trade of blacksmith to qualify himself for the ministry. Now he was giving up his training at Newcastle-Emlyn to start at once upon his spiritual mission, and to start it in that most difficult place of all—his own home—and in face of derision, scoffing, gross imputations, of doubts even among his friends of his sanity, and of questions as to what need there was for him to go when there were already plenty of ministers. And he was to act single-handed. For even his great friend Sydney Evans was unable to go with him.

The next day, October 31, he reached Loughor. His family were surprised at this sudden return from his training, and his mother warned him that if he went through Wales preaching he would have no money left for College. His family were also disturbed by his strange ways—at one time laughing, at another bursting into tears. They, too, feared that his mind was deranged. And for that reason both his brother Dan and his sister refused to go with him to the service in the evening, though both they and his mother went to the meeting for young people which he had arranged to take place after the Service.

At the close of the usual service it was announced that there would be a meeting for young people immediately after. Sixteen adults and one little girl remained. The rest left the church; the doors were closed; and Evan Roberts began his first revival meeting. No longer was he timid, shy and nervous, as in former days. Divine boldness and courage characterized his actions: spiritual happiness was visible in his face. Anxiety about the future did not trouble him: the certainty of eternity was on his side. He told his little audience of his object in coming home, and he urged them to confess Christ. Unaccustomed to this strange, new way of carrying on a service they found it difficult to comply. But after two hours, and much prayer, he induced them all to stand up and confess their Saviour.

The next night, at Pisgah, the audience had greatly increased, and Roberts spoke earnestly on the importance of being filled with the Holy Spirit, obeying Him, removing all questionable things from one's life and confessing Christ. Some of those who had confessed on the previous evening got up and testified to the happiness which had come to them. And this gave encouragement, so that six more confessed.

On November 2 he spoke powerfully at a meeting in Moriah on his four main points: (1) confession before God of every sin in our past life; (2) removal of anything doubtful in our lives; (3) total surrender and obedience to the Spirit ; (4) public confession of Christ. This was the plan, he said, which the Spirit had revealed to him. And he tells Sydney Evans that sixty-five had now stood up to confess Christ, and that some strange joy had come into their lives in consequence.

In a young people's meeting next day things were by no means so spiritual. Unbelief, disobedience and prejudice for some time prevailed. He could not get the people to bend. He urged them still more solemnly, and at last ten confessed Christ. Then he prayed earnestly for another ten. And at last slowly, one after the other, another ten stood up. He was gradually making his way. And by now the people were overcoming their prejudices against his method.

On the evening of November 4 a new element appeared. People from other denominations came to his meeting. Roberts spoke at some length and then left the meeting free for anyone to take part in. Singing, praying, confessing, giving testimony took place ; and before the meeting closed all were convinced that a certain silent, invisible power was at work among them. On the following evening, though the meeting was announced for young people, persons of all ages came, the spiritual tide was evidently rising and obstacles giving way before it. The meeting lasted till after midnight and was charged with suppressed fervour.

The meeting on Sunday, November 6, was, however, the one in which the gathering momentum was most obvious. It left its mark on the whole of Loughor and thrilled the neighbourhood with divine awe. Some irresistible power seemed to be taking hold of the people. Evan Roberts, writing the next day to Sydney Evans and speaking of it and the result of the first week's work in Loughor, says : " I am almost too full. My heart is brimming over with joy. . . . The results of last week's work are almost incredible. Peace has been made between many." His account of what happened may be given at some length as it presents most vividly the working of the Spirit :

" After the service had continued until twelve o'clock, I said I was not satisfied with it, and that we must get the blessing, even if it were necessary to stay there till daybreak. We would have to ' strive with Heaven.' ' Now,' said I, ' we must *believe* that the Spirit will come ; not think He will come, not hope He will come, but *firmly believe* it.' Then I read the promises of God, and pointed out how definite they were. After this the Spirit said that *everyone* was to pray—pray, not confess, not sing, not give experiences, but pray and believe and wait. And this was the prayer, ' Send the Spirit now, for Jesus Christ's sake.' The prayer began with me. Then it went from seat to seat—to boys and girls, young men and maidens. Some asking in silence, some aloud, some coldly, some warmly, some formally, some tearfully, some with difficulty, some with strong voices, some with tender. Oh ! how wonderful ! I never thought of such an effect. I felt the place being filled. But on went the prayer, the feeling becoming more and more intense and the place being filled more and more.

" I went to see a brother who had been weeping and sobbing, and who should it be but David Jones. ' What is the matter ? ' said I. ' Oh ! ' he answered, ' I have had something wonderful. My heart is too large for my bosom.' ' Then you have had the Holy Spirit,' I told him. The prayer had then ended its journey but not its message. ' Shall we ask for more ? ' I asked. ' No,' said David Jones. He had had as much as he could hold. But there were others who had not had enough. I told them that brother Jones had had enough, but that we could go on and ask for more and that Jones could ask God to withhold if necessary.

"Then we added to the prayer, 'Send the Spirit more powerfully for Jesus Christ's sake.' The prayer began its journey. And oh! with what effect! The Spirit was coming nearer and nearer all the while. It descended upon two sisters and they shouted aloud —shouted as I never heard anyone shout before. The people made a circle round them and looked amazed and terrified. But I smiled, saying, 'Oh! there is no danger.' And after a few minutes the sisters regained their composure. Then some young brother began to sing 'May Thy blessing,' and the meeting closed."

His second week opened with fervour. The old Moriah chapel was filled to the door on Monday evening—a thing never known before in the history of its prayer meetings—and the audience was of all denominations. After a number had confessed, the place became terrible. Almost all were moved to tears, and many cried loudly and wept in agony. A new element was that a number began to pray for those who felt hard. People were convinced they heard some powerful noise, and they felt the place filled with the Divine Presence. One after another fell in agony because of his soul's condition. The prayer for the coming of the Holy Spirit went round, and the whole audience gave way before some irresistible influence. The state of things was beyond any description. Many groaned in agony, others sighed deeply, some shouted aloud. And for the first time many prayed, sang, or spoke without being formally requested. About midnight the influence became intolerable for a

time. The meeting was boiling with fervour, and it
was not possible to close it till three in the morning.
After the boiling fervour of the Monday meeting it
was natural that the Tuesday evening should open
with a chill. But that night was memorable for the
" conversion " of Evan Roberts' mother. The meeting had lasted on far into the night without any influence coming, and some aged people, among them
Mrs. Roberts, began to leave for home. Evan accompanied his mother to the door. " It is better for
you to come back, Mother," he said; " the Spirit is
coming nearer now." " But the people are sleeping,"
she replied, " and it will soon be time for them to go to
work." With that she went home, while her son
stayed with the remainder of the people, who were
mostly young. He gathered these in the middle of
the chapel, and there they wrestled with God till the
place became awful owing to a sweeping divine influence. It was not till after six on the following
morning that Evan and his brother Dan reached home
and went to bed. A few hours later he was awakened
by a voice calling, " Oh! I'm dying, I'm dying! "
He leaped downstairs and found his mother with
clasped hands and closed eyes in a perfect agony of
soul. He swiftly saw what was disturbing her, and
throwing one arm round her and swinging the other
as if leading a tune, sang, " Praise be to Him." She
pleaded pitifully for light, and when she was relieved
of her great distress, said that what had weighed on
her mind after leaving the chapel was thinking of
Christ standing in the garden in His agony and her
not staying in the chapel till the end of the service.

Another, and perhaps difficult, convert in his family
was his sister, Mary. On October 28, before he came
home he had written to her, with more sincerity and

earnestness than tact : " I would it were possible to give you the joy I have. It would move away your sarcasm and light up your face ; and your heart would be at peace. It would be a treat for you to hear the young ladies from New Quay when they pray." He then exhorts her to pray, but first to *feel* that she is a *lost sinner*. And he recommends that they should have a family altar and she should take a part. Less than a week later we find him writing to Sydney Evans that he had begun a family altar, that Mary reads and Dan prays and that Mary has begun to pray. And a few days later he is writing that while Mary used to go to bed before he came home, now bed for her is out of the question till he arrives lest she should lose these glorious things.

And now he was receiving invitations to hold meetings outside his native place. In answer to a deputation from the Congregational chapel he went to Brynteg on Wednesday, November 9. Here the melting power of the singing was noticeable, and a minister said he had never seen anything more like a transfiguration than the look of some persons who came under the divine influence. Next night another meeting was to be held in the same place, but the old chapel proved too small, and they had to go to the new one, which was soon packed to every corner. And as this was the first meeting reported in the Press —and by a very sympathetic reporter, " Austin "— the published account may be here transcribed :

" The proceedings commenced at seven o'clock and lasted without a break until 4.30 a.m. Friday morning. During the whole of this time the congregation were under the influence of deep religious fervour and exaltation. There were about four hundred people present, of whom the majority were females ranging

from young misses of twelve to matrons with babes
in their arms. Mr. Roberts is a young man of rather
striking appearance—tall and distinguished-looking,
with an intellectual air about his clean-shaven face.
His eyes are piercing in their brightness, and the pallor
of his countenance suggests that these nightly vigils
are telling on him.

"There was, however, no suggestion of fatigue
in the conduct of the meeting. There is nothing
theatrical about his preaching. He does not seek to
terrify his hearers, and eternal torment has no place
in his theology. Rather does he reason with the
people and show them by persuasion a more excellent
way. I had not been many minutes in the building
before I felt this was no ordinary gathering. Instead
of the set order of proceedings everything here was
left to the spontaneous impulse of the moment. Nor
did the preacher remain in his usual seat. For the
most part he walked up and down the aisles, open
Bible in hand, exhorting one, encouraging another,
and kneeling with a third to implore a blessing from
the Throne of Grace.

"A young woman rose to give out a hymn and it
was sung with deep earnestness. While it was being
sung several people dropped down as if they had been
struck, and commenced crying for pardon. From
another part could be heard the resonant voice of a
young man reading a portion of Scripture. While
from the gallery came an impassioned prayer from a
woman crying aloud that she had repented of her
ways and was determined to lead a better life henceforth.

"All this time Mr. Roberts went in and out among
the congregation offering kindly words of advice to
kneeling penitents and asking them if they believed.
In one instance the reply was: 'No, I would like
to believe, but I can't. Pray for me.' Then the
preacher would ask the audience to join him in the

following prayer, ' Send the Holy Spirit now, for Jesus Christ's sake.' This prayer would be repeated about a dozen times by all present, when the would-be convert would suddenly rise and declare with triumph, ' Thank God, I have now received salvation.' This declaration would create a new excitement, and the congregation would joyously sing,

' Diolch iddo, diolch iddo.'

I suppose this occurred scores of times during the nine hours over which the meeting was protracted.

" A pathetic feature of the proceedings was the anxiety of many present for the spiritual welfare of members of their families. One woman was heartbroken for her husband who was given to drink. She implored the prayers of the congregation on his behalf. The story told by another woman drew tears to all eyes. She said that her mother was dead, and that her father had given way to sin, so that she was orphaned in the world. She had attended the meetings and on the previous day, while following her domestic duties, the Spirit had come upon her, bidding her to speak. And she did speak !—remarkably, for one who had never spoken before in public. Yet another woman made public confession that she had come to the meeting in a spirit of idle curiosity, but that the influence of the Holy Ghost worked within her, causing her to go down on her knees in penitence. At 2.30 a.m. I took a rough note of what was then proceeding. In the gallery a woman was praying and she fainted. Water was offered her, but she refused to drink this, saying the only thing she wanted was God's forgiveness. . . . A well-known resident then rose and said that salvation had come to him. . . . Immediately following, a thanksgiving hymn was sung, while an English prayer from a new convert broke in upon the singing. The whole congregation then fell upon their knees, prayers ascending from every part of the edifice, while Mr. Roberts gave way to tears at the sight. . . . This state of fervency lasted for about ten minutes and was followed by an even more impressive five minutes of silence broken only by the sobs of strong men. . . . A hymn was then started by a woman with a beautiful soprano voice. Finally, Mr. Roberts announced the holding of future meetings, and at 4.25 a.m. the gathering dispersed.

"But even at this hour the people did not make their way home. Dozens of them were about on the road discussing what is now the chief subject of their lives.

"In the course of conversation with Mr. Roberts, he said it was time to get out of the groove in which we had walked for so long. He had been praying for the Holy Ghost to come down upon him. That it had come he was certain. It was one thing for a man to be converted and quite another to receive the baptism of the Spirit. The meetings they had had were glorious experiences. . . . As for himself, he was simply an instrument in the hand of God, and he wanted men to receive the joy of religion."

This is what a newspaper correspondent reported. Evan Roberts himself, writing the next day of this same meeting to a friend, said:

"I do not know how to begin writing in the midst of this divine fire. The whole place has been moved, and my heart burns within with the Holy Spirit. . . . What a service last night! The girls and the women shouting aloud, having forgotten themselves. Over thirty were baptized by the Holy Spirit. . . . The fire is spreading rapidly and effectually. One of our deacons at Moriah has been baptized by the Spirit . . . coming on and embracing and kissing me, clapping his hands, and praising God that he had found a Saviour. . . . But what prejudice there is against the movement. Well, I have to say strange things : I have to open my mouth and speak out. And, thank Heaven, those things are very effectual. The Spirit convicts powerfully."

This was the result of less than a fortnight's work. Writing deliberately some years later the Rev. Vyrwy Morgan says of Evan Roberts that his mind was shallow and bound by conventional conceptions ; that he was not intellectual and was moved more by emotion rather than by his ideas, and had no traces of culture, no fundamental doctrine, no system of theology, no distinctive ideal ; that he was no expositor or even fluent speaker ; that his broken sentences were without depth or moral force ; that there was nothing of a colossal nature about him, and that his dimensions were small and his horizon exceedingly circumscribed. So says a Welsh minister. Yet in that short time this young ex-miner and blacksmith had of his own initiative and in that most difficult place of all, his own native township, set going a movement which was already stirring the whole neighbourhood and attracting the provincial Press, and which was eventually to draw men to him from England, France and many other countries. In spite of his being considered—even among his friends and his family—as deranged ; in spite of his being derided and scoffed at ; he was able to do in a fortnight what many an official minister would have been glad to have accomplished in a lifetime.

Wherein, then, lay the man's charm and power that he was able to achieve so much, with so meagre an equipment, and in the face of so many obstacles ? The answer is given by the reporter of these first meetings. He had an indefinable something in his manner and style. His joyous smile was that of a man in whom was no guile. And he convinced people that his belief in what he preached was impregnable. The ring of reality was in all he said. That was the secret. In those months of nightly communion with God preceding his mission there had come to him absolute certitude of the joy which may be had in this heavenly living. He had become possessed of the Spirit of God. Obedient to the heavenly impulse he had come to his homeland and spoken with the authentic voice of that Spirit. And men recognized the accent. It was the accent of a responsible agent of God. It proclaimed a living message. It brought glad tidings of great joy for all who would purify their hearts and open them, as he had, to the inflow of the same Holy Spirit. His coming had aroused dormant faculties men had not known they possessed, and had changed and enriched their whole lives. And as the glad news spread no wonder crowds flocked to hear him, and demands from everywhere came for him to appear among them.

Later, under the pressure of these demands, he was grossly to overdo himself and to break down under the stress, to lose his charming gentleness and the power to draw and sway ; and he was to develop austerity of manner and peremptoriness of address, and eventually to break down altogether. But for our present study his life up to this point is an outstanding example both of the working of the Holy Spirit upon an individual and also of how that individual can by his personality and by the power which has come into him communicate to others something of the overabounding joy which he himself has experienced and can arouse in them a passionate longing to fit and purify themselves for a like inpouring of the Spirit.

Having noted this, it will now be our business to trace the other springs of the Welsh revival and describe its course. We have already seen how Evan Roberts had met the Rev. Seth Joshua and other persons from New Quay with whom the revival may be said to have originated. And their doings we must now examine.

For some time previous to the appearance of Evan Roberts there had been a spiritual stirring in South Wales. More than one minister had been earnestly praying and working for a revival. Rev. Seth Joshua, in especial, for four years had made a revival his supreme aim. And its first actual breaking out may perhaps be dated from a meeting for young people at New Quay in Cardigan organized by the Rev. Joseph Jenkins in February 1904. A sermon of his on " Faith Overcoming the World " had produced a profound impression. And that evening a young girl, named Florrie Evans, had come to him telling him of the oppression of sin upon her. The following Sunday evening he called for testimonies and Florrie Evans got up and said : " I love Jesus with all my heart." And she said those few simple words with such burning fervency of spirit that she thrilled the whole meeting, and a few sobbed aloud. It was the spark that started the revival. From then the flame grew in volume and intensity, so that when the Rev. Seth Joshua visited New Quay on September 18, he was able to record in his diary : " I have never seen the power of the Holy Spirit so powerfully manifested among the people as at this place just now. The revival is breaking out here in great power."

Two days later he records that he closed the service several times ; yet it would break out again quite beyond the control of human power. "The joy is intense," he adds. And the next day he writes : "Every person engaged in prayer without one exception. The tongue of fire came upon each. We lost all sense of time." And of himself he writes : "I am saturated, melted, made soft as willing clay in the hands of a potter."

He was on his way to Newcastle-Emlyn on September 25. Two days later he writes of some students receiving blessing and confessing salvation and mentions one—Sydney Evans. The next day "fifteen young people came all the way from New Quay." He himself did not speak, but "allowed them to speak, pray, sing and shout as the Holy Ghost led them." "The fire burned all before it," he adds, "their souls were melted and many cried out for salvation." The following day, September 29, he writes of a "grand meeting at Blaenanerch, where many cried for mercy. . . . It was a remarkable thing to hear one young man, Evan Roberts." And we have already seen how it was at this meeting that Evan Roberts was first publicly " bent " and was caught in the spirit of the revival. That spirit had been rising in others as well as himself. And it was under the impulse which he then received that he travelled to his native township of Loughor and gave that tremendous impetus to the revival which we have already recorded.

And now that the news of the revival had been spread by the Press thousands would flock in from the villages round where the meetings were being held, and Evan Roberts himself moved from town to town holding meetings night after night, each lasting well into the small hours of the morning. Each meeting would differ from the other, as there was no fixed order of procedure. Everything was left to the spontaneous feelings of the people and to the guidance of the Spirit. But all were characterized by the same fervency, and all caught the infectious joy of the Spirit.

And a special characteristic of these meetings was the moving effect of the singing. A small band of young women singers joined Evan Roberts and were marvellously effective in melting and elevating a meeting. With their Welsh talent and beautiful voices they would sing the Welsh hymns with the most thrilling pathos. Instinctively they would choose some hymn which exactly, by its words and music, expressed the mood of the moment, and then render it with telling effect.

Chief of these singers was Annie Davies. She was eighteen years of age, with a strong, intensely spiritual, Madonna-like face, with the voice of a nightingale, and with religious fervour at white-heat within her. She had this further advantage that she had been trained by Madame Clara Novello Davies and had inherited some musical talent from her father, an underground lampman who conducted the singing at a Congregational Chapel.

Hearing that Evan Roberts was holding a meeting on November 17, she decided to go there and see what it was like. But so great was the crowd, it took her two hours to get in. The first person she saw was her sister Maggie, whose face showed that her soul was in agony. The Spirit of God was evidently working in her. Annie Davies was at this time indifferent and full of curiosity, and so continued until nearly the end of the meeting when, just before closing, Evan Roberts asked all those to stand up who could say in their

hearts that they loved Jesus above everything else.
The two sisters sat together and their first impulse
was to get up and say they did. But some power
kept them to their seats, and soon after the meeting
closed. Then Annie felt very unhappy. Her conscience spoke very loudly to her, telling her she had
betrayed her Saviour. She tried to sleep but found
it impossible. Everything seemed empty to her.
She must find peace, or die. And she counted every
hour till the time arrived for the next meeting.

When the time came and she entered the chapel
she knew a great power was working there. " My
soul," she says, " was moved to its depths. My tears
flowed freely when the Rev. David Hughes said,
' Sing something, Annie.' With an irresistible force
I leapt from my seat and sang, ' Here is love vast as
the ocean.' I could not finish it as I was sobbing too
much. And I could not refrain from weeping for the
rest of the meeting." After the meeting Miss S. A.
Jones, whom she had never seen before, came and
spoke to her and her sister. The three immediately
felt drawn to each other and desired to consecrate their
voices to their Master. They told Evan Roberts of
their desire, and he advised them to pray to be led
into the right path. They went to the next meeting.
A wonderful peace filled Annie Davies' soul. She
could not help taking part and felt convinced that
God had called her to the work.

Henceforward she was one of the leading influences
in spreading the revival. If a meeting started cold
and chilly she and her companions would melt it with
their singing ; and she developed a method of her
own of so entering into the spirit of supplicants or
thanksgivers that she would by her singing help them
to bring out, or would express for them what they

were unable to give forth by themselves. Often she would seem in low, quivering tones to be playing a touching accompaniment to a prayer. Or, again, with glorious song she would punctuate the stirring words of a speaker. Or yet again, when the meeting was in an ecstasy of gladness she would break forth into a rapturous hymn of thanksgiving and carry her hearers upward to those yet higher heights they were yearning to reach. The same hymns known to all, the same words, the same music she would use. But by using just the hymn or verse at the moment needed, and by singing from the profoundest depths of her beautiful soul, she was able to give to the music and the words a power to penetrate the souls of others which those hymns had never possessed before. And as a result of her singing reinforcing that which others were saying, what was ice at the commencement of a meeting was a consuming fire at the end.

We read how Chopin was more deeply moved by the fresh voice of an unknown singer in a minor *rôle* in an opera than by the greatest of all the others. The rare beauty which the most rigorous training and most perfect technique could not capture flowed forth naturally from the artless singing of the young girl and captured his heart. In the same way, from the singing of Annie Davies there flowed an untellable charm. For besides the beauty in her singing there was also deep and pure and passionate love for any and every human soul and a yearning that he, too, might know the joys that she had known and attain the peace that now was hers. All this it was that came out of her singing. And her exquisite voice was used for no other purpose than that it might reach the souls of others and thrill them with divinest joy.

For my own part, I have never been so moved by

any singer. The finest opera singers or the best singers in cathedral choirs—even the singers in the Salzburg Cathedral Festival—have left me cold in comparison with the singing of Annie Davies at one of these meetings in Wales, when with " unpremeditated art " and on the urge and inspiration of the moment she burst forth into some hymn of supplication or thanksgiving. There, one instantly felt, was a sweet and pure and beautiful soul yearning to draw one up with her to the loftiest height she could reach with her song; and all one's soul went out to her. The greatest artist in song could do no more. And the thrill of response an audience gives to the greatest opera singer is a tepid thing beside the emotion stirred by Annie Davies.

Her companion, Miss S. A. Jones, had not the voice or the art of Annie Davies. But she had a perhaps intenser ardency. And I recall how, when one in the meeting was praying for heaven, she threw her whole body and soul towards him as she shouted : " It is here ! It is here ! " And there heaven certainly was. It was no far-off place and at no distant time. Those present were for the moment in heaven. The Kingdom of God in that instant was theirs.

So did the revival spread. Like a fire it flamed through South Wales. Place after place was caught in the spirit. The reports in the Press helped to inflame it. It became known everywhere and everywhere talked about. Like Annie Davies, thousands of others came to see what it was like.

And it was like touching living fire. It was no light excitement. It was terrible and awesome. Too strong meat for puny souls. In comparison with the speaking, the singing and the praying at these meetings, the sermons, the music and the prayers of ordinary church services were like thin pipings.

Here was a power which pierced with terrifying force right through the crust of tradition and convention. Men would tremble in agony at the touch. They would be in a paroxysm of grief. They would writhe with pain. They would sob like children. Their hearts would break in contrition. They would wail piteously, and wrestle in prayer. And then the deeps would be released and they would burst forth without restraint—without even knowing what they were saying or doing—in a glowing rush of joy and thanksgiving. And men would clap their hands and laugh and shout and stamp with joy.

And while one was praying, another exhorting, another testifying his experiences, another singing his soul out, there was apparent confusion. Yet there were no antagonisms; no cross-purposes. Discords were blended in a marvellous harmony. And the dominant note was always joy—the exceeding joy which produces and is produced by love. Men left the meetings feeling they could love everybody.

Evan Roberts had said from the first that his belief was that the love of Christ was a powerful enough magnet to draw the people, that he himself had found a joy which was far beyond human expression and that he wanted men to receive what he had found. And now indeed they had found it. At the same time he saw that the revival could not continue at this high pitch of fervour. The time must come when it would subside again. He exhorted them, therefore, to make the most of it while he was here.

While it was at its height it was seen by Mr. W. T. Stead, the famous publicist. He, too, saw that it could not last. These seasons of spiritual exaltation which we call revivals, he said, come like the wind and vanish as mysteriously. But they are realities to those who experience them and permanently affect their whole future lives. And he foretold that this revival in the West would change, transform, inspire and glorify the lives of multitudes who till then cared nothing for their own peace or the welfare of their fellow-men.

It was a very real thing, he reported, a live thing with a power and a grip which would get hold even of spectators. It was not exactly dread that onlookers felt, but awe. There was something in it from the other world. You could not say whence it came or whither it was going, but it lived and moved and reached for men all the time. Men and women went down in sobbing agony before one's eyes as the Invisible Hand clutched at their hearts. It was pretty grim. One shuddered. Those who were afraid of strong emotions had better keep away.

The spontaneity of the whole proceedings specially struck Mr. Stead. Never was a religious movement so little indebted to the guiding brain of its leaders. It seemed to be going on its own. Another note he made was that the Gospel was sung rather than preached. Whole congregations singing as if they were making melody in their hearts to God. And women prayed, sang, testified and spoke as freely as men.

Then he observed that there was no inquiry room, no penitent form. The wrestle with unbelief went on in the midst of the people. All was intensely dramatic—sometimes unspeakably tragic. Yet he reported that the vast congregations were as soberly sane, as orderly, and at least as reverent as any congregation which sat beneath the dome of St. Paul's. A meeting would be aflame with a passionate religious enthusiasm, but there would be absolutely nothing wild, violent or hysterical, unless it were hysterical for the labouring breast to heave with sobbing that could not be suppressed, or the throat to choke with emotion as a sense of the awful horror and shame of a wasted life suddenly burst upon the soul. On all sides there would be the solemn gladness of men and women upon whose eyes had dawned the splendour of a new day, the foretaste of whose glories they were enjoying in the quickened sense of human fellowship and a keen, glad zest added to their own lives. And all this vast, quivering, throbbing, singing, praying, exultant multitude was intensely conscious of the all-pervading influence of some invisible reality—now for the first time moving, palpable, though invisible in their midst.

As to results, employers said that the quality of the work the miners were putting in had improved. Waste was less, and men went to their daily toil with a new spirit of gladness in their labour. And this public self-consecration, this definite and decisive avowal of a determination to put under their feet their dead past of vice and sin and indifference and to reach out towards a higher ideal of human existence was going on everywhere in South Wales.

If in some cases the eventual results were not up to expectation, if the subsequent lives of some have not been up to the level attained in those exalted moments, the fault may not have been entirely their own. We know that lovers do not remain at the level of their most enraptured moments. In the first case, as in the second, the fault may have been that men did not know how to capture and safely embody the lofty spirit of the moment. And it may be the task of those who recognize the inestimable value of those few precious moments to strive to recapture that spirit and enshrine it securely so that it may be ever after available and like a magnet perpetually attract men to it.

CHAPTER VI

REVIEW

I

FROM India and Persia ; from France, England and Wales ; from among Hindus, Moslems and Christians, we have drawn examples of men and women of modern times who have enjoyed the mystical experience. And the close agreement between these modern mystics, and between them and the mystics of ancient days, is remarkable. There were also differences—and without such differences there could be no unity—but the resemblance is the most noteworthy feature. And the uniformity of their testimony has great significance.

All these mystics living in such different countries, and under such different traditions and conditions, had similar experiences. All are notable for their unconquerable earnestness of purpose and crystal sincerity of character. Many of them had to break their way through crustations of conventional religion and entanglements of religious traditions, and, harder still, through the binding ties of family life and social custom. And in so doing they had to suffer excruciating agonies ; for by their very nature they were of a loving, affectionate disposition, fearful of hurting anyone—least of all their dearest. All, then, suffered far beyond the ordinary experience of mankind. Yet they shrank from no sacrifice and flinched from no suffering; and, suffer as they did, the one characteristic of all others which they displayed was unbounded joy—joy of such tremendous power as to be unbearable. Let it last a moment longer and it would be the death of them, was how some described the intensity of the joy which they experienced. Joy so overpowering that they would afterwards recoil from even thinking of it.

And this celestial radiancy of joy, unendurable as it had been at the time, had the after effect upon them of sweeping aside the least remembrance of any suffering, steadying their nerves, and bringing them the sweetest serenity and peace. After all the striving, all the suffering, all the tumult of joy there followed for them that contentment in the depths which only comes of completest satisfaction of every need, every longing and every aspiration. They had passed from a state of mere emotion into a state of profound peace —that satisfying peace of the soul which comes of finding their own souls in direct continuity with the life of the universe. A serenity which nothing on earth could ever ruffle was theirs for ever after.

Adamantine certitude also was theirs. A certitude of the trustworthiness of the world. A man must have something to hold on to and believe. And theirs was the certitude that, however bad men may appear to the eye, however much pain and evil there may be in the world about them, at rock bottom men and things are good—at the foundation of things is goodness—is a Power unceasingly overcoming the evil and transforming it into good. That mysterious Power which most men sense operating behind the ceaseless activity they find inside themselves and in all around them—that central yet all-pervasive Power which

248

holds all together in a coherent whole and gives it direction—these mystics came to regard as no mere impersonal force, but a highly Personal Person, or super-Personality, with what in men would be termed will and mind, and working with the whole might of Its being for unsurpassable good.

And a world which could produce in these mystics such joy, such serenity, and such certainty of its goodness, all came to love with a passion of adoration so intense that the devotion of a mother to her child, the love of a lover for his beloved, of a mountaineer for mountains, and of a naturalist for nature, give only the faintest indication. They were all men and women who naturally felt something in common between themselves and every other human being. Now this sense of fellowship had quickened within them to such a pitch of intensity that a hurt to any living thing would set them quivering with pain, while the joy of another would thrill them with delight. Their heart had come to beat in closest sympathy with the common heart-beat of the world. The sufferings which they had endured had helped them to enter into the sufferings of others : the untellable joy which they had known to enter into their joys. Joy through suffering had engendered in them the dearest love of the world.

Then, from this love which they bore to the world had sprung a yearning in them to communicate to all others the joy which they had known. The happiness of others is everywhere a deep concern of men. The one thing a mother yearns for and strives for daily is the happiness of her children. The ultimate aim of a statesman is the happiness of his country. All religious leaders are intent upon promoting the happiness of their flocks. This concern for happiness in parents, statesmen, and pastors became in the mystics a consuming passion. They had themselves experienced such supreme happiness that to them it was intolerable that one single human being should remain who did not know it, too. They would have all share it with them. Hence the desire which these mystics showed to communicate to others the joy and peace which they had known. They would have the whole world beaming with delight. And for this to be they would impart to others what they themselves had felt in order that others also might be partakers with them of the kingdom of heaven.

Yet they also felt an initial difficulty. Longing as they were to communicate their experience they found diffidence in speaking about it to a single other soul. It was to them something too unutterably sacred to be spoken of to any. All the mystics felt this holy reticence. Its precious fragrance might be dissipated by the utterance of a single word. To those who had already known it there would be no need of any telling. By those who had known it not it would surely be misunderstood. Why, therefore, say a word? Why not keep these deep things of the soul secret to the soul? It was only under the compelling urge of bringing happiness to their fellows that, at enormous cost to themselves, they broke through their reserve.

In all these points, then, in earnestness of purpose, in yearning after perfection, in suffering, in subsequent joy, in serenity of soul, in certitude of goodness, in longing to communicate their joy, and in the feeling of fellowship with all others, the mystics we have studied resembled each other. They had all plumbed the deeps of the soul. But they had never touched bottom : they had found their souls unfathomable, stretching down into the infinite depths of the Crea-

tive Spirit. But they had reached far enough to have
felt themselves at one accord with that Spirit. And
filled with It they had floated aloft to infinite heights.
Transported with joy they had soared to those pure
and sunlit realms of the Spirit which everywhere surrounds us, though undreamed of by pedestrians of
ordinary life. And every one of them longed to open
the eyes of his fellows to the glories which might be
theirs. That which they had always known they had
in common with others they now knew to be a common divinity. And of this they would have everyone
be aware. They would have all know that a common
humanity was also a common divinity. All were children of a Heavenly Father.

Yet with all these resemblances there are no less
remarkable differences between the mystics we have
noted. Some had visions, some heard voices, some
saw lights, some were borne on billows as in an ocean.
Some saw Christ, some the Virgin Mary, some the
goddess Kali, some the prophet Mahomed. Through
all these ways had come the joy and the serenity of
communion with the Spirit of the universe. But the
ways had been different.

So also had been the ways of training for the
mystical experience. Some had most carefully and
deliberately trained themselves for it and endured the
hardships of severest austerity. Others had had no
training whatever. And of those who had specially
trained themselves some had been on the yoga lines
of the Hindus and others on the orthodox lines of the
Roman Catholic Church.

In the ways of communicating this experience they
likewise differed. Ramakrishna remained in his

temple, but took infinite trouble to seek out a few, and especially one, to whom he could impart his message. And that one he trained for his purpose, and by personal endearment and actual bodily touch communicated to him not merely his intellectual doctrine but more particularly his very spirit. Keshub Chander Sen proceeded on much more public lines. He formed societies, he travelled all over India and as far as England preaching his message. He formulated a New Dispensation and would spread it over the whole world. The Bab had yet another way. He let others come to him, and then of those, he selected eighteen and sent them forth to proclaim his advent as the Messiah and to deliver his message. Ste Thérèse in her secluded convent had no thought of making disciples or proclaiming any new message : she simply prayed, and tried in all the little ways of a little life to show little people how heaven might be reached by the humblest. Another method, not recorded here but common in India, is for the mystic to communicate himself in absolute silence—to sit absorbed in intense meditation and to radiate his very self out to others who are attracted to him by his known saintly life, by the tranquillity of his features and the nobility of his bearing.

In their ideas on celibacy the mystics also differed. To Ramakrishna women and wealth were the twin roots of all evil—the enemies to be specially fought against. And though he was forced by social custom to marry, and had his wife living with him, no children were born of the marriage and apparently he preserved continence throughout, deliberately schooling himself to abstain. Some Hindus think, indeed, that in sexual intercourse they are expending energies which should be rigidly preserved for only the highest end. In the Roman Catholic Church, also, celibacy is encouraged, and virginity is held up as an object of adoration. Consequently, Ste Thérèse, like other nuns, took the vow of celibacy. Among our examples Evan Roberts, though he took no vows, was in fact unmarried. On the other hand, the Bab was married and had a son. Keshub Chander Sen was married and had several children. And the authoress of *The Golden Fountain* was not only married but stated explicitly that there was nothing in the married state or any of its functions to harm the highest life.

II

To these experiences of modern mystics we have now to apply the results of modern thought. Dazzled by the splendour of the vision which searchingly facing reality brings him the mystic should withdraw himself for a time from the too great radiance in order coolly and clearly to think on the significance of what he has seen and to interpret it aright. And here it is that most of the mystics cited have failed. They have been disposed to ignore the intellect. The accumulated results of centuries of thought and scientific investigation have been neglected. Accordingly, they have had but a meagre conception of the universe, and their ideal of perfection has been hazy. Of the grandeur and sublimity of the starry universe, as revealed by recent astronomy, they have been as ignorant as the ant is of the majesty of the Himalayan mountain on which it is crawling. Of the exceeding minuteness of the parts, and the intricate interplay of their relationships, they had as little knowledge as the elephant has of the eye of a midge. And their ideal of perfection has been as lacking in precision of outline and detail as the shores of a distant land are to the mariner who possesses no telescope.

True it is that the intellect alone could not have taken these mystics to the heart of the universe. Feeling was then necessary; for feeling can penetrate deeper than thought. But use of the intellect, and use of the fruits of the intellect as shown in the results of science and philosophy, would have given them a wider and deeper comprehension of the universe with which they were striving more intimately to relate themselves. Indians, undoubtedly, have a finer intuition than Europeans. They pierce more surely to the essential disposition. Yet Western science would have in no way detracted from their experience, and would indeed have widened their vision and enabled them to live the life of the universe with a larger understanding. Knowledge of the immensity of the physical universe, of the ultra-microscopic minuteness of its parts, and the exquisite delicacy of their adjustments would only have increased their awe and wonder at the Power which was ordering the mighty whole and regulating every activity. And exercise in the scientific habit of mind would only have been a help to them in testing, sifting and discriminating among their impressions and in leading them to a truer interpretation of their visions and intuitions.

Use of the intellect and the results of thought might also have helped them to clarify their conception of that ideal perfection which they would like to have before them. To prize what is most prize-worthy was their desire. And for the determination of what really is most prize-worthy the intellect is needed as well as the heart. Human experience at its highest has to be taken; and then the mystic has to see far beyond it, and with the intellect, frame in his mind in detail the ideal at which he should aim.

The intellect would also have been an aid to these mystics in getting into closer touch with the world of ordinary men. They have convictions amounting to absolute certitude. But those convictions would have had more weight in public if they were seen to be reasoned convictions. Mystics would carry men more easily with them if man could see that they were using their heads as freely and forcibly as they were using their hearts.

And if these modern mystics have in this respect been wanting may we be bold enough to try and supply this deficiency ? Making use of the results of modern science and philosophy to aid us in interpreting the mystical experiences recorded in the previous chapters, may we see how they would fit in with a modern conception of the universe ?

The interconnectedness and interdependence of all things in one coherent whole is the grand conclusion in which science and philosophy agree. The universe is not the haphazard congeries of independent units it may appear to some. There is underlying unity. The units are bound together in a whole. Not a single minutest particle is or ever can be isolated from the rest of the universe. Each atom, each star, each person is connected with the whole and is required by the whole. A mystic is, therefore, as much an indissoluble part of the universe as everything and everybody else. And he, like the rest, bears upon him the mark and impress of the whole. He is made in the image of the whole. He is as much a part of the universe as a cell in my brain is part of me.

In this view, we might interpret the mystical experience as a vivid impression of the universe as a whole.

255

In his experience the mystic has become aware of the underlying unity of the Spirit which binds together and animates the universe. The part has become aware of the whole—of the inward essence of the whole. Up to the moment of their supreme experience mystics have often spoken of there being a " wall " in between them and God. They have felt Him near but with some barrier in between Him and them. But when the experience came to them they have felt as if the wall had suddenly fallen, the barrier been removed, the veil rent asunder, and they and God had become one. The mystic had become filled with the Spirit of the universe—the part with the essence of the whole.

But how can we explain the fact that the mystical experience does not come to all ? It comes only to those who have most earnestly striven after the ideal of highest perfection and have been ready to make any sacrifice for it. But it does not come to all even of these. There is an element of favour, of grace, in it. May we explain it in this way ? We cannot suppose that the Spirit of the universe is acting with uniform pressure at every moment on every component part of the universe. More likely is it that the Spirit is work- ing, now with great intensity, then with less ; here upon this part, there upon that, just as the spirit of me, I, am acting upon my brain cells with great inten- sity now while I am thinking out what I shall write on this page, and then with hardly any pressure while I shall be asleep in the night ; and here, upon the cells of my brain, and in an hour's time there, upon the cells of my muscles as I put my legs into action to go for a walk. And supposing a particularly aspiring cell of my brain had the ambition to know me, and strove and struggled to become aware of me—of that mighty being with whom it could feel it was intimately connected. And suppose that on one rare occasion, just as the cell was striving hardest to know me, it so happened that I was trying to express myself through it in writing a page of this book, then the efforts of the cell and the efforts of myself would coincide ; the cell would find a tremendous rush of my spirit bearing in upon it : it would wellnigh collapse under the terrific strain, but it would have had the satisfaction of having attained its heart's desire of becoming aware of that power—of me—who had given it life and continually sustained it. And that certain cells of my body actually do have an impression of me imprinted on them is proved by the existence of millions of germ cells in my body, any one of which is capable of reproducing in my offspring every characteristic of me, from my fundamental disposition down to the colour of my eyes. The cells of my body do bear the impress of me. We can understand, therefore, how a man may bear the impress of the universe out of which he was born and of which he never ceases to be a component part ; and how the mystics in their supreme experience are simply becoming aware of the Spirit of the universe as a germ cell, or a brain cell, in my body might become aware of me.

The justification for considering the great mystic to represent the highest type of man here comes into view. He has developed something more than the ordinary consciousness. He has become most vividly aware of and most intimately in touch with the Central Spirit of the universe—aligned himself with the Central Line—and been lifted up to a higher plane of being. Moreover, while science and philosophy coldly assure us of the coherence and interdependence and interconnectedness of things in one whole, the mystic actually *feels* that underlying unity, and feels it to an intense degree. No one like he has such a deep sense of fellowship with the whole universe, with every living thing, with every human being.

Yet even the mystic's sense of community might be enriched, if to his wonderful experience he could add an appreciation of the world now revealed by science —of the astronomical immensities of the universe, of the innumerable unseen influences to which every creature is subjected, and of the marvellous variety of life and of the worlds within worlds in which his own life is set. So let us briefly recount these.

That the sun to which our planet is attached is only one out of other stars so numerous that if each were represented by a grain of sand, all England would have to be covered with sand to a depth of some hundreds of feet to contain them, is a statement which has become familiar to us through the writings of Jeans. And we also learn that they are so distant, that light from the nearest of them, travelling at the rate of 186,000 miles a second, takes $4\frac{1}{4}$ years to reach this earth, and light from the farthest 140 million years. This much we know about the immensity of the universe. And science now tells us marvels concerning the invisible influences continually acting upon us— of X-rays, gamma-rays, ultra-gamma-rays, cosmic rays, long electric-rays, electro-magnetic and luminous radiations, and mechanical radiations such as sounds and ultra-sounds. Ultra-violet and infra-red photography widens our vision of the world about us. And, nowadays, we are all aware of how we are being impinged upon by radio music and radio propaganda which, when we are provided with the requisite instrument to capture it, affects our minds and souls.

Naturalists have ascertained that certain animals and insects have wider powers of sensing their environ-

ment than men possess. Some can see further, others
hear more acutely, others smell more sensitively. A
bat may see little, but with its remarkable ears it
has a most delicate sense of hearing. The hawk's-eye
detects its prey with an accuracy impossible to men.
The dog can sense smells, and the antennæ of butterflies can detect vibrations which to us are quite
undetectable.

The variety of life on this planet is also yearly
becoming better known—monsters of the deep and
bacteria hardly visible through the most powerful
microscopes ; grotesque crustacea and exquisite birds-
of-paradise ; repulsive creatures of the slime and
gorgeous butterflies of the tropical forest.

And the worlds these creatures live in with their
varying organs of sense are equally various. The
world of the sightless fish in the lightless deeps of
the ocean is vastly different from the world of the
lammergeyer soaring over glittering Himalayan peaks.
The world of the mole burrowing blindly in the earth
differs as radically from the world of the bee sucking
honey from the sunlit flowers, as the world of a
parasitic tick clinging to an antelope differs from
the world of the antelope bounding joyously over the
far-stretching plain.

Yet there is a common world in which all these
lesser worlds are intimately, intricately and inex-
tricably included. And if the mystic could add to
his mystical experience what he would gain from a
contemplation of these immensities, of these delicate,
invisible influences, of this variety of life, of these
different worlds within worlds, and of the interdependence of all these in one vibrating whole, even
his vision might be widened and his sense of community deepened. And he might contemplate the

possibility, or the probability, that, in view of the interdependence of things, the manifold life of this planet may be but an epitome of a far larger life which may all the time be existing in the universe at large, just as a germ-cell in my body is an epitome of the larger life of myself—that this may not be the only inhabited planet in a universe which consists of stars as numerous as the grains of sand in the Sahara desert—that scattered over this unimaginably vast universe may be thousands of other planets inhabited by beings as different from us in outward form as men are from humming-birds but just as intelligent as we are—that on a few of these inhabited planets may be beings who in a far higher degree manifest the Creative Spirit which animates, drives and directs the whole universe—that on one planet one of these highest beings may in one part of his life be so exactly attuned to the main pulse of the universe that he would be able to make manifest and interpret the inmost meaning of the Spirit which informs it, and be, therefore, that Spirit's most perfect embodiment—and that, in such a case, this Master Mystic of the Universe might, through his mastery over the vibrations of the universe, be able to exert a commanding influence over life as a whole, and communicate to all creatures, according to their capacity, something of his own spirit and so set the tone, impart the temper, and give the direction to the great common world of all lesser worlds and of every variety of life throughout the entire universe.

If the mystic could thus contemplate the possibility, or the probability—perhaps even the certainty—that somewhere in the immensities of the universe the Creative Spirit which informs it is manifested far more fully than It has yet been manifested here, and that such manifestations may be ceaselessly influencing the development of life on this planet, just as light and heat from the distant sun affects the growth of plants, his comprehension of the world which gave him birth might be immeasurably extended. And with that expanding comprehension might go a corresponding increase in his spiritual stature. The mystic might be the bigger man for contemplating the universe as a whole.

And with the awe and wonder which would necessarily follow the contemplation of such immensities, such rich variety of life, and such glittering possibilities, there would with equal necessity go delight. And this new delight would only increase that joy which the mystical experience had already brought him.

Now that which brings a man delight he loves. And in the measure of the joy it brings is his love. A world which can produce in a man such rapture of enjoyment as the mystic feels, he loves with an intensity proportionate to his enjoyment. And love proves itself in deeds—and in deeds proportionate to his love. Hence the devoted activity of the great mystics. They have loved their fellow men—they have loved the whole world—with a tenderness and a depth unknown to ordinary men. And that is why for long years and centuries afterwards they have been loved by mankind to a point of adoration such as man gives to no other of his heroes.

And if the great mystics by the test of long centuries of struggle with other types have come to be recognized as the highest type of humanity yet reached, they may be accepted as forerunners of that higher level of existence which the onward sweep of the evolutionary process indicates must lie before the race. They may be looked upon as the feelers, or tentacles, sent out by the human species towards that higher plane of life. Therefore, by applying the results of modern science and philosophic thought to their experience we may gain some idea of what is the aim of the world-process—what is the ideal of perfection towards which we should perpetually strive.

So judging, the aim in the world-process would seem to be a state of living more intense and more ecstatic than even the joy of lovers can give us an inkling, and bringing a serenity and assurance which can only come of completest satisfaction of every need of body, mind and spirit. Yet it would be no condition of blissful ease and unending rest : it would be a stupendous living at lightning velocity ; and the love no accommodating amiability, but a God-force, elemental and invincible, as issuing straight from the mighty harmonizing principle of the universe.

The goodness to be aimed at would be something far more than goodness understood as mere rectitude —as mere correctness of behaviour. Not men of stiff upright character, unimpeachably virtuous and primly wise would men of the higher species be, but so brimming over with the divinest happiness that it would be impossible for them to be anything else but good ; and not an unctuous correctitude such as would repel men would be theirs, but a smiling loveliness which would win them.

And in this higher state all would not be alike. No two would be alike. All would be different. This is the law of the universe. And another law is that the greater is the difference of the parts the deeper is the unity of the whole. Differences, therefore, would be welcomed, and opposition regarded as a stimulus and as serving to bring out contrasts. And because of this importance of differentiation the individuality of the individual would be not only respected but reverenced. Freedom for the individual would be the watchword. On the other hand, though the individual might stoutly maintain his individuality and strenuously resist any encroachment on his freedom, he would devote himself with still more vehemence to working out the good of the various wholes to which he belonged—his family, his town, his business, his country, mankind—each whole in its turn being an individual in a still larger whole, till all are included in the only true whole—the entire universe.

Nor would there be equality. For neither is equality, any more than uniformity, a fundamental characteristic of the universe. The universe is not level. It is made up of peaks and declivities. The ocean has its lowest depth and the land its highest height. And living things are graded downward till they are scarcely distinguishable from chemical compounds, and upwards to the mystics we have been studying. Gradation is the order. Higher and lower. The lower a necessity for the higher—an absolutely necessary prerequisite. But the higher being likewise necessary to give lift to the lower. The two would be interdependent. So there would be gradation upward to the few—and to the one. And the one and the few would be perpetually changing—giving place to successors in unending rhythm.

For the Creative Spirit, though it is working in and on all men at all times, is not working always at uniform pressure. It is not working so energetically in a man when he is asleep as when he is awake, or when he is lethargic as when he is at concert pitch. And the Creative Spirit is evidently manifested in a higher degree in some of Its creatures than in others

—in men than in snails, in the mystic than in the murderer, and in some mystics more than in others, and in the highest mystics more at some times than at others.

Moreover, with gradation there would be waxing and waning. The highest would not always remain at the height of his capacity. Climbers do not remain on the summit of a mountain. A singer does not remain singing his highest note. There would be declination as well as elevation. There would be periods of absolute repose as well as of intensest activity.

In keeping with the wave-like texture of the universe we may expect rhythmic motions—culminations and depressions. At the culminations we may expect an intoxicating ecstasy of delight, and in the trough a divine tranquillity. But all will be pulsing with the Creative Spirit of the universe. All will be surrounded and permeated by that spiritual atmosphere which is engendered by the Creative Spirit as we are surrounded and permeated by the air we breathe. And every activity will derive its significance from the highest culmination as every activity of a growing plant derives its significance from its culmination in the flower.

III

Such, as far as we may judge, would be the highest state of being at which the evolutionary process is aiming—such the ideal of perfection towards which we should strive. And the methods and results of modern science and philosophy have now to be applied to other questions arising from the mystical experiences we have been studying.

Mystics, especially Hindus, make use of such expressions as losing themselves in God as a drop of rain in the ocean. In the mystical experience are mystics being absorbed in the Spirit of the universe, or are they absorbing the Spirit into themselves? At times it seems as if they utterly abandoned themselves, got rid of the self, and deliberately allowed themselves to sink into God. On the other hand, they may be looked upon as opening themselves out to the in-pouring of the Holy Spirit of God. In all cases they are overwhelmed by a Power outside themselves—if also within them—and infinitely greater. But, while a few are content literally to lose themselves—lose their lives—in this absorption in the Spirit, others, including even Ramakrishna, wished to retain their individuality in order to be able to carry on the work of God in the world.

And this latter attitude is more suited to the temperament of most Westerners. The ordinary European or American hates losing his individuality. He fights hard to retain it and to resist encroachments on it. To him the idea of absorbing the Spirit of the universe into himself would be more congenial than the idea of being merged in it and losing his identity as a drop of water is lost in the ocean.

Perhaps a truer view to take of the mystical experience is that suggested by Father Elwin, when he says that it would be better to say that the mystic was *enthralled* rather than absorbed by God. It is a good suggestion. A mystic may be enthralled by the spirit of the universe and yet retain his own individuality. He may be possessed by the Spirit and yet be himself. Undoubtedly, for the time being, while he is actually enjoying the mystical experience, he is overwhelmed by the Spirit. He is entirely overpowered; and resistance or self-assertion are then wholly out of the question. Yet he does not remain

Overpowered. He recovers himself. And on recovery he finds he is a far greater self than before he was enthralled by the Spirit.

The authoress of *The Golden Fountain* prided herself on abandoning herself, like all great lovers, to her love. Yet even she, after her experience, says that the whole of space could scarcely be large enough to hold her : she needed all of it : she welcomed its immensity. " My consciousness is alight with a new fiery energy of life ; " she writes, " it feels to extend to an infinite distance beyond my body, and yet remain connected with my body." Again, she writes : " I felt within me an immense, incomprehensible capacity for love, and the whole world with all its contents seemed totally, even absurdly, inadequate to satisfy the great capacity."

Henri Frederic Amiel says: " There is but one thing needful—to possess God." He does not say to be absorbed in God but to possess Him. And he speaks of times " in which one seems to carry the world in one's breast, to touch the stars, to possess the infinite . . . moments of irresistible intuition in which a man feels himself great like the universe and calm like a god . . . the whole creation is then submitted to our gaze, lives in our breast, and accomplishes in us its eternal work."

And the great living Islamic poet and philosopher, Iqbal, declares quite definitely and emphatically against the idea of absorption into God. " He who comes nearest to God is the completest person," he says, but adds: "Not that he is finally absorbed in God. On the contrary, he absorbs God into himself."

We may not be one with God, but we may be at one accord with God. We may be filled with the Holy Ghost.

Connected with this is the question whether God is " wholly other " than ourselves, as some maintain —Karl Barth, notably. And here also the intellect is needed. To some Indian mystics, the God whom they have experienced is most certainly not wholly other : he is not even other than themselves. They believe that in their highest experiences they *are* God. In answer to the question : " Who am I ? " they will reply : " I am Brahma, the supreme Spirit." And, just as a germ-cell in me which contains within it my main characteristics might in a sense consider itself as me, so there is nothing unreasonable in the mystic, when he is feeling himself peculiarly filled with the Spirit of the universe, believing himself in a sense to stand for God, as he is then conscious of containing within himself the main characteristics of God. In any case, he would be justified in maintaining that God is not " wholly other " than himself.

Guidance by the Spirit is another question demanding earnest consideration. Some mystics, like Keshub Chander Sen and Evan Roberts, have placed themselves unreservedly in the hands of the Spirit, awaited Its commands and implicitly obeyed them. The doubt does, however, arise whether such abandonment of the mystic's own will and intelligence is completely wise. He has to do the Will of God : that is recognized. But many will think that in order to find out what actually is the Will of God, every faculty with which the Creator has endowed him should be utilized—and to the full. Guidance has to be intelligently sought, they will say. It is not as plain as a sign-post.

A statesman representing his country in a crisis wishes to be guided by his country's spirit. He wishes to do the will of his country. It is to do it

that he has been placed in the position he holds.
But before he acts he uses all his intelligence and,
better still, his powers of intuition, to acquaint himself thoroughly with it. It would seem to be the
same in regard to guidance by the Spirit of the
universe. It is not a matter of simply abandoning
our wills and submitting our limp selves to the guidance of the Spirit. We have to do more than that.
We have to learn to know that Spirit intimately and
to use our intelligence most diligently in order to
interpret It aright before we can be sure that we
are acting in accordance with It. We have to make
a sustained effort of the intellect to determine the
precise direction in which the Spirit would desire us
to go. So, at least, it seems to some of us.

A kindred question is that of submission to the will
of God—surrendering our own wills to the will of
God. In a sense we cannot help doing the will of
God. If that Power behind and working through
the whole creative process has any will at all, our
puny opposition to it would be as futile as the opposition of a minnow to the Ganges in flood. We cannot
help being swept along by it. On the other hand,
we are endowed with certain powers of choice. Our
whole lives are spent in making choices between
myriads of alternatives. And among these numerous
alternatives we may use all our intelligence and our
own experience and the experience of others to determine which is most nearly in line with the main
stream of the creative advance.

The mystic naturally wishes to align himself with
the central line of the main impetus, impulse, stream,
fountain jet—whatever it may be called—of the world
process. And to be certain of that he has to assure
himself of what the main impetus is making to-

wards. That, we have already seen to be a higher perfection—a completer harmony. But, even though the Creative Spirit of the universe is working in the mystic and in everyone and everything about Him at every hour and every minute of the day, and is working towards this ultimate perfection and harmony, the mystic has still to use his utmost intelligence to choose from among the manifold alternatives continually presenting themselves before him the one which will most surely conduce to that perfection. He may submit his will to the will of God. He cannot help it. He has to. But it is quite clearly the will of God that he should use every faculty with which he is endowed. He will not, therefore, abrogate his reason. He will use his intelligence to the full. He will be guided by the Spirit ; but while he takes the main direction given by that Spirit he will, in the separate steps he takes, be guided by reason. A man may receive the general impulsion to proceed to a sacred city beyond the mountains, and the whole way thither he may act upon this general impulsion and in accordance with the Spirit ; but he will not expect detailed guidance in every single step he takes towards his goal : he will exercise his own intelligence and judgment as to the manner in which he shall overcome each obstacle as it presents itself and as to the particular path he shall follow from day to day. At one time it may be wiser to take a longer way round on the level, at another time to take a shorter cut over a spur. On each occasion he must use his intelligence and past experience to decide.

The question of celibacy, virginity, chastity is another problem which has to be examined in the light of what science has to tell us about the creative process. By some it is considered to be an essential for the higher spiritual life. Virginity is extolled. Vows of celibacy are taken. But, as has already been noted, many of the mystics whose experiences are here recorded were married, and the fact of being married did not prevent them from having the mystical experience or from leading a saintly life. And one of them, the authoress of *The Golden Fountain*, herself a married woman, has stated quite definitely her conviction that there is nothing spiritually objectionable in the married state. After showing how all affections go up to and are enclosed in the love of God she says : " In this is included, in a most deep and mysterious fashion, marriage-love in all its aspects. In every way it can become a sacrament : there is nothing in it which is not holy, in no way does the marriage bond of the body separate the spirit from acceptableness to God." She came to regard marriage as the prototype in this physical world of the spiritual union with God in the spiritual world. She reminded herself that this relationship between men and women was His thought and His plan and not ours, and that our part was only to keep the bond of it pure and clean and sweet. This bond of earthly marriage is of the flesh and can be kept by the body and yet the heart, mind, and soul can all the time remain in lovely, perfect charity. This was her view.

And it is strongly supported by modern science, which is directly opposed to the old view that there is something inherently shameful in the bodily connection of man and woman. Modern science holds, on the contrary, that such union is both bodily beneficial and spiritually elevating—and to both the woman and the man. This opinion and the grounds for holding it have been amply set forth by Douglas White, a practising medical man, in his *Modern Light on Sex and Marriage.* He is in favour of abstinence as a preliminary to obtaining in the end the prize of an all-embracing love, both physical and spiritual. But he places no value on abstinence as a thing in itself, and says, indeed, that continuous suppression of normal sexual activity constitutes a severe strain on a normally sexed man, and that the denial of the maternal and conjugal satisfaction is a still more severe loss to a normal woman. Further, he regards sex-activity as the most potent moving force in personal life and what should be its main elevating, refining, and beautifying influence. It ought, he says, to intensify spiritual love. The corporeal intimacy should be the sensible manifestation of the spiritual relation, body, mind and spirit all fitting into each other with a glow of satisfaction. For a true and energizing love for the mate alters and sweetens the whole outlook on life, spreads like a ripple in ever-widening circles of friends, relations and acquaintances, and diffuses itself further still in a general good-will to all mankind. Frankly sexual though the love of man for woman and woman for man is, there is nothing unseemly in its physical expression, nor is it in any sense necessarily tainted with evil. It is, he holds, the most beautifully spiritual thing the world has ever seen—radiating its beauty even to those who are not experiencing it. The spiritual irradiates the physiological function, and the physiological intensifies the spiritual. Each interprets and satisfies the aspirations of the other. And each of the partners in a well-suited marriage calls into life what is fine and beautiful in the other, and in great

271

moments comes into touch with that great Love
which lives at the centre of the universe. For these
reasons, Dr. White considers marriage as the most
profound sacrament of life. It should be regarded
with an increasing sense of sanctity.

Similar—even more pronounced—views are held by
Havelock Ellis as a result of a life-long study of this
problem. He allows that in rare and gifted natures
transformed sexual energy becomes of supreme value
for its own sake without ever attaining its normal
physical outlet. But he says that in the effort to
achieve complete abstinence we are abusing a great
source of beneficent energy. For the sexual activities
of the organism constitute a mighty source of energy
which we can never altogether repress, though by
wise guidance we may render it an aid not only to
personal development and well-being but to the moral
betterment of the world.

" It is passion, more passion and fuller, that we
need," he says. " The moralist who bans passion
is not of our time. . . . It is more passion that we need
if we are to undo the work of Hate, if we are to add
to the gaiety and splendour of life, to the sum of human
achievement, to the aspiration of human ecstasy."

Through harmonious sex-relationship he believes
that a deeper spiritual unity may be reached than
can possibly be derived from continence in or out of
marriage. Sexual activity may be the stimulus and
liberator of our finest and most exalted activities.
For it fortifies and enlarges the whole personality.
And for Havelock Ellis, as for Douglas White, the
love of man and woman for one another is something
unspeakably holy.

When, therefore, we combine the conclusions of
modern science with the experiences of the mystics

we see no actual necessity for the state of celibacy. There may be rare individuals to whom it may be preferable. But married persons as well as celibates can attain the highest spiritual condition. In any case, marriage is not to be decried. Rather is it to be lauded. There is no actual need for men to seclude themselves in monasteries or women in convents.

So it seems as if the glory of the holy state of matrimony will come into its own, and be regarded no longer as a drag and hindrance to a man or woman's spiritual development, but as a sweetening and uplifting power. The procreative urge will not be looked on as coming from the Devil but from God. It will be worshipped as divine. Woman will not be thought of as the temptress and beguiler to evil but as the wondrous evoker of good, and as necessary to the full development of man as he is to hers. Not virginity, but matrimony will be the fit object of worship, though the wedded state will be treated with increasing solemnity and entered on with no less fear and trembling than gladness and rejoicing. At no time in their lives more than in their infinitely delicate approach to each other and in their final choice, will the man and the woman need a surer intuition, a finer wisdom and a more sustained courage. Nor will the exercise of these qualities be permitted to lapse when the wedding is consummated. Perhaps then, even more than ever before, they may be required, if, as in the old story books, the pair are "to live happy ever after," and if they are to attain that highest happiness of all which should be their aim. Married love is the most natural way, and it may prove the best way of reaching the highest perfection. By the long-continued loving of one another in the spirit of the universe, the man may

273

evoke from the woman, and the woman from the man, the highest capacities of each.

IV

One last subject remains for discussion—and that is of the greatest importance. Joy and gladness, happiness to the point of ecstasy, goodness to the point of saintliness have so filled these pages that it is time to take count of the sorrow, the evil of all kinds—the downright wickedness and awful brutality, bestiality, and cruelty there is in the world. These the mystics may seem to ignore, or run away from into the temple or the cloister or the jungle. But ordinary people have to face the realities of life. The pains and troubles and wickednesses of ourselves and our fellows cannot be ignored. They are right on top of us and everywhere around us. At any moment death may remove our dearest. Sickness may come upon us without a warning. An accident may kill or cripple us when in the full stride of life. Our daily newspaper is full of murders, robberies, crimes of every kind, desertions and adulteries; of strikes in one country, political assassinations in another, civil war in a third, and actual or threatening war always in some part of the world; and of awful natural calamities, an earthquake in Japan, a famine in India, floods in China, and everywhere the misery of men and women just on the edge of starvation, hopelessly seeking employment and the wherewithal to keep themselves and their families alive.

If we face such stark realities as these straight before our eyes, how is it possible to go into ecstasies of delight like the mystics, or to believe that the world is governed for good? it will be asked.

To this the mystic would reply that the evil is there sure enough—and it is not easy to see how there could be good if there were no evil. But what he feels with such intensity of conviction is the existence of a Power at work in himself and in the world redeeming the evil, actually transforming it into good and using it as the very means to achieve the better.

The daily newspaper is concerned more with the abnormal than with the normal. The normal has no " news value." It is not worth reporting day by day that in respect to the greater number of countries there are no earthquakes, or famines or floods. The normal honesty, civility and goodness of people the newspaper-reader is not concerned to read about. Yet even in the daily paper, alongside the descriptions of horrors and calamities, there also appear quite as frequently, stories of heroisms and endurances, and of excellence achieved in many fields of human endeavour in sport, in art, in science, in religion. And in notices summing up the life of a man or a woman in its entirety it is the good and not the evil in that life that is primarily insisted on. Afterwards will come the " realist " writer who will tell us that the person so be-praised was no stained-glass window saint but could lose his temper, have his animosities, indulge his prejudices, and in general be as wicked as his neighbours. But this fashion of belittlement is already wearing thin. True enough, Queen Victoria did have her prejudices, and even George Washington, notwithstanding the legend, may have told a lie. Yet in spite of these blemishes there is the plain fact that the good in most heroes not so much outweighed the ill as waged a life-long struggle against it and usually came out victorious in the end.

The world is not a perfect world : it is a world in process of perfecting itself. No man is perfect : all men are in the act of improving themselves. Some lamentably fail ; others miraculously succeed. The mystic would not contend that there is no evil in the world. But if he be asked to face reality, he would reply that he has faced it and found that the profoundest reality in life is the existence of this drive to perfection of which he has become so acutely aware. As he looks out on the world about him he sees suffering and wickedness, certainly ; but he sees far more of quiet, unreported, unsuspected, yet heroic struggles against adversity ; he sees the sublime patience and invincible good cheer of that most numerous class in every country, the humble workers on the soil ; he sees poets, painters, musicians agonizingly struggling against every discouragement to give expression to the deepest things of the soul. Above all, he sees everywhere about him, not only among human beings but among birds, animals and even insects, that most purely good thing in life— the unselfish love of a mother for her offspring. And seeing these things with that clearness of vision so characteristic of mystics, and with their faculty of discriminating between the essential and the un- essential, he recognizes that the good in the world about him is of far deeper significance than the more obvious evil. He sees the universe actuated by a love akin to the love of a genius for his work—a universe which is only the visible and tangible aspect of the spirit of mother-love. The evil, however great, is, in the view of the mystic, the transient. In com- parison with that ultimate perfection towards which the world-process is driving, it is of utter insignificance.

And in this view he would have the support of

science. For science tells us how life as we see it to-day on this planet has evolved from a tiny primordial germ which came into being roughly about a thousand million years ago. At that time the land surface was as bare as the most barren desert and the waters were devoid of any life whatever. Now it may have its suffering and its evil, but this planet is obviously a better place than it was then. Or, take only the last million of those one thousand million years—take only the single million years since man appeared : the planet to-day, in spite of the wars and jealousies and strifes and general wickedness of man, is very clearly a better place than it was at the first appearance of man. And though amongst those who have never lived in a great forest and seen what jungle life really is there is an idea that wild animals pass their whole life in terror and that cruelty reigns supreme, naturalists who have studied life in the forest tell us that it is a vigorous, happy life, that birds and animals, while always aware of danger, are not so much terrorized by it as kept ever alert and at concert pitch of efficiency, and that wild animals do not kill out of sheer cruelty, but from hunger. Happiness is the outstanding feature of wild life in the jungle. And we in civilization can confirm this for ourselves by watching the birds and animals in the woods and fields about us. Compared with the sluggish domesticated animals protected from every danger, wild animals and birds kept by the keen struggle for existence at the top of their capacity, are at their fittest and alertest and obviously enjoying life. Death when it comes, comes swiftly. Alive they are happy. And when besides this joy in life among the birds and animals we see the beauty of plant and tree life continually renewed year after year, it is in the highest degree reasonable to suppose that the activity about us is a beneficent activity— that there is a power for good at work in the world.

And if it be objected that the existence of even one act of cruelty, one piece of suffering, one evil deed is a blemish on this Power showing that it is either not completely good or not completely powerful, the reply would be that the universe is not a static universe on a dead level which, because of its levelness, could be neither good nor bad; it is a dynamic universe—a dynamic process making for higher and higher perfection, and displaying a constant struggle of the good with the bad, and of the better with the good. Goodness lies in the struggle. Without the struggle there could be no goodness. The existence of the evident evil in the world need deter no one from believing that the world is ordered for good, or from having faith in the essential goodness of things. It should only spur men on to overcome it. So, the sight of evil is a goad to the mystic. It incites him to his best. It is intolerable to him that it should exist. And by his efforts he does actually succeed in transforming evil into good.

V

Thus there are grounds for the mystic's faith that the world is ordered for good and that a drive towards perfection runs through the world-process. Progress is made. Yet it is also clear to the mystic that that progress has to be achieved: it does not come of itself without effort on the part of the individual. Men are the instruments and agents through whom the progress is brought about. The drive to perfection is operating through each and all. And there is a mighty Will and Mind behind that drive which will ensure that perfection after perfection will in the end be achieved. Yet experience shows us that within limits liberty is left to the individual to avail himself little or much of this Power for good which is working in and around him. Running through every country—through France or Italy or Russia or India—is this urge to better the country. All Frenchmen or Italians feel their country expecting of them to do their best to better France or Italy. But some are better agents than others for the purpose. Some, like Mussolini or Briand, feel the urge with an intensity which drives them forward through every obstacle and opposition ; and they achieve much. To others it is but a faint inclination : they make little effort to respond even to that, and they achieve but little. So also is it with regard to the world-urge. The world will go forward. Progress will be made. Perfection will be achieved. But not by all—not by sluggards. Sluggards—whether nations or individual men and women—will be dropped out, just as slugs have been left behind. Progress will only be made by those who brace themselves for effort, who open themselves to the full inflow of the drive to perfection, and who use their intellects at their brightest to visualize that ultimate perfection towards which the world-process is driving, and then determine with the whole of their wills to make bad good and good perfect—first in themselves and then in the world.

The truth of these things we may test for ourselves. If we can from time to time of set purpose withdraw from the busy rush of life, and in solitude deliberately ponder on the ultimate significance of what science reveals of the orderliness, the intelligibility, and the

progressiveness of the universe ; what astronomers
tell of the mighty scale on which the universe is
built ; what physicists say of the microscopic minuteness of the units of which it is constructed ; what
biologists relate about the nicety of their adjustments
into a whole and the architectural intricacy of even
the lowliest living thing ; what the evolutionist has
to record of the emergence of higher and higher types
through a thousand million years and of the variety
and adaptability of manifold species ; what anthro-
pologists observe of the development of man from
ape-like beings in merely family groups to cultured
men in great civilized nations ; what sociologists note
of the transmutation into good of the horrible evils
of war, pestilence and famine ; what we ourselves
can observe of the all-pervading beauty of the world,
the glory and the splendour of a sunset, the tranquillity of starlight, the freshness and the radiancy of
dawn, the purity of rain-washed skies, the majesty
of snow-clad mountains, the vastness of the ocean,
and the tender loveliness of flowers ; and, lastly, what
we know of those highest products of the evolutionary
process on this planet, the abounding happiness of
wild life, the ecstasy of perfect marriage, the devotion
of maternal love, the gentleness of Buddha, the pro-
fundity of Plato, the wisdom of Confucius and the
utter holiness of Jesus—if we can think these things
out right through to their final implication, and
ponder again and again on what these ascertained
and observable facts in the end imply—if we can thus
face real realities, not confusing the solid, palpable,
tangible, surface actualities with the underlying real,
but sensitively divining the truly real shining through
the superficial actual, as a man's soul shines through
his outward features, and divining also the Eternal

which lies beyond yet in the temporal—if we can thus penetrate to the true heart of things, can we not see a Something before which we are only able to bow in reverential adoration ? For what else can it all ultimately imply than the existence at the base of things of a Mind, a Spirit, a Personality, or a more than Personality, with the exactitude of a mathematician, the imagination of a poet, the sense of beauty of an artist, the capacity for love of a mother, the holiness of a saint, all combined in one, raised to the highest pitch of perfection, and possessed of invincible power, as the mystics contend ?

And may not this mysterious Power—this dominating personal Power—so tremendous yet so compellingly attractive, be the motive power of that all-encompassing, all-pervading, all-creative Activity in which our lives are set ? And may not what this Power is driving at be what the mystics unite in describing as a mode of living so exalted, so intense, so rapturous as to be endurable only for rare moments by even the most spiritual and yet characterized by all the surety, the serenity and the poise of harmonized activities in perfect equilibrium ?

CHAPTER VII

CONCLUSIONS

I

HAVING now recounted various mystical experiences and judged of them in the light of modern science and of the ordinary experiences of life what can we say as to their use in the practical affairs of the world ? Of what good is the mystical experience ? What can the mystic do for those millions on the point of starvation, for those other millions who have fruitlessly sought for employment ? What good would this highly emotional mysticism be to them ? And apart from these extreme cases, what good would it be to the normal man and woman engaged in the everyday work of the world with its unending worries, disappointments, sorrows and disillusions ? What to the clergy fighting a forlorn hope against the materialism and soul-withering indifference of the day ? Or to the poet with precious things to say and striving to get heard above the clamour and clatter of the street ? Or to the statesman borne down by an accumulation of the gravest possible issues ? Or to the soldier with death and disaster immediately threatening ? Or to the financier facing crisis upon crisis in a bewildering complexity of economic entanglements ? Or to the young wife who had staked all and found her marriage a ghastly failure ? Or to the poor mother responsible for rearing her children, keeping the home together and making two very far-off ends meet ? Of what good is this very sentimental mystical experience to such as these ?

And what can it do for us practical-minded Europeans and Americans who are so suspicious of the dreamy and the emotional and who are perpetually wanting to be doing things—to be seeing something solid springing up before our eyes—building the biggest ships, erecting the highest buildings, constructing the fastest motor-cars ; or, at least, to be promoting tangible social and political reforms ?

To all such questions the mystic might reply that what he has to communicate should be of obvious value in practical life, for it was out of the midst of life that he had himself obtained his experience. It was no dream or illusion, he might say : it was an actual personal, healthy, normal experience of proved value to himself as enhancing a hundredfold his normal enjoyment of life, and being of value to himself of value also to others, as he was no more than an ordinary man. Some mystics might add that it was out of extreme poverty that they had gained their experience—out of a self-imposed poverty resulting from a deliberate renunciation of all worldly goods. Further, the mystic might remind the inquirer that even for the most practical kind of work, spirit is what is ultimately required. Whether a piece of practical work is well or ill done depends in the last resort upon the spirit in which it is done. In the Great War all in the end depended upon the spirit of the combatant nations, and the final aim of statesmen in each country was to fortify the spirit of their own country and break the spirit of the enemy. Even for seeking employment much depends upon whether it is sought in a gloomy and despondent or in as cheerful and hopeful a spirit as can be summoned up for the occasion. And it was through lack of the spirit to make precautionary efforts that thousands died in the Indian famine. Always it is the spirit that counts. And it is because the mystical state refreshes, reinforces and refines the spirit in a man that it is of such value in practical life.

As practical men we have to cultivate the spirit and seek out whatever will strengthen it within us. And what like mysticism will meet such a need ? Philosophy, science, may supply the cold knowledge of what the world is like and the clear wisdom as to what to do. They may point the way. But where, save in mysticism, will be found the drive and passion, the glad courage, the sure intuition and the flaming conviction that will make men not only follow the way that wisdom shows, but leave the beaten track and strike upward to unscaled heights ? And where, save in mysticism, can be found that radiant serenity which can, with a smile, face all disaster ?

Science and philosophy may give the bare information that all things are interdependent, interconnected and cohere in one living whole ; the recent experience of mankind in the World War and World Depression may have shown the political and economic interdependence of nations ; but what like mysticism can make men feel that kinship with such intensity that they will sacrifice their lives to deliver their fellows from pain and evils and fill them with those joys which they themselves have known ?

For rousing, sustaining and elevating the spirit we rightly look to great preachers and orators, to poets and musicians. But all—and more than all—that

284

these can do to elevate and fortify the spirit, the mystic claims that the Spirit which is working so vehemently in him can do. If great poetry, great music, great art of any description can be of value in stirring men, putting heart into them, and raising them out of themselves on to a higher and more lovely plane of the spirit, all this and more the Spirit of which the mystic is the manifestation can do for men. So the mystic would claim.

Then, at the base of all things the mystical state must surely be of most practical worth ? For if a man is given certitude at the centre, poise to his whole being, and made at peace with himself, that must clearly be something of untold value to him in the tossings and turmoils of life. If, in addition, he is set brimming over with an abounding joy which buoys him up, enables him to buffet his way against the fiercest storms, to breast wave after wave and carry him triumphantly through seas of misfortune, then that value is redoubled. And if this invigorating joy goes further still—gives a mighty impetus to all he does, attracts men to him, unites them together, and shines from him with a radiance that dispels fear, avarice, jealousy, hatred and all uncharitableness, then that value is again redoubled. If, lastly, he discovers that something new has come to birth in his soul, that his whole soul is set going out to others, that he has become endowed with a new truthfulness of spirit and an intuitive insight which enables him to look straight into the hearts of his fellows and instantly detect the real thing in a man —that hidden best thing about him which is much more truly real than that worst which is so glaringly obvious on the surface—if a man finds himself possessed of such intuition then the value of the mystical state is once more redoubled. Such surety, such serenity, such all-conquering gladness, such insight, must necessarily be a supreme asset to a man in practical life. In his business, in professional, official or public life he has against all provocation, and at every cost, to keep his equilibrium, retain his composure, control his temper, maintain a sense of proportion, and preserve his intellect unclouded ; and, beyond this negative necessity he has the positive need of being able to see into men and carry them gladly with him in the work before him. And for what will infallibly do these things for him he would deem no price too heavy to pay.

The same is it with women in society and the home. Women, as well as men, in the common-day life of the world, would find the combined serenity and buoyancy of inestimable value. To them the inexhaustible *joie-de-vivre* would be as a pearl of great price. All that they had they would give to possess it.

This, then, is the measure by which the mystical experience may be valued.

Now, if the mystical experience is of such paramount value in human life—if it is a pointer in the direction of that higher state towards which the evolutionary process is progressing, and an impetus as well as an indicator, we would suppose that everyone would be eagerly pressing forward to attain it— that there would be a rush for it as for a goldfield. We would imagine that everyone would be panting to train and fit himself for entry into the new state. We would think that in every home and every school and every university in every country the training for it would be the one main aim of all education and all home upbringing.

But is it ? Universities are the seats of learning.

They set the standard of education throughout a country. They honour those outside their gates deemed most worthy of honour. But whoever heard of a university honouring a mystic ? In what university is there a faculty for promoting mysticism ? From universities have come learned scholars, able statesmen, efficient civil servants, brilliant scientists. Where is the university that looks upon it as far and away its chief and highest business to impart the temper and the spirit which should animate these and give aim to all their activities throughout their lives ?

Through education we want to send our young men and women into life able to cope with the world, equipped with a sound working philosophy of life, capable of distinguishing between the worthy and the worthless and of appreciating what is unquestionably of most value and therefore most worth striving after. They will be put to the most searching tests. Temptations we know will assail them—temptations to extravagance, luxury, indolence, bad company, vice. Terrific contingencies they must be prepared to meet —family bereavement, accidents, loss of health, loss of employment, loss of money, heart-breaking disappointments in love, war, disasters of many kinds. We know, too, they will have to forge their way through a perfect maze of staggering complications, conflicting interests, opposing sentiments—through cold criticism, hot anger, hard prejudices, hatred, suspicion and mistrust.

We know all this to a certainty. We know only too well the temptations and catastrophes and hostilities that await the young as they launch out into the world. But we are confident, too, of the good in them and we want their utmost best to be brought out of them. This, we would suppose, is the final purpose of all education.

We would expect to see them trained to inure themselves against whole seas of adversity; their fibre strengthened so that they may be able to take the incessant rubs and worries, the vexations and petty disappointment of life with cheery composure as all in the day's work; their temper steeled till they are able to bear the heaviest responsibilities, take the cruellest decisions and act upon them with unflinching courage. Yet, also, we would wish for them much more than passive endurance. We would wish them made active and forthcoming, quick in discrimination and eager in response to every rightful impression. Whether it be in earning a living, in choosing a mate, in making a home or in conducting great affairs of state or of business, we would want them able to do consummately well whatever they undertake. As their lives mature we would want them to become increasingly refined so that they may have grace sufficient to allay antagonisms, appease resentments and compose differences. We would wish their eyes trained to discover fresh beauties in the world around them and their souls quickened to a full appreciation and enjoyment of all such beauty. Most fervently would we wish that they should know how to choose friends well and keep them fast. And while we are aware of the dangers of sex we are still more acutely aware of its benefits—of the good a woman may elicit from a man and a man from a woman. So we would desire the intercourse between men and women to become increasingly intimate in order that the most fit mating may be assured. And all this we would desire for those going out into life because we believe that only as their whole selves, body, mind, and spirit, are satisfied can they ever have that highest happiness we would most of all want for them and which alone will bring with it final peace and contentment.

This is how we would like our young to be provided for as they launch out into life. But in all that concerns these deepest things in life where is that wise guidance and expert training given ? In most European and American homes, schools, and universities, attention is paid to bodily health, to training the mind, to forming character, and to fostering patriotism ; but how much is there given to the fundamental things of the soul and to that wider patriotism—the love of that whole great world which gave humanity birth ? Technical training of the most perfect kind is often provided for the various sciences, and for such arts as music, drawing and painting ; but where is there to be found any technical training for that mode of life for which the human race is so obviously destined ? A smattering of religious education may be given in the schools and by the churches at the time of confirmation ; but where is to be found that highly expert and prolonged education of the soul which the progress of mankind so urgently requires ? Where is fit spiritual nourishment provided ?

For the science and art of mysticism almost no provision is made in our education. And as no such training is available we have to grope our way towards it, recognizing that we have to train ourselves not only for intellectually knowing the great Creative Spirit of the universe but also for feeling It in the same way as a patriot feels the spirit of his country —in the same way only to a far intenser degree. May I therefore put forward a few tentative suggestions evoked by this study of present-day mystics and by personal intercourse with a few of them, but put them forward only as supplementary to what has already been so fully expounded by such authorities as Poulain, Evelyn Underhill, and Rufus Jones, and by Hindu yogis.

II

The crucial point to be first decided by all embarking on life is whether the universe is to be considered friendly or indifferent. For upon a man's view of the nature of the world he lives in must depend his fundamental attitude to life. With all our hearts we would long that those going out into the world should feel assured in their hearts that the world they live in is governed for good, and that in every effort they make towards the good they will have the whole weight of the universe behind them. Yet we recognize how natural it is for them, when they see so much evil about and are being so continually warned of the evils to be on their guard against, to have periods of doubt, depression, and disillusionment. So, while we would afford them every opportunity of learning what is the true view of the universe and would imperatively compel them earnestly to *consider* it and their attitude towards it, we know how important it is that having done this much we should also leave them to make their own decisions in the matter. For only as they make their belief on fundamental matters their own will they be able to act on it with conviction and force. Moreover, however much faith they may have, it will be the stronger for being confirmed by thought; and whatever their courage may be it will be strengthened by judgment. They must decide for themselves, therefore—and may take years about it, so long as they are seriously deliberating and not merely letting themselves drift—whether the universe to which they belong is simply a blind mechanism grinding relentlessly on without a thought for them or their fondest hopes and ambitions, or whether it is a living universe, a loving and a lovable world which will sustain them in every effort they make to accomplish what is good and beautiful, and will reward with unspeakable joy every perfection they achieve. They must make up their minds whether they will go into life as Bertrand Russell did, believing that physical laws ultimately prevail and that what we hope for and achieve is destined to final extinction ; or as Cecil Rhodes did, assuming that the chances are even whether there is a God or not and that the survival of the fittest is the rule by which the universe is guided ; or like McTaggart did with an intellectual as well as an emotional certitude that the universe is essentially a spiritual universe animated by love.

Those who have not been able to satisfy themselves that the world is governed for good will presumably not desire to fit themselves for attaining the mystical experience. But those who really have convinced themselves of the goodness of the world will want to experience the goodness of things to the full. They will have heard from the mystics of the feeling of intense beatitude which it brings and they too will want to experience this overflowing joy. They will want to have direct, immediate experience of the effects on them of the working of that Creative Spirit which they have assured themselves drives and governs the world.

Fear of pain may deter them from adopting a wrong course. But it is no sufficient incentive for high adventure. Vision and imagination are required for that. Anticipation of the joy of achievement is what lures men upward on the dangerous climb. And it is anticipation of the bliss of the mystical experience that will be the irresistible lure for those who would now desire to attain the mystic state.

But in order to gain that experience they must obviously have to fit themselves. Some indeed have acquired it without any definite training. The authoress of *The Golden Fountain* is an instance ; and even the great Indian mystic and philosopher of ancient times, Sankara, prided himself upon never having deliberately trained himself in yoga practice. Yet assuredly some technical training would be beneficial, and the time has come when a psychologist who can bring his mind without prejudices to this crucially important subject is distressingly needed to steer groping humanity through the uncharted realm of the spirit which it has now to explore.

In the meanwhile, even if no technical training be available, there are certain obvious steps which all who seek to obtain experience of the Universal Spirit may take. All might set their affections on things above. All might set their whole hearts upon attaining higher and higher perfection, upon ascertaining and assuring themselves of what are the most valuable things in life. All might school and discipline their powers of attention. All might daily spend some portion of their time in deliberately focusing their whole selves upon the Highest Perfection—praying to God as it is usually described—purifying their minds of any lesser thought or desire ; selecting from time to time first one and then another particular perfection, meditating carefully upon it, appreciating with discrimination what precisely constitutes its perfection, whether of goodness, beauty, or truth, and then using their full will and intention to achieve that perfection.

And the modern explorer of the high and holy realms of the spirit will take modern ways of preparing himself. And he will start with this advantage—that there is about him in these days a demand for the better of which he would be wise to take full benefit, and turn into a passion for the best. People are demanding better food—not necessarily more luxurious, but fresher, more wholesome and more varied. They are wanting better clothing—not necessarily finer but warmer for winter and cooler for summer. They are seeking better houses—not necessarily more sumptuous—but lighter, more airy, more beautiful and better adapted to house-keeping needs. They are calling out for better means of locomotion—a faster train service or 'bus service or bicycle or motor-car. They want, too, better means of communication—a better telephone service or radio set. Better conditions of labour they are crying for too—better conditions in the factory and more leisure. More air and sunshine they are wanting in their lives. In every way they are trying to better their lot.

And here and there one succeeds. And by what the one does to achieve perfection the whole benefits. The millionaire is decried, but he may have initiated or developed a new enterprise and benefited the whole community. He who builds the fastest motor-car or aeroplane helps the builders of ordinary motor-cars and aeroplanes and through them the general public. The climber of the highest mountain encourages the climbing of all lesser peaks and thus adds to the enjoyments of all.

In this atmosphere of striving after the better and the best the modern spiritual explorer will make his start ; and of it he will have to take advantage, filling his lungs with as much of it as they will hold. What men are everywhere doing in games and in sport in striving at least to see, even if they cannot play, the finest cricket, or football, or lawn-tennis, or golf, he will do likewise in the higher realm of the spirit. He will seek at least to be acquainted with what is the most perfect in poetry, or drama, music or poetry, oratory or preaching, and in holiness of living. Thus will he discover for himself what really is of most worth and get to know what true excellence is, so that he may infallibly recognize it when he sees it—and infallibly also recognize what just falls below it. And once having known the best he will never be finally contented with anything less. A yearning for that best will remain within him. With nothing short of the best will he ever after be really satisfied. And with him a striving after perfection will soon become a habit.

And nowadays through the progress of science it is easier than ever before at least to see or hear examples of what the highest perfection really is. The modern spiritual explorer has but to decide for himself what is most worth striving after, making his own, treasuring and developing—he has only to make up his mind as to what is the most precious thing in life and he can at least see it if he will only make full and proper use of the mastery which modern science has made over matter. If he will neither spurn the modern machine on the one hand, nor on the other, let the machine master the man, he will find in it an inexhaustibly useful extension of his body. For through the instrumentality of the modern machine his eyesight has been extended till he can see objects 140 million light-years distant and others a thousand times finer than a spider's web; his hearing has been so extended that he can hear voices from the Antipodes; and his power of locomotion till he can travel from England to India in a day through the air at two or three hundred miles an hour. And with this capacity of his body thus expanded his soul may be proportionately enlarged if he will now learn to make the fullest use of the machine which the skill of science has placed in his hands. Through it he should be able to track down perfection however remote it may be and however obscurely hidden. And reciprocally, perfection will be using the machine to reach him. Not only is the power of hearing increased but the power of speaking also. The King's voice is heard at Christmas all round the world, carrying messages of greeting and good-will to his subjects. Both the seeker and the promoter of perfection have much to gain through the instrumentality of modern science.

May we suggest a few of the ways in which modern material development may thus be of aid to the spiritual researcher? Take, for instance, broadcasting. The radio brings perfection of music, preaching, oratory, straight into the home. Then again, cheap books, free libraries, good newspapers, bring him the best literature. The railway, the omnibus, the motor-coach, will take a man inexpensively to where perfections of other kinds may be seen or heard. A town-dweller has the advantage of easy access to theatres and cinemas where he can, if he choose wisely, see good drama, to museums where he can see fine pictures and other works of art, to churches where he can see fine architecture and hear good preachers and singers, and to public parks where he can see the many beauties of flowers, trees and shrubs.

Temporary exhibitions, too, he may see of the best producible in many spheres of art and science. The country dweller has not these particular advantages ; but he has others of his own. He has the benefit of quietude and tranquillity and of close touch with the glories and beauties of nature, of his own garden and of neighbouring meadows and woodlands. And with the growing facilities for locomotion the advantages of town-dweller and countryman may be interchanged—the town-dweller benefiting by the repose and beauty of the country and the countryman by the more vivid life of the town.

And both may use these swifter and easier means of transportation and communication to seek that best thing of all, the best society. Not indeed the smart society of London or Paris, of Rome or New York ; and not only the most intellectual society or the most art-loving. Not this, but the society of those few who are closest to the ground of things and who may be found in tiny villages as well as in great towns—those joyous children in spirit, however aged in years, whose company gladdens all who are privileged to share it.

Thus will the spiritual explorer make use of science to cultivate a flair for perfection, first assuring himself of what is the highest perfection, then rigidly restricting himself to attempting only what is really worth while, and finally determining to do that thing to perfection—to do it with finish—to make of it a real work of art.

And concrete examples of perfection will be helpful to him here. For, besides wanting some principle to hold on to and believe in, a man wants also some person. And living are better than recorded examples. It is for that reason that the Hindu de-

votee travels over India from one Swami to another
in search of the one who will most fully fulfil his
ideals, while Roman Catholic nuns have to be content
with reading lives of saints long since dead. And in
searching for living examples modern means of transportation and communication will again be a help.
Hindus attach the greatest importance to the actual
bodily touch of the disciple by the master. In the
case of Vivekenanda we have seen what a thrilling,
almost intoxicating, effect the touch of Ramakrishna
had upon him. But such bodily touch cannot always
be expected. What however is fairly accessible for
those who set their heart on it is at least the sight
at a public meeting or the hearing on the radio of
one or other of the most spiritual men and women
of the day. This is not all : but it is a little. It
is a little of the living touch which means so much in
spiritual matters. And we have seen how much even
the sight of Pope Leo XIII did for the Protestant
authoress of *The Golden Fountain* in showing her what
holiness meant.

III

By heroic examples of the past, and by living touch
with examples in his own day the modern mystic's
imagination will be fired. He will be stirred to
emulate them. He will dare even to surpass them.
Why not ? For he starts with the advantage of their
example. Where they had pioneered the way he may
more easily follow after. He should therefore be able
to outstrip them.

Profiting by their example he will fit himself rigor-
ously for the venture, schooling himself with the
sternest discipline to stand the fearful strains which
lie before him, yet also quickening his sensitivity till

his soul is able to register the subtlest impressions, surely discriminate the good of them from the bad, the better from the good, and the best from the better, and then to the best instantly give the liveliest response.

And the modern mystic will not seclude himself from life : he will live in its very midst. He will not live the hermit life in the mountain or the jungle or seclude himself in a monastery. Nor will the woman mystic think it necessary to retire into a convent. Rather will the modern mystic live the full life of the world. Convinced of the divinity in men and women he will love to be among them to be stimulated by that divinity. He will not adopt artificial penances to discipline himself : he will let the only too many rubs and disappointments and endurances of life do that for him. He will not inflict uncalled for sufferings on himself, he will let the sufferings of life do their own work in sensitizing his soul. In bodily health, in mental alertness, in tenderness of heart, and in sensitivity of soul he will keep himself as fit as an athlete or a concert pianist for the stern yet delicate work that lies before him. And he will let the usual battling through the oppositions and rivalries of his fellow-men do what is necessary for tautening his fibre, and sharpening his intelligence, and will let sharing in their joys and sorrows deepen his sympathy and quicken his intuition. Assuredly, he will find necessity for brief periods for retreat and solitary communion with himself and with the Spirit. But in the main he will live in the world ; and in his fellow-men he will find his chief inspiration.

Being already convinced that the Creative Spirit of the universe is no separate person living outside of and apart from the world and watching with a

Judge's eye our puny efforts to please Him, but is a Power unceasingly at work in us as well as in all about us, fashioning us into more God-like beings and more effective agents for carrying out Its vast purposes, the modern mystic will prepare to let himself melt into that Spirit of the Whole, absorb It till he is at more than saturation point, as a lover is overflowing with joy or a patriot with love of his country. Thus will he become increasingly aware of the divinity in himself and increasingly disposed to credit his fellows with what he himself so vividly possesses.

In his earlier days his efforts may be more exclusively concentrated upon perfecting himself But in maturer years his thoughts will be set more upon helping his fellows, his country, and mankind. Eschewing pure selfishness as sheer self-destruction he will yet jealously preserve his own individuality, for he will know the necessity of differentiation in every unity and the value of the contrast which variety affords. He will not be selfish, but he will be himself to the full, as must be every singer in a choir. But with his individuality he will develop his sociality, as only in the society of his fellows can his individuality develop to the full. So he will cultivate *esprit de corps* in all its forms—patriotism, local patriotism (such as love of Parisians for Paris and Devonians for Devon), comradeship, that fellow-feeling which all throughout the world have for others engaged in the same kind of work, the artist for all artists, the scientist for all scientists, the lawyer for all lawyers, the manual labourer for all hand-workers, the peasant for all peasants. He will share in that common admiration all have for perfection in the other—all artists for perfection in the scientist and all scientists for perfection in the artist. And in developing at once his individuality and his sociality self-assertion will be as necessary as self-surrender and self-surrender as needful as self-assertion. Times there will be when he must have the vision, the wisdom, the initiative and the courage to assert himself for the sake of the divine that is in him. Other occasions there will be when, for the sake of his family, or his child, or his country, or out of love for humanity, he must surrender all—even his life. The mother, the soldier, the captain of a sinking ship all know such occasions and instinctively act on them.

With feeling and reason a like adjustment he will have to make. He will learn to be as aware of the danger of feeling without reason as of the chill of reason without feeling. While illimitably deepening his love and affection he will not disdain the intellect but increase its power and add to his knowledge. Judgment and good sense he will value as well as affection, till feeling is tempered by wisdom and wisdom warmed by feeling.

And with reason thus combined with feeling the modern mystic will take a very different view of the passions than have many mystics of the past. Passions he will not regard as evil in themselves but as good—good as furnishing the driving force for all great effort. They need not degrade : purified and refined they will only elevate. So not suppression but control of the passions will be his aim. Not mortification but sublimation. Not celibacy but marriage—marriage with one who is capable of eliciting from him the divinest potentialities in his passions and of making them heroic.

He will put his whole heart into whatever he does, but first he will put the Holy Spirit into his heart. By prayer and meditation he will strive to align himself with the central drive of the universe and to imbibe its Spirit. By sternly focusing his entire attention upon some perfection of beauty or goodness and meditating deliberately upon it—upon the various elements that go to make its perfection—he will pierce to the inner essence of its beauty or its goodness and eventually reach the Source of all perfection.

He would cultivate the nicest appreciation of the exact worth of each object and would recognize that each such perfection was only a part. He would see it as a part but with a feeling for the whole. He would realize that a single perfection pursued to the exclusion of others would become a defect. Each must be viewed in relation to the whole and as but one aspect or attribute of the Spirit which animates and sustains the whole. And he would not, while seeking the good, ignore the evil. But he would view the evil also with a feeling for the whole. He would see it in proportion to the whole ; and he would not allow himself to be unduly obsessed by its presence in the world. He would not shut his eyes to death the inevitable, to the prevalence of disease, and to the existence of vice, malice and cruelty. But he would note that in the long result death has been beneficial as opening the way to the evolutionary emergence of higher and higher forms of life—that without death there could have been no progress. And rather than let his mind dwell disproportionately on the obvious evils of life he would remind himself of the skill men display in battling disease, of their heroism in enduring unavoidable suffering, of their self-sacrificing devotion in the removal of vice, and of their determined attempts to beautify what is mean and in every way better the lot of mankind.

Then realizing the deep significance of the everyday things of life he would take those common objects as the subjects of his meditation. One or other of these he would take according as it might present itself to him or according to his mood of the moment. But once having made his selection he would devote his whole self to it. Each would be taken in turn day to day, year to year, and for the period of meditation, whether that period be a minute or an hour, it would be profoundly and intensely meditated upon again and again till the would-be mystic had saturated himself with its particular perfection—till he had absorbed it into his being and become absolutely possessed by its excellence.

Such everyday subjects for meditation might be the grandeur of a thunderstorm, the magnificence of mounting monsoon clouds, the gladness of spring, the glow of autumn, the solemnity of night, or the infinity of far horizons. Or they might be the beauty in form or colour of some tree or flower: the stateliness of a deodar, the loveliness of a rose, the purity of a lily, the distinction of an orchid, the delicacy of a primrose, the grace of a clematis. Or they might be the sweetness of a robin's song, the daintiness of a wagtail, the heroism of a mother-bird, the attraction of young things, the loyalty of a dog, the dignity of a stag, the keenness of a hawk, or the sagacity of an elephant. Or again they might be the intuition and spontaneity of a child, the charm of a woman, the virility of a man, the light in lovers' eyes, the holiness of perfect mating, or the joy of motherhood. Or, more in particular, they might be the art of Shakespeare, the greatness of Napoleon, the daring of Nelson, the nobility of Lincoln, the sincerity of Darwin, the chivalry of Bayard, the humanity of

Wilberforce, the compassion of Catherine Booth, or the gay saintliness of St. Francis. Or they might be any of these high qualities typified in living examples of the day.

The duration of the meditation might vary from a few impulsive moments as an object might suddenly impress itself on him to long unhurried hours as the complexity of the interrelated elements which go to make a particular perfection came into view. In any case, the meditation would for that period be concentrated and intense. And as it grew in intensity it would rise to admiration. And as admiration for some specially high perfection intensified it would grow to adoration. And adoration would culminate in emulation. Emulation of what others had achieved would then become the governing motive of the meditator's life. As they had done, so would he do : nothing less. He would model himself first on this and then on that one who had achieved some high quality and then step by step creep up to and eventually surpass him.

Nor would he stop there. In addition to meditating upon high qualities separately he would further ponder on them in their togetherness. For his sense of proportion would show him that each was only a part—only a part of a whole—and that in the whole there may be other and higher things than in the parts separately. In selected times of secure leisure, away on the mountain side or by the fireside in the quiet of the night, he would more particularly concentrate his most earnest attention on that which lies behind all and includes all—that stupendous ultimate of which these high qualities are the different attributes and manifestations. He would meditate on the universe as a whole. He would collect himself together and, undistracted by any other interest, meditate deeply, penetratingly, upon the sublimity of the starry universe as a whole, upon the utter interdependence of every single part with every other part and with the whole ; and upon the possibility, nay, the probability, that many other stars than our sun may have planets attached to them, inhabited by intelligent beings, far higher in the scale of life than ourselves. By thus from time to time deliberately recalling what we know of the immensity of the universe and reflecting most deeply on its sublimity, on the infinite beauty of the world with which he himself is so tightly connected as an integral part, and on the possibility that it contains beings far higher than himself, his horizon will be widened, his sense of the whole developed, and his feeling for the infinite and the sacred quickened and intensified. And as he meditates long and often throughout his life on these greatest of all things, awe and wonder and reverence will grow and deepen within him ; though too deep for words his feelings may then become, and only through the greater art in the solemnity of public worship may it be possible for mankind in the smallest degree to express them.

When he descends from these heights and goes back into life he may quickly become aware of the sufferings and evils about him. But he will notice that the most poignant sorrow is invariably matched by the profoundest sympathy and the direst calamity by the highest heroism—the one evoking the other. And his newly acquired sense of the whole will have shown him how in the process of time evils are slowly dissolved, as impurities are by the sunshine. Though he will also recognize that it is only through the active instrumentality of himself and others, as rays from that sun, that evil is redeemed. The evil and misery round him will therefore only stimulate him to action, as calamity spurs to heroism.

Thus will he seek to clear and complete his vision of the world, to obtain a more truthful picture of the universe, to store his mind with more beautiful images and to attain sublimer heights of perfection. And such meditation to be most fruitful would be made in the very midst of life, in periods of leisure purposely and at all costs made for the purpose. For this experience of the fundamental realities of existence gained in meditation is life itself—not merely the means to it, as is that part of life concerned with bread-winning and the ordinary social amenities. It is of the very essence of life. And for that reason, of an early morning or an evening, on walks or amongst crowds, or during a holiday—whenever or wherever leisure may be found or made—the modern mystic would be wise to resort to meditation.

Thus will he concentrate his faculties and control his powers. And having in this way gathered himself together occasions will from time to time arise when he will feel himself impelled to go beyond meditation —when he will feel driven to throw out his whole collected self in yearning aspiration towards that Supreme End which has also been the Source and Inspiration of all his striving. In gratefullest thanksgiving for whatever he has so far enjoyed, but with passionate prayer for yet higher favours to come, he will feel constrained to fling himself upward to the Most High and Holy, the final Bestower of all good gifts.

Then one day his prayer will be answered. The culmination of all things will be reached. The climax will have come. Of a sudden a rending crisis will be on him—a fearful upheaval within him, a breaking down of all barriers, a tearing assunder of that which encases him and keeps him together and separate, and a sudden inrush from without. A rushing mighty wind will sweep through his soul. He will be filled with the Holy Ghost. Caught up in a hurricane of unendurable rapture he will no longer be able to contain himself. He will be beside himself with unbearable joy.

In one breathless leap he will be exalted beyond the utmost he had prayed for or expected. What Columbus must have felt on reaching the New World, what the Everest climber will feel on attaining the summit, what every mother feels on first seeing her firstborn—all these combined and surpassed he will now experience. Before he was self-conscious, now he will be world-conscious, cosmic-conscious, God-conscious.

A slow settling down will necessarily follow this terrifying convulsion of the Spirit. And in that calm a great peace will fall on him. Cleansed, purified, redeemed, he will at last be really himself. He will be sure on his pivot. His nerves will be steadied. He will have emerged as a new man, breathing a new air, bathed in a new light. Life in a new world will have begun. It will be the same world to which he had always belonged ; but he will be seeing it in a new light. The scales will have fallen from his eyes. What kept him to earth will have been unloosed. Wings will have come to his soul and he will soar away to infinite heights.

Yet, though no longer tied to the ground he will still belong to the earth. He will still love to be among his fellow-men. And now more than ever.

For in the new light he will see a beauty and a goodness in their hearts he had never suspected before.
He will see what they too are capable of becoming.
And he would open their eyes to the new world that
is theirs for the seeing. But how can he do this?
How can he make the blind to see? How can he
make them aware of the encompassing glory?

Of himself it would be impossible. But no man
works of himself alone. In all men is working what
was working in himself. He, too, used to be blind
like they. But working in him was the incessant
urge to break through to the light. Prompting him
was this urge to high adventure. And it is the same
with some of them. They, too, are possessed of the
same urge to perfection, and all he will have to do
is to help them to come to themselves. A skylark
would find it hard to tell her still blind and feather-
less chicks of the glories of life in the sunshine. Yet
she can provide the conditions that will enable them
to see. She can keep her chicks warm in the nest,
bring them food, aid them in developing the powers
within them till they, too, have won their wings and
their eyesight and like her can soar to the skies. And
the mystic's task will be the same. He cannot of
himself make men see. But he can help men to
see for themselves. He can put faith into them,
subtly communicate to them something of his own
confidence, give them confidence in themselves, confidence in their fellow-men, confidence in the beauty
and goodness of the world in which they are immersed and with which they are inseparably connected. That much he can do. And it is enough.
For the world itself will do the rest. The Creative
Urge of the universe will do its work.

As a result more and more men will reach extreme

tension, pass the crisis, burst through their encasement and come to full consciousness of the glorious world in which they are immersed—more and more will have the new vision and see the world in the new light. And among those who will be pressing forward to the conquest of the new realm there will spring up an ardent rivalry. Each will be eager to surpass the other in advancing the kingdom of heaven upon earth. Thus will the higher species of man come into being and steadily spread over this planet, till the earth is peopled by a new type of men—men capable of enduring the lightning intensity of a new standard of living as high above our present standard as that is above the standard of monkeys ; and an all-embracing charity will have become as much the order of mankind as *esprit de corps* is the rule of a regiment.

For the future habitability of this planet science allows a period of time far more than a hundred times greater than the, roughly, one thousand million years it has taken life to develop from the proverbial amœba to man. And of what such vast period of time means we may form some faint conception if we adopt and adapt a method used by Jeans to illustrate what a million is. He points out that a book of 500 pages, each page of 330 words of an average length of six letters, would contain about a million letters. Taking this scale and applying it to a proposed history of life on this earth and allowing one letter for each year, that is about sixteen words for a century, and half a page for a thousand years, we find that the history would occupy a thousand volumes. And only in the last of those thousand volumes would the history of man commence, and only in the last page or two of that last volume would the story of civilized man be told. But a new era has already dawned. The spiritualization of man has begun. The first page of a new volume is being written. But ere the history of life upon this earth has been completed another thousand volumes—perhaps ten or even a hundred thousand volumes—will have to be written even though the story is so condensed that only half a page would be allowed for a thousand years. And the stage for the drama which the new series of volumes will record will be very different from the tiny terrestrial stage upon which the drama so far has been played : it will extend over the entire stellar universe. And it will portray the conquest not merely of the land and the air on this planet but of that spiritual realm which is co-extensive with the universe itself. When we think of the wonders already written on the first page describing this new era of the spirit we can see no limit to the height of development which will be described before the final page of these thousand of volumes is reached. If life has developed from a microscopic single-celled organism to man in a thousand million years imagination reels at the thought of what it may develop into in a period ten or a hundred times as great.

Ten thousand million years hence we may well conjecture our far descendants will have fashioned the minerals of this planet into instruments of such surpassing range and nicety as would enable them to detect the subtlest vibrations of the ether and most delicately yet precisely respond to messages from the universe at large borne on them as the eye responds to light from distant stars. And they themselves may have developed such sensitivity of soul, such fineness of perception and response, that with the aid of these instruments for extending their powers of hearing and seeing they may be able to recognize influences emanating from any living beings there may be on other planets of other stars. And by thus establishing contact with any such living beings they may be able with them to form a close community of celestial beings throughout the universe.

We may likewise suppose that the Creative Spirit, working as It will be on this planet day and night through every second of those ten thousand million years, will by then have brought into being here on this earth a Master Mystic who will embody It in supreme degree and most perfectly make manifest Its sovereign purpose. Then through the powers of transmission which science would by then have developed this Master Mystic would be able to exert his master influence over the whole community of living beings throughout the universe and, for the period of his ascendancy, be the central directing power of the world holding them together, controlling them and alluring them upward. This planet would for that period occupy the key position and be the dynamic focal centre for the spiritualization of the whole universe.

This indeed is pure speculation. But it is legitimate speculation. And speculation is necessary. For the human species is on the move. It is on the upward grade. It is not tied down by inexorable instinct like the bees, who through being thus bound have remained in their present state for millions of years. Man is endowed with an intelligence which enables him to profit by experience. Through this intelligence hide-bound instinct is being broken up and more pliable intuition is taking its place. Using his intelligence and powers of direct intuition man is looking ahead. A few of the more venturous spirits are advancing into new ground. They have to watch their every footstep lest they fall. But an explorer's attention is not always on the ground immediately beneath his feet. From time to time he halts on some eminence. Then he lifts his eyes to scan the far horizons for those distant snowy peaks which mark the climax of his journeyings. A glance may be sufficient. But that glance is a necessity. It maintains his sense of proportion and assures him of the right direction. And so is it with those who are pioneering the way into the new realm of the spirit. They, too, have to look ahead. Like born explorers they have to divine instinctively what may lie before them and thereby shape their course.

So the sum of it all is this. As life, which originated in the sea, first conquered the land and then the air, so will it now conquer that enveloping realm of the spirit which extends to the farthest confines of the universe and has been there from all time and will remain there for all time, world without end. Evolution will remain. Natural Selection, the Struggle for Existence, and the Survival of the Fittest, will remain. But the drive to evolve will derive, as it always has derived, from the informing Will in the deeps of the Universe as a whole; the " Nature " which selects will be, as it always has been, the informing Mind in its infinite heights; the struggle will not be for bare existence but for higher existence; and the fittest to survive will be the fittest to endure the intensity of this higher form of living. Then through the operation of this struggle for a higher existence men will be kept on the razor edge of their capacity.

311

And through being forced to be at their best, the keenest enjoyment of life will be theirs.

Men will become aware that their great days are before them. No longer will they look back to a golden age of the past. They will turn their whole minds to the glories of the future. The promise of that future is already working in them. A great Hope is dawning in their hearts. That hope will brighten into Expectation. And expectation kindles Effort: men will vie with one another to bring it to Fulfilment. The many will fail: the few will succeed. But the few will acknowledge that without the many fulfilment could never have been achieved. And Joy will be to all who genuinely strive. For joy is in the struggle. Great gladness infallibly comes to all who courageously strive to be to the full whatever is in them.

And he who means to be more than his best will win most.

INDEX

INDEX